The Politics of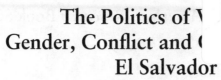
Gender, Conflict and
El Salvador

The *Bulletin of Latin American Research* Book Series

The *Bulletin of Latin American Research* publishes original research of current interest on Latin America, the Caribbean, inter-American relations and the Latin American Diaspora from all academic disciplines within the social sciences, history and cultural studies. The BLAR/SLAS book series was launched in 2008 with the aim of publishing research monographs and edited collections that compliment the wide scope of the Bulletin itself. It is published and distributed in association with Wiley-Blackwell. We aim to make the series the home of some of the most exciting, innovatory work currently being undertaken on Latin America and we welcome outlines or manuscripts of interdisciplinary, single-authored, jointly-authored or edited volumes. If you would like to discuss a possible submission to the series, please contact the editors at blar@liverpool.ac.uk

The Politics of Violence
Gender, Conflict and Community in El Salvador

MO HUME

WILEY-BLACKWELL

SLAS
SOCIETY for
LATIN AMERICAN STUDIES

This edition first published 2009

Editorial organisation © 2009 Society for Latin American Studies, text © 2009 The Author

Blackwell Publishing was acquired by John Wiley & Sons in February 2007. Blackwell's publishing program has been merged with Wiley's global Scientific, Technical, and Medical business to form Wiley-Blackwell.

Registered Office

John Wiley & Sons Ltd, The Atrium, Southern Gate, Chichester, West Sussex, PO19 8SQ, United Kingdom

Editorial Offices

350 Main Street, Malden, MA 02148-5020, USA

9600 Garsington Road, Oxford, OX4 2DQ, UK

The Atrium, Southern Gate, Chichester, West Sussex, PO19 8SQ, UK

For details of our global editorial offices, for customer services, and for information about how to apply for permission to reuse the copyright material in this book please see our website at www.wiley.com/wiley-blackwell.

Library of Congress Cataloging-in-Publication Data

Hume, Mo.

The politics of violence : gender, conflict and community in El Salvador / Mo Hume. p. cm. – (The bulletin of Latin American research book series ; 2)

Includes bibliographical references and index.

ISBN 978-1-4051-9226-2

1. Violence–Social aspects–El Salvador. 2. Women–Violence against–El Salvador. 3. Violence–Political aspects–El Salvador. I. Title.

HN190.Z9V545 20

303.6097284–dc22

2009038776

A catalogue record for this book is available from the British Library.

Set in 10 on 13pt and Palatino
by Laserwords Private Limited, Chennai, India
Printed and bound in the United Kingdom by Page Brothers, Norwich

Contents

Dedication

For my parents, Pat and John

Preface

The Politics of Violence: Gender, Conflict and Community in El Salvador

BY MO HUME

University of Glasgow, UK

Bulletin of Latin American Research Book Series

SERIES EDITORS: DAVID HOWARD, JASMINE GIDEON, GEOFFREY KANTARIS, TONY KAPCIA AND LUCY TAYLOR

The *Bulletin of Latin American Research* (*BLAR*) has a distinguished history of publishing primary research from a range of disciplines in Latin American studies. Our readers have long been able to draw upon ideas from History, Geography, Politics, International Relations, Anthropology, Sociology, Economics, Gender Studies, Development Studies and, increasingly, Cultural Studies. Many of our articles have addressed thematic topics and debates of interest to all Latin Americanists, such as *mestizaje*, populism or the politics of social movements. This is one of the great strengths of being an area studies journal rather than a discipline-based publication. The current book series thus aims to complement the multidisciplinarity of the journal by publishing original and innovative research from scholars who are working across disciplines, raising new questions and applying fresh methodologies. The series seeks to develop into a major forum for interdisciplinary work in Latin American Studies.

This second volume in the series arose from the author's longstanding engagement with El Salvadorean society as a development worker and researcher. Mo Hume has incorporated her depth of experience and knowledge to produce a new perspective on the processes of violence in the Americas, developing an original feminist standpoint on the multiple aggressions that shape the 'everyday'. Her work both illuminates previous studies on violence across the region, and builds on the importance of detailing a gendered ethnographic approach to reveal the overt, as well as more hidden or silent, spaces of violence in society.

Acknowledgements

This book is a product of my evolving thoughts on violence. It has been enriched by conversations with many people and engagement with a broad range of existing work on violence. The analysis presented in the pages that follow does not pretend to be definite or complete. I am also very conscious that it is not an optimistic book.

Without the tremendous generosity of the research participants who shared their stories, this book would never have been written. To them I owe a huge debt that cannot be adequately expressed in words. Unlike me, they cannot retreat to the comfort of academic life to ponder on ambiguities and epistemologies. Instead, they must engage with the politics of surviving and resisting violence on an everyday basis. I particularly wish to acknowledge the students of the school in 'El Boulevar'. The drawing on the cover of the book is by 'Ruben', a thirteen year old boy from the community. It is entitled 'Mi Comunidad' (My Community).

I have been very lucky to work with a great editorial team at Wiley Blackwell and the *Bulletin of Latin American Research*. First, I owe a big thank you to the journal's editors, Jean Grugel and David Howard, whose support and encouragement has been consistently generous. Thanks also must go to Matt Jenkins, Ken Lestrange and Jacqueline Scott who have been very helpful throughout the different stages of production. I would also like to thank an anonymous reviewer whose insightful comments on the manuscript were very helpful.

The book began its life as my doctoral thesis. The research would not have been possible without the financial backing of the University of Liverpool, the Society for Latin American Studies and the Economic and Social Research Council. I learned a lot from the tutelage and friendship of my supervisors, Nikki Craske and Andy Davies, whose faith, guidance and support were invaluable throughout. My dearest friend and office mate, Anne-Marie Smith shared much of the angst—existential and otherwise. She also shared also a lot of laughter. *La otra mosquatera*, Luz Estela Villarreal, did not live to see this book finished. I will always think of our friendship with a smile. Lewis Taylor, my 'mentor' offered valuable advice despite the fact that I had strayed beyond the Peruvian border. Anita Schrader keeps the debate alive with regular conversations about Central America. Ronnie Munck has both challenged and supported this project intellectually. I am grateful to him on both counts. Felix Zamora brought Chilean song to the darkest of English winters. Thanks also go to my good friends in Liverpool: Sarah and Joe Penny, Ian Sharpes and Diane Breeze.

My interest in Central America began many years ago and, like many others, I was attracted to the region because of its politics and its poetry. The words of Ruben Darío and Ernesto Cardenal led me to Roque Dalton, Claribel Alegría and Manlio Argueta. Thanks must go to Lorna Shaughnessy for making the introduction! In recent years, Stuart Cullen generously advised me on making contact with the police in San Salvador, and I have very much enjoyed our communications and debates. Jenny Pearce has offered invaluable support–both practical and intellectual–for which I am very grateful. The study of Latin America remains vibrant in the UK. I have benefited greatly from the comradeship and exchanges with many members of the 'community'. In particular, I would like to acknowledge: Laurence Allen, Jelke Boesten, Cath Collins, Cathy McIlwaine, Ulrich Oslender, Dennis Rodgers, Rachel Sieder, Polly Wilding and Ailsa Winton. Across the Irish Sea, I cannot forget my old and dear friend, Barry Cannon.

The Department of Politics at the University of Glasgow is a highly supportive and friendly environment in which to work. Special thanks to Maurizio Carbone, Chris Corrin, Kelly Kollman, Ana Langer (not least of all for her advice on aesthetics), Kurt Mills, Sarah Oates, Cian O'Driscoll, Barry O'Toole, David Stansfield, Vikki Turbine, Myrto Tsakatika and Alasdair Young. Our administrative team deserves extra thanks. Thanks also to Orian Brook and Karen Wright who endure nights out and weeks on remote Scottish islands with the Politics 'gang' with unwavering good humour and to Teresa Flavin and Geraldine McDonald. All of the above help make Glasgow an extra lovely place to live. Thanks also to my old(er) friend, Roma Cassidy who provided very welcome distractions with her daily updates and culinary brilliance.

In El Salvador, the list is long and without the kindness of many people, this project would never have been completed. I wish to thank everyone at FLACSO (the Latin American Faculty for Social Sciences), who gave me office space in San Salvador and very useful guidance throughout fieldwork in 2001–2002. Carlos Ramos raised certain 'epistemological suspicions' that have benefited my analysis. Special thanks to Kay Andrade and Wim Savenije. The exchange of ideas has been stimulating and the friendship continues to be invaluable. I am very grateful to my dear friend, José Manuel Ramirez, who sparked many an idea and accompanied me on some of the interviews. I wish to thank Gilma Henriquez, Guillermo Garcia and Mirna Peralta for facilitating prison visits and interviews; I have enjoyed conversations with José Miguel Cruz, whose own work has inspired me in many ways. Special thanks also to Edgardo Amaya, Augusto Cotto, Martin Dwan, the marvellous Conor Fox, Jorge Granadillo, the 'fantabulously witty' Helen O'Malley, Sally O'Neill, Gustavo Pineda, Hugo Ramirez, Elin Ranum, Vladimir Solórzano and my former colleagues in Movimeniento de Mujeres Mélida Anaya Montes and Progressio.

In 2007 and 2008, I carried out some research for Oxfam America in the municipalities of Ahuachapan and San Marcos. I very much enjoyed working with the whole team and I am very grateful that they allowed me to use some of the material here. Particular thanks go to Marilyn, Gloria, Allison, Mélida, Isabel, Ana Ruth, Blanca Edith, Yanira and all the women who made the research possible.

The Guadron Hernandez family–Margarita, Alfonso, Mauxy, Jim and most recently, Mercedes–have provided a home from home in San Salvador and I can never thank them enough. Margarita's *frijoles* are legendary. More important has been the friendship and laughter shared over many years. Gloria, Fernando and Manuel Enrique Romero Domiguez have indulged my love for the sea and I treasure the moments shared. Gilberto Arriaza and Mercy Cornejo came to Ireland to paint murals and to share their dreams of a life beyond violence. Thank you. I was extremely lucky to meet Helene Van Acker during my first week in El Salvador. We worked together for a while and I learned a great deal from her. I have been humbled and inspired by her courage and her unfailing belief in the power of humanity. Gracias mujer! Rhina Clará Salinas sends me a *crónica del mes* and has been a guiding inspiration to this project. She has reminded me that that idealism is not only possible, but worth the struggle.

I am grateful to Tess and Mike Featherstone for their generous hospitality in their wonderful wee corner of Wales and for the 'proper' letters that provide a lovely distraction to a Glasgow morning. I also wish to acknowledge Marni who shares happy moments of 'girlie time' that I find go very well indeed with my feminist politics.

Most of this book was written in the wonderful space provided by my parents in Donegal. I am grateful to my lovely sisters, Thérése and Áine, who patiently read various chapters and to my brothers, Aidan and John, who have inspired much of my critical engagement with masculinities! They and their partners have been the source of much love, laughter and support. A special thanks to my brother-in-law, Kevin Abbott, for the rather perfect location of the hammock and to all the (not so) baby Abbotts, Humes and Brittons for whom I struggle for the position of favourite aunty! Most of all, I wish to thank my parents, Pat and John, who gave so much and have always been unconditional in their love.

My partner, Dave Featherstone, has been an unfailing source of love, support and engagement throughout. He is my first–and favourite–reader and he has enriched the experience of writing this book in immeasurable ways. He also provided the musical soundtrack to the writing and I can only apologise if I was not always the most receptive audience!

Notes on previously published sections of this book:

Elements of Chapter 5 were previously published as:

Hume, M. (2007) 'Mano Dura: El Salvador Responds to Gangs'. *Development in Practice* 17(6): 725–738

Sections of Chapters 3 and 4 have appeared in the following:

Hume, M. (2008) 'The Myths of Violence: Gender, Community and Conflict in El Salvador'. *Latin American Perspectives* **35**(5): 59–76.

Hume, M. (2006) 'Contesting Imagined Communities: Gender, Nation and Violence in El Salvador' in W. Fowler and P. Lambert (eds.) *Political Violence and the Construction of National Identity in Latin America*. Palgrave Macmillan: London, 73–90.

Introduction

The bus that used to go up the hill, well they killed the [bus driver]. They're always killing people up there and they're people from the same area and they charge them 'rent' ... They killed him. They always kill up there. There used to be another bus that took people up but they killed him too ... My brother goes from work straight home but they have followed him from work several times. Before, nothing happened to my brothers, they killed my cousin, but the violence here is down to the problem of poverty that there is in the country and that is why there is so much violence because they are even charging 'rent' to the shops, and the worst thing is that there is no work and a lot of violence. (Ana, San Marcos)

In October 2007, I returned to the municipality of San Marcos, a satellite town on the outskirts of San Salvador. I had previously worked in some of the communities on the steep slopes of the Cerro San Jacinto in San Marcos in the late 1990s as part of my work with a local women's organisation, *Movimiento de Mujeres Mélida Anaya Montes*. My role at this time was to work alongside the women of the communities as they articulated their development concerns and tried to lobby local institutions for their resolution. The issue that struck me most about the process was how different forms of violence shaped and constrained both women's livelihood concerns and their strategies to overcome them. In San Marcos, access to water in the communities was limited and the communal tap that served the neighbourhood was locked by a local resident who charged her neighbours for each *cantaro* or container of water. This was an issue of primary concern for the women, but not an issue that they felt they could address. The woman who controlled the water had two well-armed sons who 'protected' her interests. In addition, she was a member of the governing ARENA (National Republican Alliance Party) party that was in power from 1989 until 2009 and it was felt that she had contacts in important places that afforded her additional 'protection'.

In community residents' minds, this meant that she was untouchable and free to act with impunity, restricting their access to water. Attempts to lobby Administración Nacional de Acueductos y Alcantarillados (ANDA), the national water company, had proved futile and the women were resigned to the fact that they would continue to pay for the use of the tap. Another issue that concerned the residents at this stage was the need for a bus route to take them to the top of the hill. This was for security as well as practical reasons. Not only did women have to walk up a steep hill and often with heavy loads, but there were points on the hill where local youth congregated. Frequently they asked women for a *colon* when they walked past and there was some concern about the growing gang presence in the area.[1] In response, local women lobbied the Ministry for Public Works to fix the road and they petitioned the local transport companies to provide a minibus service (see MAM, 1999). Their petition was successful and a minibus route started in 1999. Almost ten years later when I returned to San Marcos, the service had just stopped. The narrative cited above is from a focus group with women in late 2007. The women explain that the bus driver had refused to pay local gang members *renta* or protection money. As a result, he was killed.

This is a book about violence. It is a story of how different forms of violence affect everyday lives in post-war El Salvador. The site of a brutal civil war from 1980 to 1992, El Salvador's peace remains characterised by violence and insecurity. The introductory narrative exposes a vicious circle of developing violence in which problems of fear, inequality and corruption continue to shape citizens' experiences and understandings of everyday life in the post-war period. It points to a world in which constant levels of threat have deeply destructive effects on individuals and communities, not only resulting in physical harm, but restricting livelihood opportunities. The women interviewed indicated that the perpetrators are local residents known to the community. Many are neighbours and friends. Restricted access to water not only highlights local corruption, but also the perceptions of impunity that are linked to national politics. In this context, the threat and actuality of violence does not come from a nameless stranger or group, but from the very people that form part of the community. Such experiences and perceptions of violence expose the immediacy and proximity of violence to everyday social interactions of many citizens of Latin America.

The episode of localised violence above uncovers some of the complexities of conflict and community in El Salvador. While the study is situated in localised structures of power in El Salvador, the stories that the research participants tell reflect larger narratives of oppression that are shaped along

---

1   The *colon* was the national currency of El Salvador until the US dollar was introduced in January 2001. Officially the *colon* is still in circulation but, in practice, the dollar has replaced it.

class, ethnic and gender grounds. The pages that follow are not merely a story of El Salvador; they offer insight into the lives of communities who must negotiate high levels of violence in Latin America and beyond. The empirical assessment of the multiple and often contradictory meanings of violence in everyday life provides important insights into the wider politics of violence. Without applying this knowledge 'from below' and reclaiming this interpretative space, the theorisation of violence is limited. Multiple expressions of violence overlap to shape everyday life and responses are often contradictory and confusing. This book challenges some of the socially accepted myths that contribute to the reproduction of violence, in terms of both its meaning and its material effects. By using the term myth, I do not wish to discount individuals' interpretations of their own realities. Instead, I am referring to the accepted (and often unquestioned) norms and values that shape both the ontological and epistemological appreciation of violence. How do individuals and communities live with the painful and emotive forces of violence in everyday life? How do individuals and groups come to understand and recognise violence in their own lives? To what extent do gendered norms and identities colour this process of definition? What dominant discourses within society inform and shape this process of making violence both visible and hidden?

The proposal here is to generate knowledge about violence in El Salvador beyond that which is deemed 'official' or that which relies on dominant voices. In this exercise, I draw on the methodology of subaltern studies which proposes an alternative historiography to that of dominant or elite groups (Guha, 2000; O'Hanlon, 2000a, 2000b; Rodríguez, 2001). Given the particular ideological and moral potency of narratives of violence, I am concerned with foregrounding the voices of those subaltern groups who have been historically ignored and excluded from 'official' definitions of violence and will examine the vocabularies of violence used by those people who live with it on an everyday basis. The analysis is informed by life histories of men and women from low-income communities. This approach is based on the critical understanding that an episode of violence only contains the *potential* for being defined as violence and whilst some actors may define the actions as violent, others may not (Cavanagh, Dobash, Dobash and Lewis, 2001).

The study is grounded in the politics of feminism and contributes more broadly to the critical theoretical propositions that question how knowledge is produced, for whom and by whom. My position is informed by a feminist interpretive methodology whereby a theoretical examination of violence is both framed and unsettled by empirical realities. In other words, I am concerned with 'how' violence becomes possible rather than the direct causal analysis of 'why' it becomes possible (Jansen and Davis, 1998). Knowledge from below can offer critical insights into how violence is understood, mediated and legitimised in other contexts. Locating the analysis in local structures of power and oppression also uncovers organic strategies for surviving and resisting violence, those behaviours that James Scott (1990) might call 'hidden transcripts' of resistance. This contributes to feminist debates about situating theory in lived experiences. Edward Said (1986) reminds us that knowledge is more than self referential; it is always a product of power relations. I am therefore concerned with the gendered politics of violence: the recognition of an act as violent, contestation over meaning and the missing stories of violence. Feminism has provided a much necessary perspective from which to question and critique what is said about violence; crucially, it also demands an engagement with what is not said, particularly concerning violence against women (Radford and Kelly, 1998). Its intellectual rationale is rooted in silence and absence.

Important to this exercise is the recognition of the heterogeneous nature of subaltern histories that are themselves productive of competing narratives based on localised hierarchies of power (Gidwani, 2009; see also Scott, 1990). The central argument of this book is that this is a particularly gendered process whereby violence against women and children is normalised and rationalised under 'acceptable' codes of men's behaviour. This not only demands an analysis of women and children's experiences of violence, but a critical engagement with men and masculinities. Mainstream approaches to violence have failed to acknowledge or simply ignored the gendered politics of violence in both public and private realms. A key contention of a feminist approach has been that historic epistemologies of violence have been constructed on a reductionist and binary logic of exclusion/inclusion, with a clear distinction between what counts as violence and what does not, ignoring its important ideological and discursive dimensions (Kelly and Radford, 1996). Most analytical endeavours and political responses to growing citizen insecurity in Latin America are heavily reliant on an exclusively public reading of security. This belies the fact that much of the violence that affects women and children occurs in the home. The result of this separation between 'public' security and the safety of women and children has multiple implications. This approach misses historic practices of violence and keeps them hidden from public scrutiny. It also offers an incomplete analysis of violence, ignoring important linkages between violence in the home and violence in the street. More than a mere intellectual bias, it is a statement about the politics of power (Ramazanoglu, 1992: 341). In this vein, I hope that the book will contribute to a debate that moves an analysis of gender to the centre of the theorisation of violence, rather merely as a particular type or subset of violence.

El Salvador: Situating Violence in History

El Salvador provides a brutal case study about the use of violence by the state, its agents and within wider society. Salvadoran history does not make for comfortable reading; it is a history 'defined' by violence (Huezo Mixco, 2000). The small Central American republic was the site of a civil war between 1980 and 1992, which claimed over 75,000 lives and led to the displacement of more than a million men, women and children in the region (United Nations (UN), 1995; Ardón, 1998). Following a military stalemate by the end of the 1980s, the reduction of military aid from the United States, and increased pressure from the international community, the UN brokered the January 1992 Chapultepec Peace Accords, signed by the high command of the Frente Farabundo Martí para la Liberación Nacional (FMLN) and government members. The accords brought a very real hope of replacing violence with meaningful peace for Salvadoran citizens. Nonetheless, the reality of this peace remains contested (Popkin, 2000; Hume, 2008a). In an analysis of the ten years after the peace accords, the Central American University's Human Rights Institute (IDHUCA, 2002: 2) stated: 'there is little discernable difference between the point of departure and the point of arrival; the issues are the same: the majority of the population is excluded and vulnerable'.

Economics, politics and violence have been a potent and destructive combination in Salvadoran history and continue to undermine citizens' well-being. Historically, El Salvador has been one of the most unequal countries in Latin America and socio-economic issues are seen to be at the heart of political conflict. Nonetheless, the peace accords and subsequent government policies systematically failed to address the social and economic fault lines that had triggered the war. Pearce (1998: 589) disputes the idea that the region's conflicts have been 'resolved'. This may be true at the 'formal level of peace accords between armies and insurgents, but is less so at the real level of people's everyday lives', which remain marked by exclusion, poverty and violence. Rather than dissipating after the war, violence has characterised El Salvador's peace. The post-war period has seen a dramatic rise in crime, youth violence and so-called 'social violence'. Between 2004 and April 2008, there were 15,153 murders. In 2007, the year that registered the lowest murder rate since 2002, this averages out at 60.78 murders per 100,000 citizens (FESPAD, 2008).[2] In peace, the country stands out as one of the most violent countries in

---

2   2007 census figures estimate that the population is 5,744,113, significantly lower than the figures that had been managed by National Census and Statistics Directorate, which estimated that the population in 2006 was 6,980,279 (DIGESTYC, 2007: 3; FESPAD, 2008). This changes the per capita murder rate for previous years, which had been based on the higher estimates. These new figures indicate that the problem

the world. This continued context of violence demands a critical analysis of the 'ideological continuities' of conflict and difference with a view to moving beyond reductive discussions of the 'metamorphosis of violence from one domain or form to another' (Binford, 2002: 205).

The war has proved a key moment for the analysis of social and political processes. It has become the single most important focus for studies on El Salvador and the country's history is regularly divided into 'before' and 'after' (Mason, 1999). While the armed conflict invariably constituted an intensity of violence that transcends all aspects of social and political relations to the present day, it is much too simplistic to reduce the analysis of violence to a post-war phenomenon.[3] Extreme terror was used by the Salvadoran state from Independence onwards in order to ensure the continued social and economic hegemony of a small agro-export elite: 'one of the smallest, most omnipotent, pugnacious and reactionary in the world' (Dunkerley, 1982: 7). This group, popularly referred to as the 'fourteen families', created the conditions in El Salvador to assure maximum control over the resources of the country at the expense of the masses. Wood (2003: 22) stresses the significance of the clientelistic relations between local economic elites and peasants for the maintenance of this order. The cost of transgressing these local rules of engagement was 'everything: work, food and home'. A key way of ensuring peasant subordination was through the use of overt violence, often with the active collaboration of state agents in the form of the National Guard and local residents (Alvarenga, 1996).

Far from being a response, the excesses of violence perpetrated by the state were strategic and calculated in order to demonstrate the existence of a threat to the privileged position of the economic élite. 'Extreme repression helped create an impression of extreme danger' and not the other way round (Stanley, 1996: 53). In this way, violence became functional, allowing the military to justify its usefulness to the oligarchy and at the same time maintain its control of the state (Williams and Walter, 1997; Mason, 1999). Elite groups not only appeared content to ignore the excesses of military brutality in order to maintain hegemony, but actively bought into the rationalisation and legitimisation of force as a political and economic tool. Historically, therefore, violence and economics have between intertwined. Lauria-Santiago (2005: 90) notes that a distinguishing feature of El Salvador is an occurrence of '*all* the structural elements that might be seen to generate a violently repressive state' (emphasis in original). This is developed further in Chapter 2.

---

of violence is actually more serious than previously imagined. I return to this issue in Chapter 2.

3   For an interesting debate on this issue, see the dialogue in the journal *Ethnography* between Philippe Bourgois (2001) and Leigh Binford (2002).

One of the most brutal examples of the spread of violence was the killing of some 30,000 indigenous people by military forces after a tentative uprising in January 1932, mostly in the western part of the country. At a rough estimate, this constituted some 2 per cent of the population (Stanley, 1996, citing Paige, 1994: 2). This episode, *la Matanza*, has been judged as: 'perhaps the single most important event in Salvadoran history; it is indelibly etched into the nation's collective memory both as a momentous occurrence in itself and as the matrix through which all succeeding developments have been understood' (Dunkerley, 1982: 9). For citizens, *la Matanza* demonstrated not only that the state was willing to employ genocidal tactics, but provided a reminder of the cost of dissent that was 'unique' to Central America (Dunkerley, 1988: 340). The official explanation of this event as a 'necessary massacre' in order to prevent the spread of communism provided for future generations 'an echo chamber, a language, and a confirmed justification for what was perceived as the necessary solution to problems of social and political mobilisation from below' (Lauria-Santiago, 2005: 92). Following *La Matanza*, the Salvadoran military took control of the apparatus of the state, while the financial elites maintained control of capital. Sustained repression and an indiscriminate use of violence became an element of everyday life for citizens during the decades of military rule, reaching a peak in the 1970s and 1980s, coinciding with the outbreak of the war in 1980. The collective and competing memories of this repressive political economy have proved important for the development of social relations in contemporary El Salvador and remain important to understanding contemporary political polarisation.

This history of El Salvador is still 'contested' and the interpretative domination of El Salvador's 'official' history is grounded in silencing important sections of the population, particularly those who were victims of state violence (see Gaborit, 2007). Historically, fomenting violent conflict and a politics of fear was an important tool for the political survival of the Salvadoran state on both discursive and material plains. A bipolar construction of society between *los malos* (the bad) and *los buenos* (the good) has been used as important political rhetoric by the state to spread fear and legitimise repression (Martín-Baró, 1983). This judgemental and moral tone appealed not only to the fears of El Salvador's elites, but its emotive content spoke to a wider citizenry. Historically ordered within a logic of 'anticommunism' that had predated the 1932 massacre and continued throughout the war, a rationale was provided for state-sanctioned force. The official discourse of violence was therefore employed strategically to legitimise state terror. In this way, violence was constructed as being functional and necessary for the national interest.

To relocate Allen Feldman's (1991) reading of violence in Northern Ireland, the 'dominant morality' in El Salvador was about legitimising one form of violence over another, rather than rejecting its practice. For state violence to achieve a degree of effectiveness in El Salvador, it had to engage local populations. The perpetrators of violence were therefore not only invisible death squads and uniformed combatants, but local networks of neighbours, family members and friends. Those who live in contexts of violence 'do not escape unscathed' and their responses are reflective of broader relations of power within society (Bourgois, 2001: 30). I am interested in how historic 'explanations' and indeed justifications of violence continue to resonate in contemporary discourse. These not only make their mark on official processes of memorialisation, but affect how violence is recognised and awarded meaning in the contemporary scenario. Echoes of these historic rhetorics of oppression based on class, gender and age still reverberate in current debates in the post-war context on violence.

Both government and citizen responses to growing violence in the post-war context have been, at best, fragmented and, at worst, have exacerbated existing tensions within communities and across society more generally. Responses to violence are not merely random ways of 'reacting'; they are purposeful and calculated (Cavanagh, Dobash, Dobash and Lewis, 2001: 698–699). A politics of fear continues to shape responses on different levels and fear itself is now considered a major threat to democracy (Balan, 2002). Fear is rarely 'objective' and often it does not respond to actual levels of threat or levels of victimisation (Lechner, 1992). The 'talk of crime' among citizens and the political mobilisation of a rhetoric of fear have pushed societies to extreme polarities. Such 'talk' invokes a moral discourse that creates illusory distinctions between 'good' and 'bad' citizens, much in the same way as 'anti-communist' rhetoric did in previous years (see Snodgrass Godoy, 2006 on Guatemala and Calderia, 2000 on Brazil). Many 'good' citizens respond to fear by demanding greater security and hard-line policies, which appear to contradict and undermine the process of democratisation. This is evidenced in public policy response at national and international levels whereby governments adopt a heavy-handed or zero tolerance approach to crime. In practice, this usually means targeting or criminalising certain groups within society such as youth or the poor in displays of 'punitive populism' (see also ECA, 2005). I develop this line of argument further in Chapter 5.

One of the main targets for such policies are youth gangs, or *maras* as they are known in Central America. Since the end of the war (and notably since the late 1990s), youth gangs have emerged as one of the most visible and feared expressions of violence in Latin America (Rodgers, 2006). Various theories have been put forward to explain their emergence, though it is generally accepted that there is no single identifiable cause and that gangs are an evolving and increasingly sophisticated phenomenon (see, for example,

Rodgers, 1999; Winton, 2004; Aguilar and Miranda, 2006). The emergence of gangs in El Salvador has been attributed to problems of social exclusion, patterns of migration and the fragmentation of families because of economic imperatives, and few livelihood opportunities for youth (Savenije and Van der Borgh, 2004). Research from the region links *maras* to localised drug provision and consumption, sexual violence and extortion (IUDOP, 1998; Cruz, 1999; ERIC, IDESO, IDIES and IUDOP, 2001, 2004). Research in the late 1990s and early 2000s, suggests that the gang provides an important sense of belonging and identity for many young people (Smutt and Miranda, 1999; Miranda, 2000; Santacruz Giralt and Concha-Eastman, 2001). This is an identity based largely on the use of violence and is particularly notable in the behaviours and attitudes of young male gang-members who display aggressive notions of maleness or 'hegemonic masculinity' (Connell, 1987). The male role model here is based on a reproduction of domination and aggression. Violence against women in the gang is common, both as part of the general *modus operandi* of the gang, but also in particularly gendered forms. Young women often face highly sexualised forms of violence from within. The use of violence within the gang has evolved and become much more sophisticated in the 2000s. This is in no small part a result of state responses to gangs.

The series of heavy-handed anti-gang measures adopted by the Salvadoran government since 2003 are a case in point. El Salvador's *Mano Dura* ('Heavy Hand') policy was introduced in July 2003 and is reflected in many similar initiatives across Central America. The plan advocated the mass arrest and immediate imprisonment of gang members or suspected gang members. The vagueness of the criteria meant that the plan was reliant on stereotypes of poor urban youth, who can be arrested 'simply for having gang-related tattoos or flashing signs' (Boraz and Bruneau, 2006: 38). Although no longer an official policy and widely regarded as a failure, little has changed in the practice of targeting poor urban youth. On a more extreme level, cases of police brutality, summary 'justice' and revenge killings have been reported in recent years. These should be contextualised as an endpoint in a broader continuity of exclusion and polarisation, not as something outside *normal* social relations. They are indicative of the endurance of a hegemonic political project that continues to silence alternatives to the use of force. Few preventative strategies exist. Neither violence nor many of the responses to it displace the historic logic that repression and the form of control it generates is functional. It is therefore important to situate this study of everyday violence within an analysis of state and social responses.

A Feminist Interrogation of Violence in Latin America

Increasingly, the problem of violence has been at the forefront of research on Latin America and other countries emerging from political conflict, such as South Africa and Northern Ireland (for example, Scheper-Hughes, 1998; Monaghan, 2008). Crime and violence have emerged alongside and been seen as antagonistic to democratising processes in many parts of the world. This blurs the boundaries between 'war' and 'peace' (for example, Pearce, 1998; Keen, 2000; AVPI, 2004; Moser and McIlwaine, 2004; Pugh, Cooper and McDonald, forthcoming). In many countries of Latin America, violence and crime have 'acquired alarming proportions and dimensions' (Concha-Eastman, 2001: 37). High levels of violence are regarded as 'inconsistent' with democracy and the emergence of non-state violent actors is now considered a major threat to democratic stability in the region (McCoy, 2006). This threat is rooted in both the scale of the phenomenon as well as the incapacity of democratically elected governments to address it in any effective manner (Howard, Hume and Oslender, 2007). However, the problem of violence is not new to Latin America. Issues of conflict and inequality have dominated research on the region for decades. Earlier work focused principally upon issues of political violence; for example, military rule and the role of the state as a violent actor (for example, O'Brien and Cammack, 1985; Stanley, 1996; Williams and Walter, 1997; McClintock, 1998). Other work has looked at revolutionary struggles and guerrilla groups (for example, Wickham-Crowley, 1992; McClintock, 1998). More recently, in an effort to understand the place of violence in the emergent democracies, there has been an outpouring of research on its 'new' and criminal expressions (for example: Kooning and Kruijt 1999, 2004; Méndez, 1999). Notwithstanding these important and rich debates, existing frameworks for understanding violence in the post-war period are limited and a new analytical vocabulary is needed urgently to begin to comprehend growing levels of violence in what Bourgois (2001: 5) has termed 'a neo-liberal version of peacetime'.

Moser and McIlwaine (2004) develop a continuum of social, economic and political violence in order to highlight the connections between each type. In this way, social and economic violence cannot merely replace political violence. This allows us to understand how, for example, violence against women can be both a weapon of war and a pervasive force in times of peace. Others authors have suggested that contemporary forms of violence are also political, since they result from political choices, such as policies that have exacerbated inequalities and the continued failure of governments to address structural problems (see, for example, ECA, 1999 on El Salvador; Tedesco, 2000 on Argentina and Pinheiro, 1996 on Brazil). Rotker (2002: 18) understands current levels of violence as an 'undeclared civil war' in major

Latin American cities, seeing them as rooted in protest, albeit random and unorganised, against pervasive structural inequalities:

> This undeclared civil war clearly engages elements of fear and rage, but it is no longer a question of planting bombs or hiding in the mountains to take up arms against a dictator or corrupt government. It deals instead with a violence that resists a whole system, creating it in a more profound way, at the heart of its social relations (Rotker, 2002: 18)

Viewing the response of marginalised groups as violent political protest offers a plausible and politically committed framework for analysis (see Bourgois, 2001, 2002). I do not discount this approach, but wish to foreground my concern with overly simplistic linkages between historic forms of civil society protest and contemporary violence. Violent political protest in previous decades was generally motivated by collective and emancipatory goals to dismantle structural inequalities and the mechanisms of state repression. Much contemporary violence, on the other hand, is more individual in character and tends to be motivated by consumption rather than redistribution. Further, the particular violent forms of masculinities that are mobilised suggest that this 'protest' also mimics patriarchal and misogynistic tendencies of hegemonic groups. This caution does not, however, discount the fact that contemporary violence continues to be rooted in and against continued exclusion and dispossession.

Given the centrality of this theme to the study of Latin America and repeated calls for a 'holistic' approach to research, it is perhaps surprising at how knowledge remains characterised by a certain 'disciplinary fragmentation', and 'under' theorisation (Moore, 1994; Moser and McIlwaine, 2004). Increasing violence has presented a challenge to the region in both theoretical and practical terms. It has been characterised by its 'ubiquity', its 'banality' and its 'everydayness' (for example, Pécaut, 1999; Torres-Rivas, 1999; Rotker, 2002). Informed by this existing research, this book situates contemporary forms of crime and violence in their wider historical and political context to ask to what extent has violence become 'banal' or more crucially, which types of violence are termed 'banal'? What are, as Pécaut (1999) asks in the context of Colombia, the historic continuities and discontinuities that provide the clues for understanding this increasingly 'prosaic' phenomenon? Can it not be framed as new moves in an old game, in which violence may not be understood as new but different? (Peireira and Davis, 2000: 4). What is the distinction between 'old' forms of violence that challenged the power of the state and the 'new' violence that is characterised by its arbitrariness, its 'democratisation' and its location in 'non conflict zones'? (Kooning and Kruijt, 1999, 2004; Rodgers and Moser, 2005). These questions underscore some of the central concerns of this book.

In this exercise, my approach is self-consciously feminist. Many scholars now claim the validity of cross-/inter-/multi-/transdisciplinary approaches to the study of violence notably, though not exclusively, in Latin American studies (Levine, 2003, Moser and McIlwaine, 2004; Oxhorn, 2008). Feminism has historically invoked vocabularies and methods from different disciplines in a critical manner in order to promote a transformative and politicised knowledge: a way of telling 'new stories' (Scott, 2004: 24; see also: Pryse, 2000). The analysis that follows is based on a concerted attempt to move beyond the boundaries and 'exclusivities' of any one discipline and enter into a dialogue between social science research and the rich empirical debates within area studies (see Jackson, 2006). Rather than telling the 'new stories' about violence, I hope to forge a space for old and often unspoken stories to be articulated. A project grounded in key principles of feminist research involves more than 'adding' women into existing violence research and 'stirring': 'it is not enough rhetorically or theoretically to "add women and stir". We need to completely change the empirical focus' (Zalewski, 1995: 348; see also: Chesney-Lind, 1986: 81). It requires a process of deconstructing existing patterns of knowledge to reveal the centrality of muteness and silence that discipline what we know. In other words, I am invoking the broad critical methodology of feminism to challenge how the 'story' about violence has been monopolised by dominant groups in El Salvador.

Researching Violence: The Personal is Political

The research started out as a personal and political response to having worked in low-income communities in El Salvador. Echoing Dunkerley (1982: 1), this book is 'the product not only of study and political conviction but also outrage'. Although I am writing at a very different political moment, I continue to empathise with Dunkerley's 'outrage' when I listen to the life histories of Salvadorans and witness their continued struggle for justice, security and quality of life. 'Para que?' (For what?) was the question asked by a peasant mother of five in northern Usulutan when I interviewed her in 1997 as part of my work with a local women's organisation. She had lived for many years in refugee camp in Honduras; two of her children were killed by the military and she still lived in abject poverty. Other women shared her despair. Binford (2002) recalls similar sentiments in Morazan where people felt in worse economic, physical and social shape than before the war. Materially little has changed for El Salvador's poor with the socio-economic factors that sparked the conflict 'remarkably absent' from the peace accords (Stanley, 2006: 109). In 2005, poverty levels stood at 47.5 per cent with 19 per cent living in extreme poverty (ECLAC, 2007: 11). In 1980, the number of poor was 51 per cent, growing to 56 per cent in 1986, so although figures have not 'worsened since the end of the war, ... neither have they improved significantly' (Pearce, 1998: 592). The United Nations Development Programme (UNDP) puts the GINI coefficient, which measures income distribution *per capita*, at 0.48 in 2006 (UNDP, 2007: 350). Phillips (2007) speaks of a new political economy of dispossession and inequality in the region where the population is increasingly reliant on family remittances for survival. Indeed, some citizens feel that the contemporary situation 'is worse because before if you did not get involved in politics, you did not get killed; now it is different: you could be at home and you could be killed there' (Cruz et al., 1999a: 3, citing IUDOP, 1996: 240). Violence has certainly evolved in recent years and the promise of the new institutions has not been realised. The peace process and its expected dividends appear to have eluded them, and, although the actors may have changed, insecurity and fear are still a routine element of daily life.

The effects of armed conflict and preceding decades of state terror should not be underestimated. They continue to reverberate in economic, political and social terms throughout El Salvador. The country remains one of the most politically polarised in the region. Politicians from the left and right continue to trade historic insults in the Legislative Assembly. The consequences of limited (post-)transition politics, thwarted opportunities for transforming the landscapes of conflict and aggressive neoliberalism have combined to deepen historic structural inequalities. Dollarisation was introduced in 2001 to the advantage of the country's financial elite, but with harsh effects for its poor and the sectors that generated most employment such as agriculture and manufacturing (Towers, 2004; Stanley, 2006). Migration to the United States has become a key strategy for combating poverty on both macro and micro levels: remittances reached over $2.5 billions in 2004 and accounted for an estimated 16 per cent of the GDP. This is more than double the annual budget for social spending in the same year (IDHES, 2005). Over 20 per cent of the population live outside the country.

It is against this backdrop that I understand outrage not as a destructive emotion that prejudices the analytical process, but as a force that needs to be 'contextualised, theorised and politicised' in order to rupture the silences that so often underpin the research endeavour (Pickering, 2001: 486). Emotion in research has been described by elements of the academy as 'intellectually irrelevant' and positivist notions of 'objective' and value-free research are still held up as an attainable goal by many (Pickering, 2001: 485; see also, Tickner, 2005; Waylen, 2006). A distinguishing feature of a feminist methodology is its central concern that research is not and cannot be a value-free endeavour;

rather it is shaped by our 'personal, political and intellectual biographies as researchers' (Ribbens and Edwards, 1997: 120). Hearn (1998: 56) argues that, 'violence is a potentially powerful topic to research because it connects with other powerful experiences in researchers own lives'. 'Knowledge' cannot be presented as separate from the process through which it was made (Stanley and Wise, 2000). Opening up emotional engagements and seeing them as creative elements of the analytical process, rather than something to be excluded, both challenges and stretches existing theoretical approaches to the study of violence.

As such, I believe that it is paramount to foreground the emotions and implicit 'moral tension' in our research, particularly on 'sensitive' subjects such as violence (Renzetti and Lee, 1995; Bourgois, 2001; Rodgers, 2001). Post-colonial feminists have been critical of the historic tendency of Northern women to 'speak' for and about women in the Global South (Mohanty, 1991). This tension demands recognition of the 'power differentials' among the participants of the research, with the understanding that violence 'does not just occur between two independent individuals . . . [it] is located in a complex set of relations . . . [that] affects the way individuals use and give meaning to experiences of violence. Any research on violence therefore is ultimately a narrative on the morality of social space and social privilege' (Liebling and Stanko, 2001: 428). As researchers, we are not immune from these structures of power and we invariably seek explanations for violence. Donna Goldstein's (2003) powerful ethnography of women in a Brazilian *favela* (slum or squatter development) urges us to locate our analysis of violence within the context of power in which it operates and not from a middle-class Northern perspective. In particular, she (2003: 172) refers to a mother's–Gloria - administration of extreme punishment to her kids, arguing that it should be judged within the 'harsh survivalist ethos that drives her' and that the practice of Gloria's domination should be seen within wider structures of domination. Goldstein speaks about her struggles with her initial feelings of disgust and endeavours to find a framework in which to make sense of Gloria's 'cruelty'. I agree with Goldstein that violence should be interpreted within its local discursive and material context, but feel that it is disingenuous to assume detachment from who we are is either possible or desirable. Rather than sidestep feelings of disgust when confronted with particularly brutal accounts of violence, I found it useful confront these directly. In my struggle to 'make sense' of violence, I am conscious that there is a fine line between explanation and apology. In response to this challenge, I attempt to analyse how the rules of engagement are forged in particular contexts, but am politically committed to critiquing violent and unequal power relations within these.

While I am conscious about my identity as a Northern feminist, I believe it problematic to close down the dialogue that can be opened by cross cultural research from an explicit feminist standpoint.[4] Engaging in critical discussion of these uneven power relations that underpin dominant vocabularies of violence is an important theme of this book and shapes the framework for engagement with my subject. This does not mean we do not challenge our feelings and make explicit our judgement of violence; rather, I propose that the act of seeking explanation is in itself an act of judgement. Lundy and McGovern (2006: 49) argue that it is 'morally reprehensible' for researchers to remain detached and silent in situations where political violence and marginalisation have occurred (see also Green, 1995; Scheper-Hughes, 1995). Torres-Rivas (1999: 286) argues that a 'dispassionate' analysis of violence is not possible: 'one can never analyse dispassionately the phenomena related to death without the anger and sadness inspired by death itself'. He concludes that the classification of violence–both theoretically and politically–is made from a normative point of view. This raises important questions about the norms of violence and, specifically, what is classified as violence in the context of the research. Following a feminist standpoint, I argue throughout this book that the normative construction of violence is essentially public and masculinist. This has profound implications for classifying those forms of violence that take place in the 'privacy' of the home that are largely against women and children. Like Harvey (1998: 74), I found myself 'far more horrified' than the research participants about the frequency and severity of domestic violence. While I attempt to contextualise this violence against women within a wider structure of patriarchal relations, I cannot ignore its emotional and material effects. As a woman and a feminist, I find violence against women abhorrent and that subject position invariably guides my interpretative process.

Throughout the research process, I found myself continually referring to and questioning episodes in my own life to enhance my understanding of the realities that I was researching. I grew up in the North of Ireland and my formative years were embedded in the political turmoil that surrounded me. Certain periods of the political calendar invariably meant high levels of violence and, thinking about it in retrospect, I grew up expecting/accepting bombs, riots and shooting as a normal element of daily existence. As a member of a community that was marked by high levels of violence on an everyday basis, I was versed in holding horror and terror 'at arm's length' in order to survive the 'permanent "state of siege"' of my locality (see Scheper-Hughes, 1995: 416 on South Africa). From a very young age, I was attuned to the localised vocabularies or 'euphemisms' that we use to insulate

---

4   See Mohanty (1991) and Shope (2006) for further discussions of the tensions in cross-cultural feminist research.

ourselves from the harshness of everyday reality in an extreme situation (see Bourdieu, 1990). My capacity to recognise, feel and question the violence that surrounded me was hampered by its everydayness. It would be wrong to say that I was oblivious to the violence of my surroundings but I had learned from an early age to negotiate such a context, so much so that it seemed instinctive. This does not mean I was not affected by violence nor does it mean that I was unfeeling to abuses and suffering. What I conceived of as normal had been shaped by structures within society such as the family, educational system and political rhetoric. My reading of violence was almost exclusively of political conflict because there appeared to be no room for other types (see McWilliams, 1998). My role as a researcher of violence cannot be divorced from my lived experience. Listening to the narratives of violence of my research participants chimed with some of my lived experiences of my own context. This is not to claim that experiences of political conflict can be universalised, nor do I assume that I am better qualified than others to research violence. Rather, I believe that my own identity and socialisation in a situation of political violence have nuanced my understandings of the violence in the context of study, invariably shaping the interpretative process. In a similar manner to that articulated by the Basque anthropologist Begoña Aretxaga (1997: 22) on researching nationalist women's resistance in Belfast, in order to understand El Salvador's history, I had to explore my own. Aretxaga describes the 'forgotten history, full of silences, gaps and repressed memories, at once personal and collective' that she encountered in Belfast and how this forced her to think about her Basque identity.

The more time I spent in El Salvador, the more I became interested in these silences, gaps and repressed memories. Reading powerful accounts of violence in Northern Ireland by academics from 'outside' (for example, Feldman, 1991; Aretxaga, 1997; Pickering, 2001) while writing about El Salvador as an 'outsider' raises interesting questions with relation to the study of violence. In some senses I inhabit a contradictory space – both 'reader' and 'read' – breaking down rigid notions of insider/outsider research that are deemed so problematic in cross-cultural research. By revealing aspects of my own identity here, I do not claim to erase power dynamics of research. Rather, I argue that this can contribute to a more 'honest' debate on what we claim to know (Shope, 2006). Situating myself as a researcher between these different contexts of violence undermines the possibility and indeed pretence of any detached analytical space. Importantly and despite very real differences between conflict areas, this is also suggestive of the possibility of drawing on theoretical and empirical assessments of violence in one context to inform our studies of another. Although violence may be historically contingent, it is surprising (or perhaps not) that there are many parallels in the stories of survival of those men and women who must face violence on an everyday basis. This opens up localised or bounded interpretations of violence to a larger political stage.

I therefore draw on other contexts of violence to inform my analysis of El Salvador. Speaking of Bloody Sunday, a key historical event in my own home town of Derry in 1972, Dawson (2005: 153) suggests that the killing of fourteen civilians by British paratroopers is a 'contested past' in which 'official' readings of the event are at odds with local understandings.[5] I was born in the shadow of this event–nine months later in the same neighbourhood–and grew up in a context where meanings of violence and history are continually contested. I am attentive to the dominance of certain narratives, and the contestation between different readings. In particular, I am conscious of how 'official' versions can silence demands for justice and recognition. Wood (2003) documents how similar 'contested' events in El Salvador have a profound effect on shaping historical memory and how this process is reflective of the political loyalties of the teller. This contestation over meaning takes place within broader relations of power in which certain voices stamp an 'official' meaning on events that excludes alternative readings (Gaborit, 2007). Consequently, I am particularly conscious of how certain ideologies of violence–namely political violence–interact with and silence other forms of conflict and aggression.

Silence is a productive element of violence and consequently an important theme in this book. Following Foucault (1984: 27):

> Silence itself–the things one declines to say, or is forbidden to name, the discretion that is required between different speakers–is less the absolute limit of discourse . . . than an element that functions alongside the things said, within them and in relation to them within over-all strategies. There is no binary division between what is said and what is not said; we must try to determine the different ways of not saying such things, how those who can and those who cannot speak of them are distributed, which types of discourse is authorized . . . There is not one but many silences, and they are an integral part of the strategies that underlie and permeate discourses.

I understand silence to be multi-layered, contradictory and complex. It is complicit with fear, threat and alienation to become a tool for the subaltern who use silence as a strategy to negotiate and survive the hostile world

---

5 In an inquiry into the murders by the British state, the Widgery Report (Widgery, 1972) found that the military were guilty of no wrong doing. A subsequent inquiry was launched in 1998 precisely to challenge the 'official' version as defined by Widgery. See: [WWW document]. URL http://www.bloody-sunday-inquiry.org/index.htm (accessed 31 July 2008).

around them. Growing up in a context of political violence, I am all too aware of the old adage 'whatever you say, say nothing'. Speaking about violence is dangerous, but not speaking about it or more accurately, not being allowed to speak about it, denies individuals and communities a voice. It closes down the possibilities of justice and constitutes an important element of repression and impunity. It is no coincidence that much of the political work on historical memory in violent situations has focused on 'speaking out' and 'breaking the silence'. The move towards truth commissions throughout Latin America and in other conflict zones and the ongoing struggle for historical memory has been a concerted attempt to subvert the official mobilising of certain political narratives. These struggles are also rooted in a bigger search for justice. Historically, silence has been a tool of the powerful, an important political strategy (and indeed goal) in an arsenal of terror and brutality. Apathy and indifference were necessary elements that both sustained state violence and protected citizens against it (Torres-Rivas, 2000). This is discussed further in subsequent chapters. Silence therefore is an important thread of the history of violence in El Salvador and of Latin America more generally.

Situating a Study of Violence

Most of the research for the book takes place in two urban communities on the outskirts of San Salvador, which I call El Boulevar and La Vía.[6] The bulk of this research was carried out between 2001 and 2002 when I also conducted interviews and focus groups with men in a prison and in a self-help group for men convicted of domestic violence. A brief history of the communities is provided in Chapter 3. Researching marginal groups is not in an attempt to make simplistic linkages between poverty and violence that appear to have garnered such currency in many public debates. Instead, I am interested in how those people who live outside the many gated communities and security cordons cope and survive in a hostile environment. I am committed to foregrounding the vocabularies of violence of those who are so vulnerable to its effects. These people resist and survive harsh and even brutal realities on a daily basis. They forge organic alternatives to violence on a micro level in order to resist and survive their hostile realities.

The broad methodological approach is qualitative. I chose to mix methods, collecting individual life histories and using participatory research

---

6   These are pseudonyms. The two communities were also the locations for research carried out by the Latin American Faculty for Social Sciences (FLACSO). I was affiliated to FLACSO between June 2001 and June 2002 and FLACSO assisted me with access to the communities. For more information on these communities, see Savenije and Andrade Eeckhoff (2003).

workshops. I collected a total of 21 life histories across the different sites, which meant multiple interviews with the same people. This was supplemented with a series of focus groups in El Boulevar where I used techniques associated with participatory urban appraisal. These involved collecting community histories from adult residents who drew community timelines to trace the history of El Boulevar (see Chapter 3). Young adolescents drew their communities as a way of initiating discussions on violence in a non-intrusive way (an example of these sketches appears on the cover of book). Adults and adolescents also mapped out different types of violence inside and outside the community and in the household and discussed the ways in which different types of violence affected them. These groups were divided by gender and age, because I was interested in determining the ways in which violence affects different groups.

I began the field research by speaking to the men in prison and in the self-help group who have been labelled 'doers' of violence by the state. This alerted me to different ways in which men talk about violence (Hearn, 1998). It also undermined some of the pre-existing normative notions of violence that I had brought to the research, principally surrounding perpetrators, an aspect discussed more fully in the following chapter (see also Hume, 2007a). This was a useful lesson in being open to the varied and contested vocabularies of violence. It is for this reason that I sat in on weekly meetings of a self-help group for men convicted of domestic violence and interviewed some of the participants and inmates in a prison in a rural town. This is supplemented by additional interview-based research carried out on various trips to El Salvador since 2002. In this period, I have interviewed over 30 policy-makers, practitioners and representatives of civil society organisations, often more than once and across several years. I have chosen, unless unavoidable, to make all interviewees anonymous by using either a pseudonym or by stating the interviewee's profession or the organisation in which they work. Between 2007 and 2008, I carried out research for Oxfam America on women's perceptions of gender-based violence in one urban and one rural municipality, San Marcos and Ahuachapán. Elements of this are included in Chapters 2 and 5. These different threads are woven together throughout the book.

The process of recognising and ascribing meaning to violence is a central concern of this book and offers the intellectual frame for many of the chapters. The aim is to demonstrate that a gendered analysis of violence is not reducible to the private sphere, but demands a critical examination of its social and political context. Such an approach not only broadens our understanding of this highly negative force, it uncovers certain social and political myths that serve to reproduce violent realities. Chapter 1 reviews some of the different debates on violence from various disciplinary perspectives to argue that there is an implicit tension between actual violence and its representation both in theory and practice. This chapter foregrounds the contribution of feminism in order to think about ways in which violence is embedded in unequal power relations. This discussion is carried over into Chapter 2 where I explore two enduring fault lines that have historically characterised Salvadoran social and political relations: violence and an unequal political economy. An interrogation of the patterns of state terror and unequal political economy challenges neat separations between the state and citizens in the production of violence. Attempts at peace building have been undermined by neoliberal governance, limited democratic reform, weak institutions, and the role of formal and informal structures in the continued promotion of authoritarian values. This provides a foundation for further discussion of empirical research in subsequent chapters.

Chapter 3 introduces two communities whose lives are marked by violence on many levels. It traces both the intersections and the development of different types of violence in El Salvador, from particularly brutal political expressions in the past, to criminality and gang violence in the contemporary context. These stories of violence pinpoint the existence of scarce alternatives and other means of dealing with conflict. I argue that survivalist strategies such as silence and isolation should be regarded as important ways for resisting violence. Rather than mere passive victims of violence, this approach emphasises the agency and courage that citizens display on an everyday basis when they confront high levels of violence. Their stories also point to a life where solidarity and violence coexist among neighbours. This approach renders problematic simplistic notions of the community as harmonious and homogeneous. The different stories of violence from El Boulevar and La Vía indicate that violence discriminates within communities. Men, women and children feel its effects in different ways. They also use it to different ends.

This moves the discussion of violence into issues of accountability, complicity and hierarchy in Chapter 4. I unpack gendered hierarchies of violence to advance the notion that intimate partner abuse and violence against children is a public secret as opposed to a private matter. Cultural norms and gendered roles shape who uses violence and how and when they might use it. The prevailing gender order prescribes identities and relations that accept and even prioritise the use of physical violence, particularly among men and against children. Issues of sexuality, power and machismo are explored here to frame the discussion of ways in which certain types of violence are normalised and legitimised. This discussion sets up the debates that are further explored in Chapter 5 on responding to violence from state, community and civil society perspectives. A key issue for concern that has emerged in both policy debates and community level research is the issue of youth gangs. Arguably, one of the most misunderstood expressions of violence in the contemporary era, this chapter offers a detailed analysis of the politics of fear that surround gangs. This context of fear restricts the space for alternatives to violence to emerge. Nonetheless, it does not close them down completely. In this vein, I explore community responses to violence, which can be both productive and counterproductive. I also look at alternatives emerging from civil society, emphasising the important contributions of the feminist movement to challenging violence.

Finally, in the conclusion I draw together the key arguments of the book. Thinking about violence in gendered ways opens up a concern with how violence is interpreted from a range of different standpoints. Violence is rarely judged only by its material consequences or the harm it generates. The processes of attaching meaning to violence are contested, but citizens do not compete for this interpretive space from equal positions. For this reason, I have sustained a commitment to critically engaging with subaltern voices throughout. This approach opens up possibilities for theorising violence from the perspective of everyday life. It is important to gender our analysis of the interactions between the local, the national and the global, rather than restricting gender to an analysis of women and the private sphere. Engaging with violent masculinities, sexualised and domestic abuse, and violence against children rejects notions of violence as removed from everyday power relations. The analysis in the book is localised within the context of El Salvador. The conclusion draws out critical insights for other transition/post-transition situations.

1

Questioning Violence: Meanings, Myths and Realities

It is not difference which immobilises us, but silence, and there are so many silences to be broken. (Lorde, 1984: 44)

The purpose of this chapter is to examine how knowledge about violence is produced in order to promote a critical dialogue between the theorisation of violence and its contextualisation in the everyday life of post-war El Salvador. How do the empirical findings that will be explored in later chapters enhance and question existing understandings of violence in both situated realities and theoretical frameworks? I sustain my earlier claim that there is no such thing as a 'morally and politically neutral' account of violence. All studies of aggression, conflict and war are produced by engagement with emotion, history and competing political ideologies. These forces invariably 'encroach' upon the interpretative process to direct the meaning we attribute to any discrete act or process of violence (Burman, Batchelor and Brown, 2001; Lawrence and Karim, 2007: 6).

This process of opening up an emotional and political dialogue with violence can be productive as well as destructive to the task of recognising violence. Such a dialogue can generate previously hidden and silenced knowledge and create a potential for transforming violent relations. More dangerously, if we do not make explicit our positionality and subjectivities, our thinking on violence is stunted. It is precisely this tension between what is presented as 'truth' about violence and the ideological and political undertones that go to the core of theorising it that I wish to explore here. The theoretical argument centres on an engagement with the disciplining practices of epistemologies of violence. I am interested in disentangling the interlocking axes of violence and gendered power relations as a way of opening up a critical dialogue between competing theories and practices of violence. I argue that violence is an inherently relational process and should be understood within the context of unequal power relations. Power is productive of both material and epistemological effects. In this sense, our knowledge about violence is both limited and limiting. In this exercise, I organise the chapter into three broad sections: epistemologies of violence; power and violence and gendered hierarchies of violence. Before this, I offer some critical reflections on my approach researching violence. By setting my argument up in this way, this chapter will provide a theoretical framework for the remainder of the book.

Positioning Violence

It is now largely agreed within academic and policy circles that the gendered ordering of society affects how we live and how we experience social and political relations. I argue here that gender is central to how and what we recognise as violence. Violence does not affect all people in the same way and a theory of violence that is representative of this essential difference is both politically and practically necessary. This speaks to the broader aim of the book, which is to outline aspects of a gendered theory of violence. Interpreting violence in this way foregrounds gender as essential to the theorisation of violence generally, and undermines the reduction of 'gendered violence' to a subset of violence or particular expression of unequal power relations. There are tensions in attempting to craft such an approach, not least of all the risk of sidelining issues of class, ethnicity and age as productive of important and overlapping inequalities. However, the account here seeks to be attentive to the intersections of violence with these multiple and intersected power relations. This opens up possibilities for more inclusive and critical interpretation of violence.[1]

On a practical level, the very decision about the location of the research, who to talk to and what questions to ask betrays normative ideas about violence. Like all researchers, I asked these same questions on embarking upon this project. As I stated in the introduction, one of my principal motivations was to uncover the silences that shroud violence. The issue that interested me was the gendered dynamics of violence, particularly questions of masculinities and men's use of violence in the post-war context. At the outset, and wondering where to start, I thought that perhaps it would be interesting to conduct my research in a prison. The logic seemed straightforward: prisons held men that have been convicted as having committed some form of crime or violent act. I was persuaded initially

---

1 I agree with Kinsella's (2007) caution that untangling the multiple and deeply intertwined discursive sites of inequality is an important, if hugely challenging exercise. She suggests that it is impossible to do this in its entirety. I also agree that this should not undermine the attempt.

by Cruz, Trigueros Arguello and González's (1999a: 57) argument: 'All in all, the persons interned in the penitentiary for delinquential acts make up the population closest to the kind of people who tend to practice criminal violence and who can be approached with less difficulty considering their situation as prisoners'. After much thought and in light of a radical revision of my research plan, the simplicity of this approach reveals limitations. It not only belies my own lived experience in a context where the rule of law has been consistently questioned, but it also disregards the fact that I had lived and worked in El Salvador for several years and was highly sceptical of its security apparatus and judiciary. It also betrays a crude approach to my subject matter: by wanting to carry out research on violence in a prison, I was locating violence in a context that is forcibly separated from wider society.[2] This is not to underestimate the significance of studies of prisons and prison violence, but merely to reflect upon the short-sighted rationale in my own approach and the particular institutionality of prisons outside the realm of everyday life.[3]

The initial desire to order my research into a realisable project around prisons is revealing of broader tensions that underlie our ideas about violence that are more than merely the confessional spirit of self-reflexive research. I am concerned by my own readiness to name those within the prison system as doers of violence, while sidelining other more everyday conflicts that are deeply corrosive to citizens' well-being (Hearn, 1998). At its most basic, this desire fitted into a neat and binary construct of reality where it is possible to separate the 'them' from the 'us', the perpetrators from the victims or the 'bad' from the 'good'. Such a split is dangerous in its seductiveness. It offers a false ordering of social reality that eliminates the possibility of ambiguity and is reliant on the construction of a dangerous 'other'. As an everyday narrative, it insulates citizens from the complexities and closeness of violence. In this way, it is both reflective of and complicit with bigger exclusionary narratives that operate to sanitise and stamp an 'official' value on violence. I was, in a sense, removing violence from its everyday social and political circumstance and relying on what Rachel Pain (2001: 899) has termed a 'currency of stereotypes' that define and limit what we know about violence. This is a theme I wish to emphasise as central to this book. The power of these stereotypes acts as an organising discourse, providing the certainties and received truths of violence at the level of popular epistemology or everyday social interaction. Its potency lies in the fact that certain stereotypes become so taken for granted that they go unquestioned. In this way, the widely held 'myths' of violence

---

2　I am grateful to colleagues in FLACSO El Salvador who encouraged me to think more critically about my research plan, especially Kay Andrade Eeckhoff, Carlos Ramos and Wim Savenije.

3　Examples of powerful studies of prison violence include Toch (1998) and Salas (2002).

are generated. To borrow from Hannah Arendt (1969: 8): 'no one questions or examines what is obvious to all'. However, Arendt was writing before the outpouring of feminist research on violence that is inspired precisely by the goal of questioning what appears 'obvious to all'. My initial approach was not forged in ignorance of the pervasiveness of violence, nor without regard to my concern with its gendered dynamics. At the time, it just seemed like a relatively straightforward option in order to gain access to 'violent' men. It is reflective, however, of the effectiveness of hegemonic notions or 'myths' of violence, to which researchers are not immune.

The notion that a prison might be a good place to study violence is indicative of several issues for discussion in this chapter. I am interested in how we go about naming violence. This is not with a view to reaching a conclusive definition of my own that I think is neither possible nor desirable. Rather, it is informed by a desire to unpack the process by which understandings of violence are reached. I am interested in uncovering the 'myths' or 'fictions' that sustain and produce our commonsense appraisal of violence. My rationale for questioning violence in this way is shaped by broad debates in criminology and critical theory. In particular, I am interested in feminist contributions to these. I should emphasise that I am not suggesting a singular feminist analysis or pushing the notion that feminism offers a superior knowledge of violence. I contend here as I do throughout the remainder of the book that the questions posed by feminist analyses (as opposed to any notional answers) are critical to the study of all violence. The sidelining of feminism and violence against women as a 'peripheral' concern has very real material, political and epistemological repercussions. By refusing to acknowledge the radical challenges feminism poses to existing theories of violence, not only are our understandings of violence in its multiple forms limited, but so too are our responses. The following section draws out some of these concerns by examining how violence is defined, awarded meaning and situated within its political and economic context.

Epistemologies of Violence

The discussion above proposed that research on violence must determine its parameters, yet also explores some of the tensions in this exercise. Here I examine some of these tensions in a discussion of the literature on violence. I am interested in three broad questions. First, what is defined as violence? Second, how are these definitions made operational and, third, in what conditions do they gain meaning? The first step in this exercise is to identify what we understand by violence, a term that is both obvious and 'slippery' at the same time (Taussig, 1987: 241). Carolyn Nordstrom (1997: 115) suggests that violence is 'essentially defined' because we all assume that we know what it is. Rather than an issue of definition, I suggest that (following a feminist logic), we need to look at how violence is named and awarded meaning. This demands an interrogation of the institutional regulation of violence, whether this is symbolic or overt. I discuss the tension between legal definition of crime and the more generic term 'violence'. I also engage with the work of Pierre Bourdieu, who is concerned precisely with what is recognised as violence. Finally, this takes the discussion to the context of violence and to how violence becomes possible. Johan Galtung's threefold theorisation of violence as structural, cultural and personal/direct opens up the discussion to issues of inequality and social justice.

John Keane states that violence is 'any uninvited but intentional or half-intentional act of physically violating the body of a person who had previously lived in peace' (Keane, 1997: 6). Keane's definition is narrow, but not uncommon, in that it only recognises the physicality of the act of violence, without addressing either its non-physical forms or the context in which it occurs. Violence certainly invokes a notion of physicality because it is fundamentally an embodied experience. The term 'violence' is used to refer to a multitude of behaviours, but also to render judgement on these behaviours. It conjures up images of war and political conflict; crime and domestic abuse. It evokes images of victims and perpetrators, weapons and bodies. Munck (2008) argues that violence should be studied as a 'politics of scale', because the local and global increasingly interact. New technologies and unequal economic relations deepen the lethality of violence and change theatres of conflict on a global scale (for example, Duffield, 2001).

An important characteristic of research on violence is 'the blurring of the boundaries between the terms "violence" and "crime" [which are] often used coterminously due to the violent nature of much contemporary crime' (McIlwaine, 1999: 455). Although common, the elision between these two concepts can be misleading, because all crime is not necessarily violent and all violence is not considered a crime. Crime is narrowly defined by the distinction between legality and illegality. Defining an act as illegal may be an important step, but responses are dependent on a functioning and fair legal system. Continued impunity and the criminalisation of certain groups within societies in Latin America undermine the very premise of the rule of law. Muncie and Mc Laughlin (2002: 1) warn that: 'the formal concept of crime is an inherently unstable and shifting definition of fear and insecurity ... What is conceptualized as crime changes over time and circumstances and is rarely consistent across different societies.'

In theory, legal codes operate to regulate the limits of acceptable or what is deemed *normal* behaviour. The implication is that if something is deemed criminal, it is sanctionable by law. In practice, however, crime is both more and less than 'acts prohibited by criminal law' (Sparks, Girling and Loader, 2001: 887). For example, domestic violence may be illegal in many countries, but it is rarely analysed specifically as a criminal act. Even when it is, Macauley (2005: 111) argues that the criminalisation of domestic violence in many countries in Latin America has not effectively assisted women survivors: 'the real problem lies not in the designation of the competent judicial authority, but rather in the understanding of domestic violence as a distinct offence with a unique relationship between victim and aggressor, and therefore requiring a specific mix of protection, redress and rehabilitation measures'.[4] In El Salvador, the law operates a distinction between 'serious' and 'minor' injury in domestic violence cases, yet only the reported episode of violence is considered in case files. Individual incidences of 'minor' violence are understood as separate and not as part of repeated abuse. 'Serious injury' is deemed as that preventing victims from going about their normal activities for a period of at least twenty days. This 'snapshot' model does not consider the process of violence that so often characterises intimate partner abuse (Saraga, 2002: 108). A critical effect of this is that often such cases do not enter the criminal system. Female interviewees in Ahuachapan interpreted this as women being expected to produce 'physical' proof of violence, such as bruises that last several days, but that many men were aware of this so took care how they hit their partners. This example is illustrative of how the combined effects of a 'snapshot' approach or popular understandings of crime can undermine both state response and women's struggle for justice.

Rather than impose strict definitional boundaries, both 'violence' and 'crime' are used concurrently throughout this book. This is not to evade distinction between the two, but is reflective of the elision in common parlance and the limitations of both terms. By referring to the overlapping categories of criminality and violence, I am not suggesting that they are the same, or that one is a category of the other. Instead, from the outset I wish to draw attention to the labels attached to different types of violence. These are invariably limited, but also have a very powerful effect on levels of visibility, fear and, crucially, response (Winton, 2004). The task of defining such a broad range of actions on a conceptual level is mirrored in the sometimes confusing and contradictory narratives of violence of individuals and groups in relation to their own life experiences that are explored in subsequent chapters. Violence is essentially rooted in experience or, more pointedly, the politics of that experience that require interpretation and articulation. It is for this reason that I concentrate on the process of attaching meaning to violence rather than squabbling over definitions. This exercise demands an interrogation of the

---

4 See Saraga (2002) for further discussion on this point.

macro-political context and localized structures of power and knowledge (Cavanagh, Dobash, Dobash and Lewis, 2001; Moodie, 2006). Pertinent here is Raymond Williams's (1977: 61–62) reminder to us of the impossibility of separating 'consciousness' from the 'development of men' [*sic*] and from 'real knowledge'. Knowledge (consciousness) and its production are always part of the social process. Williams calls for a critical examination of the 'assumptions, concepts and points of view, whether received or not, by which any knowledge has been gained or not'. This approach demands engagement with competing arenas of political subjectivity at both individual and collective levels.

Subjectivity is clearly important to violence (see Das et al., 2000) and raises important questions about the possibility of reaching a unified definition of violence in a context such as El Salvador where perpetrators, victims and witnesses all compete for a space in which to tell their story. The classic division between victims and perpetrators produces very different stories of violence. This is particularly evident in the manufacturing of competing rationales and the struggles for legitimacy that have been central to El Salvador's political history, but is also true of everyday conflicts that inform this research. It is hardly surprising that empirical accounts undermine these strict categorisations between perpetrator and victim; legitimate and illegitimate; and even legal and illegal (see Bourgois and Scheper-Hughes, 2004). This does not mean we should avoid making clear what we understand by the term 'violence', but it does call for attention to how these understandings are reached.

Raymond Williams (1985: 329) warns that violence is 'clearly a word that needs early specific definition, if it is not to be done violence to'. Important to Williams is the meaning or significance of the act and not its specific definition. However, he sees meaning and definition as recursive, which directs us to one of the central questions of research on violence: how should the gap between 'actual' violence and its representation be negotiated and understood (Levine, 2003: 129)? This critical space between lived experience and articulation – the ontology of violence and its epistemology – has the potential to be both productive and destructive. I sustain throughout this book the claim that the meaning of violence is never random or incidental; rather, it is actively informed by particular interests within the social and political order. It is precisely this challenge that I am interested in exploring through this book. Certain types of violence appear obvious and even 'palpable' – a punch, a stabbing or a robbery are cases in point. These are acts of violence rooted in clearly identifiable bodily harm (Keane, 2004). Yet a central question remains: is violence necessarily judged against the harm it generates?

Ellen Moodie's (2006: 65) study of the differentiated symbolic values ascribed to violent deaths in post-war El Salvador refers to this as a process of forging 'hegemonic definitions of publicly meaningful violence'. She argues that a series of values inform the definition, recognition and identification of violence that are based on age, class, gender and nationality. It is therefore impossible to dislocate the process by which violence is defined and awarded meaning from matters of political economy. It is because of these differentiated meanings, and also in light of the discussion above with regard to my initial approach to the research that I propose that adopting an 'early specific definition' potentially undermines the questions we ask (see also Daniel, 2000). Bounded definitions assume that we can achieve a clear distinction between what is violent and what is not and that a range of behaviours can 'fit' a particular mould. The reality of violence is altogether messier and the process of definition is not only an issue of contestation, but one of competition.

To put it crudely then, there are no 'pure facts' in the study of violence; rather, we are dealing with competing interpretations of facts. This is why violence is not reducible to easy definitions or labels, but should be viewed within a broader process of interpretation. The stories of violence do not evolve randomly; instead they illuminate systems of values and beliefs to form the 'myths' of violence. Myths work to create the 'commonsense' accounts of violence and to naturalise certain types of violence. They are full of internal contradictions, such as people condemning violence and using it at the same time. In order to understand violence, we must foreground these inconsistencies. A central contention of this book is that the stories help forge meaning: they appeal to stereotypes and they organise patterns of fear and terror within society, shaping identity and also interaction among different social groups. To a certain degree then, Allen Feldman's (2000: 55) argument that 'meaning' is 'prepared in advance' before the violence actually occurs is a tempting one. Feldman refers specifically to politically motivated violence in Northern Ireland, but his analysis is useful more generally:

> In terms of the sheer materiality of violence, these acts are basically undifferentiated in terms of their concrete human consequences. They are polarized and differentiated through the instantaneous infusion of idealising national, ethnic and other cultural codes into material performance and its debris, rendering the latter inexcusable. (2000: 55)

Feldman argues that in order to understand violence, we should be alert to the 'recognition codes built into any violent enactment'. These set the 'facts' of violence and demand an interrogation of how meaning is connected to both political discourse and popular memory. In this way, past violence provides a justification for present conflict, while the invocation of history and tradition provide a potent moral framework for certain types of aggression. Rather than defined by its experiential element, this opens up an understanding of how violence engages with morals, norms and symbolic codes. While a useful critical framework from which to explore the pull of violence for certain groups, it is worth pointing out that not everyone accepts the meaning of violence as fixed and even the most embedded stories of violence can be disrupted.

Nonetheless, the normalising tendencies of the accepted stories of violence reduce the possibilities for naming violence, and also for contesting pre-established definitions of it. A central question of this research centres on whose voice is heard in the telling of violence, and also how the stories themselves are shaped by considerations such as gender, class and age. Men and women do not compete for this interpretative space from a position of equality. Historically, women's voices have been muted or their stories of violence distorted. Likewise, the naturalisation of men's aggression undermines a gendered account of male violence (see, for example, Connell, 1987; Hanmer, 1990; Bowker, 1998; Hearn, 1998; Jacobson, Jacobs and Marchbank, 2000; Moser and Clark, 2000). Listening out for the silences and gaps then becomes as important as listening to what is said in the study of violence. Feminist scholarship and activism have met this challenge directly by questioning the way that the stories of violence are told and, specifically, arguing that the masculinist bias in accounts of violence has led to a very real censorship in what is and what can be known about violence.[5]

At its most basic, feminist research presents a challenge to the underlying assumptions behind social inquiry and how it has been approached. While this is true of other critical perspectives, feminism foregrounds gender relations 'as a salient form of oppression in the way that other forms of critical theory have yet to do' (Eschle and Maiguascha, 2007: 286). It is about taking women's lives 'seriously': paying attention, listening carefully and digging deep (see Enloe, 2004: 3). By emphasising a feminist perspective, I wish to emphasise the intersections between gendered oppression and other forms of injustice. I also wish to highlight the continued pertinence of the historic questions of feminism to the study of violence. Feminism is not based only on exploring women's and men's lived experiences, but on undermining a whole range of social and political structures and ideologies that are used to sustain male

---

5   Second-wave feminist research emerged in the late 1960s and 1970s as a response to the hitherto 'masculinist' bias manifest in the social sciences (Roberts, 1981; Stanley and Wise, 1990). Early research aimed to 'make women visible', claiming that 'not only is women's experience often ignored, but also where it is noted it is distorted' (Stanley and Wise, 1983: 15). Initial efforts to 'correct' this bias sought to explore different aspects of women's lives in order to fill in the 'gaps' in our knowledge. One key issue for research was in the area of violence.

privilege or patriarchy.[6] A principal question of feminism centres on what is regarded as 'normal' behaviour for men and women regarding their use and experience of violence. This book is therefore not only interested in the material *facts*, but the understandings and explanations that work to undermine and sanitise the destructive potential of violence. This contributes to the broader aim I articulated previously of thinking about violence in a gendered way (as opposed to categorising certain types of violence as gendered).

In the context of political conflict in Northern Ireland, McWilliams (1997: 82) is critical of the distinction between politically motivated and 'ordinary decent' murders. 'Ordinary decent' is the euphemism that the police used to refer to the murder of women by their spouses or partners. These localised vocabularies alert us to the differing interpretations for what are arguably similar acts, both defined as illegal within that particular context. McWilliams interprets these different types of murders as operating along a continuum 'that ranges from the least to the most acceptable type of murders'. The notion of the continuum is useful here, for it allows us to unpack the ways in which the same crime is viewed in different ways. It also alerts us to the shortcomings of the legal system with regard to defining and interpreting particular forms of aggression.

Implicit in McWilliams's critique is the way in which hierarchies of meaning emerge. The concept of continuum suggests this difference in meaning, and we need to make explicit that this difference is not neutral. It is premised upon the differentiation in value attached to these distinct forms of murder. They are not incidental. In this vein, I would expand McWilliams's notion of continuum to include the concept of gendered hierarchies of violence. I am not suggesting hierarchy as a static or singular formulation, but rather a moving scale in which certain forms of violence are rendered more meaningful than others. These crimes may be undifferentiated in terms of intent – the desire to harm; and consequence – its physical effects or psychological harm. Nonetheless, their symbolic value or public significance betrays the potency of intersecting systems of prejudice.

Emphasising the importance of recognising the existence of hierarchies of violence along gendered lines is not to argue that some types of violence are more important than others. It is precisely against this hierarchical

---

6 For example, in her groundbreaking study of sexual violence, Liz Kelly (1988a: 35–36) identified six myths that inform popular epistemologies of domestic and sexual violence: women enjoy/want violence; women deserve/ask for violence; violence occurs only in certain types of families or to certain types of women; women tell lies/exaggerate violence; women could have prevented it; the violence is caused because men are under stress/ill.

interpretation that I am arguing. Notwithstanding, we must recognise and name the process by which such inequalities become endemic in order to challenge them. Chapter 4 develops this notion further by examining the apparent acceptability or inevitability of violence within intimate partner and familial relations that stands against the public condemnation of 'stranger' violence. I cite the example of Alfonso, a young man from La Vía who is open about beating his wife, yet feels bad when members of a local gang attacked her: 'it makes me feel bad. Maybe if she were a man, I would not feel bad because the man can take it [*aguanta*] but the woman can't.'

The process of interpreting violence, then, can never be clear-cut, nor is it necessarily dependent on the degree of force used. This takes us to our second question: how is the meaning of violence managed and how do particular definitions become operational? The debate around issues of what is recognised as violence and what is included in its theorisation is addressed in the work the French sociologist, Pierre Bourdieu. Throughout his work, Bourdieu contends that the very recognition of violence poses a challenge and cannot be taken for granted. He distinguishes 'overt' violence – that which is obvious and physical in its manifestation – from 'symbolic' forms of violence. His elaboration of the concept of 'symbolic violence' provides a compelling framework for understanding how ideologies of violence are internalised and replicated by both elite and subaltern groups (Bourdieu, 1977, 1990, 2001). Understood as a means of naturalising unequal power structures to the point of rendering them inevitable, these are not simple or static hierarchical structures, but engage the active complicity of both elite and subaltern groups.

The process by which violence is recognised (and therefore named) is cod-ified in legal statutes and implicit in community 'rules' and family relations to define the limits of acceptable behaviour. These 'symbolic' rules are not necessarily overt (as in a legal code, for example), but are embedded in pro-cesses of both epistemology and ontology – how we understand and interact with the world. Rather than by the harm it generates, violence is implicitly, if not explicitly, measured by the reaction it generates. An important strategy of symbolic violence is therefore to manage the response. It is precisely in the denial of violence, in its censorship and 'euphemisms', that violence gains currency (Bourdieu, 1977). Bourdieu (2001) identifies male domination as a paradigmatic form of symbolic violence that defines the acceptable limits of male behaviour whereby the gendered order of things often excuses or explains the use of violence as 'natural' elements of masculinities. Analysing violence as the recursive relationship between its overt and symbolic forms draws out a critical examination of the material and discursive effects of power relations to understand how violence is misrecognised rather than necessarily recognised. Misrecognition is not accidental, but serves to embed 'symbolic violence' so that the 'dominated' accept as legitimate their own condition of domination and act as agents in its reproduction (Bourdieu and Wacquant, 1992: 167). Philippe Bourgois (2001) uses this concept to analyse why young working-class men in El Salvador have become agents in their own destruction through engagement in violent crime. He argues that the poor internalise blame by pinpointing their failings rather than focusing on issues of uneven political economy as causal factors (see also Binford, 2002; Bourgois, 2002). I develop the analysis of symbolic violence in the following chapters in order to glean a fuller understanding of when violence is accepted or what violence is regarded as legitimate by those who must live with it on an everyday basis. This is particularly pertinent to an understanding of violence against women who often blame themselves for men's violence.

The fact that marginalised groups internalise and even become complicit with the systems of domination demands an analysis of the context in which violence becomes possible. This addresses my third concern in this section. In what conditions can violence become possible? Johan Galtung's (1969, 1990) work is useful here in order to understand the political and economic conditions that both create violence and sustain it.[7] He argues that there is no singular form of violence; instead, he proposes a threefold conceptualisation that includes structural, personal/direct and cultural violence. The differentiation between the three is important, but even more so is their complementarity. Structural, personal/direct and cultural violence are the three interrelated, multi-directional and multi-layered elements that are regarded as reproducing and sustaining violence in any given context. Structural violence refers to the economic and political structures that constrain human potential. It occurs whenever people are disadvantaged by political, legal, economic or cultural traditions. These are not always obvious or even perceptible and 'may be seen as about as natural as the air around us' (Galtung, 1969: 173). This analysis is of particular consequence for those who suffer its effects and who do not readily indentify their lived experiences as violence. Its purpose is to understand the 'social machinery' of oppression (Farmer, 2004). His second type of violence is more obvious; personal or direct violence 'shows' and the victim is aware of it. It refers to, as the term suggests, violence from one person or group of people to another in a clearly identifiable situation, such as murder or wounding.[8]

---

7   Coming from the conflict resolution perspective, Galtung uses this model to unpack the concept of peace to give it more meaning than merely 'the absence of war'. Pearce (1998) uses this model in order to assess the limitations of the peace processes in Central America in the context of endemic poverty and violence.

8   Galtung (1969) uses the term 'personal' violence, although in his later work (1990) he prefers the term 'direct' violence, with little definitional variance.

Cultural violence does not have direct physical effects like direct or structural forms, but the concept brings together those aspects of culture – such as language, religion or ideology – that can be used to justify or legitimise the other two types to make them, 'even feel, right – or at least not wrong' (Galtung, 1990: 291). Galtung (1990) envisions these as three points in a triangle, which reinforces the notion that violence does not begin with one particular element but that three types nourish and feed off each other.

Galtung's typology permits an understanding of violence as a manifest action that can be identified by its object (victim); he also nuances our understanding of the conditions – both material and symbolic – within society that serve to maintain and reproduce inequality and injustice. Violence is both physical and psychological. It contains 'avoidable insults to basic human needs, and more generally to *life*, lowering the real level of needs satisfaction below what is potentially possible: 'threats of violence are also violence' (Galtung, 1990: 292). This approach departs from most analyses that emphasise the intentionality of an act of violence to address its consequences (for example, Keane, 1996; Concha-Eastman, 2001; Nordstrom, 2004). Galtung understands violence as both that which intends to cause harm (such as physical violation) and that which causes harm yet its manifest intention is not necessarily such. This approach is particularly compelling in that it allows for an analysis of the many subtle and barely perceptible forms of violence that affect a society. This is pertinent to this book, where I am interested in how certain types of violence are normalised or rendered invisible. Without interrogating the recursive dynamics between overt and symbolic or structural, personal and cultural violence, it is difficult to understand how violence so powerfully shapes human relations.

Galtung has come under much criticism for this broad conceptualisation. Specifically, by using the concept of structural violence to address issues of social justice, he has been charged with effectively rendering the concept 'nonsense'. John Keane (1996: 66), for example, argues its broadness 'effectively makes nonsense of the concept, linking it to a questionable ontological account of "the satisfaction of human needs" and making it indistinguishable from "misery", "alienation" and "repression" '. Of interest here is not whether injustice fits into a neat definition of violence, but that Galtung highlights the inter-relatedness of the two. More pertinently, Galtung alerts us to the ways in which patterns of economic development are not 'benign' and they have yielded winners and losers across time and space (Pugh, 2006). Processes of economic development can be both constitutive of and constituted by violence, whether this is overt or symbolic (see, for example, Taussig, 1987; Escobar, 2004; Coleman, 2007; Howard, Hume and Oslender, 2007). The effectiveness of these processes has been in their portrayal as neutral, or disguised as taking place in the interests of the universal good that effectively ignores the centrality of violence to its success. To name such injustices 'structural violence' is an explicit recognition of and challenge to such forces. Not to do so is to embrace the definitional hegemony of powerful interests.

This challenge is particularly pertinent in the context of El Salvador, where the structural conditions that limited access to land, a decent wage and basic labour rights provided the historical roots of conflict (for example, Dunkerley, 1982; Pearce, 1986; Wood, 2003). Both direct and structural violence worked together in El Salvador to reinforce the deeply unequal society and, ultimately, these factors are seen as principal causes of the outbreak of massive political violence in the 1970s and 1980s. The aggressive neoliberal model of post-war El Salvador has done little to break down these historic inequities or the hegemony of economic elites (Robinson, 2003; Moodie, 2006). I explore this in greater detail in the next chapter.

I have argued here that it is rare that violence be regarded merely as the simple act that causes harm to an individual or group. Indeed, acts of violence are seldom judged simply on the damage they cause. There is a politics of violence that is productive of different reactions that are seldom based on material effects. Different institutions mediate the act of violence and construct its meaning. I propose here that examining these processes of misrecognition are beneficial to moving towards a theory of violence that is representative of difference rather than one that is peddling false assumptions of universality. This is premised on the fact that not everyone can name and define violence from the same position of power. This approach makes possible a critical interrogation of hierarchies of violence from a gendered perspective. It also intersects with issues of class, age and ethnicity. A hierarchy of meaning (as opposed to any notional degree of harm) is operated by institutions such as the media, the family and the state. Violence does not affect all groups in the same way. Likewise, some forms of violence are simply viewed as more acceptable than others. A necessary element in determining the processes by which this takes place is to examine the interconnectedness of violence and power.

On Power and Violence

Our understandings of both power and violence have gone through a radical revision over the last few decades, not least of all because of the contribution of feminism. Nonetheless, the fact that normative views of power still hold a hegemonic place in accounts of violence indicates that there is still a need to be alert to them and challenge them. These comprise what Michel Foucault (1980) has labelled a 'juridico discursive' model of power, a power that is possessed, coercive and from a centralised source (see also Sawicki, 1991). Power, in this sense, is frustrated and narrowly understood as coercive: 'power over'. This is 'obvious power, and is what we usually think of when imagining power. It is the power of one person or group to get another person or group to do something against their will' (Townsend and Zapata, 1999: 26).[9] Such notions of power or, indeed, the idea of power as material rarely reflect the complex nature of human relations that are fluid, diffuse and consistently challenged. A quest for power is a common, if not unique, explanatory factor for the use of violence. Žižek (2008: 63) argues that violence is an 'implicit admission of impotence'. Arendt (1969) differentiates power from violence, viewing them as opposites. In her view, violence occurs when power is missing, as having real power does/should not necessitate the exercise of violence. Cruz (1999) associates the proliferation of youth gangs or *maras* in the Salvadoran transition to a search for social power that has been lost, or, indeed, never held. Others explore the complex and indirect linkages between violence and social exclusion (for example, Ramos, 2000; Savenije and Andrade-Eekhoff, 2003). Within this logic the relationship between power and violence explains why individuals use violence to rebel against their perceived lack of social, economic and/or political power with the use of force. This is not an unproblematic analysis and demands a closer interrogation of different forms of violence and their location within relations of power.

The suggestion that violence only occurs in situations where power is absent or frustrated is reductive on two interlocking fronts. It is also reflective precisely of the process by which certain types of violence can be misrecognised. First, a focus on the violence of the 'powerless' assumes that power can somehow be missing from human relations. This implies an exclusively material and indeed unidirectional notion of power that is not rooted in processes of human interaction, but that both and indeed power are discrete actions. Second, it fails to acknowledge the violence of the powerful and the resultant centrality of violence to the maintenance of unequal power relations. Violence against women, for example, is an extreme reminder of gender inequality and functions precisely as a statement of male power,

---

9   A key task of feminists has been to unpack and challenge historic patterns of power and domination (Corrin, 1999). Townsend and Emma (1999: 30–33) have developed a multiple typology of power that moves beyond coercion or 'power over'. This comprises: 'power from within', 'power with' and 'power to'. 'Power from within' is the recognition that 'one is not helpless, not the source of all one's own problems, that one is restricted in part by structures outside oneself'. 'Power with' represents the transformative possibilities of collective action and 'power to' involves gaining access to a full range of human abilities and potential. This is central to empowerment. Power is, therefore, not only important in the exercise of violence to force an individual or group to do something against their will (power to), but it is also key to resisting violence (power from within/power to/power with).

not of powerlessness. Some studies have, however, argued that men's loss of power in one context leads to their use of violence against women as an expression of their frustration. Philippe Bourgois's (1996: 412) study of marginalised masculinities among Puerto Rican crack dealers suggests that men develop a 'street culture of resistance' that 'celebrates a misogynist predatory street culture that normalises gang rape, sexual conquest and paternal abandonment. Marginalised men lash out against the women and children they can no longer support economically or control 'patriarchally'. It is worth remembering that not all 'marginalised' men use violence in this way and the men who choose to 'lash out' against women and children do so precisely because they can. While their violence may be analysed as a response to an unequal political economy, their violence towards women should be seen as a statement of power in intimate gendered relations. The effectiveness of male power to discipline women's bodies and actions, however, is not solely reliant on the use of physical violence. Male power as symbolic violence works through and within different institutions to reinforce and naturalise 'patriarchal privilege' (Connell, 1987; Bourdieu, 2001). Further, despite their position of disadvantage compared to men, evidence suggests that women have historically used less violence than men (for example, Hearn, 1998: 36).[10] This undermines neat explanations of the relationship between violence and power. It requires both a more nuanced appreciation of how power works and how violence is used by different groups and to different ends.

The relationship between power and violence is not unidirectional; one does not automatically produce the other (Savenije and Andrade-Eekhoff, 2003). Even when power is taken to mean coercive power or 'power over', violence is not a necessary element (Townsend and Zapata, 1999). Instead, there exists a whole range of subtle, even unspoken, social rules that enforce the will of the powerful without the explicit use of force. It is this hidden nature of power that is key to understanding its effectiveness. As discussed earlier

---

10 I am not suggesting that women do not use violence. Indeed, Chapter 4 highlights the very severe violence that women use against their children. I share Kelly's (1996) preoccupation that by exposing women's use of violence, there is a risk that this will overshadow the enormity and extent of women's repeated subjection to violence at the hands of men. Throughout the course of the research, men referred constantly to women's violence and their role in reproducing machismo. Women themselves spoke of physical and psychological violence between neighbours and family members. I do not sidestep this issue. Other women spoke about how women's violence against children is a reaction to men's violence: 'she takes it out [*se desquita*] on the children' (focus group, La Vía). Nonetheless, I wish to emphasise that understanding violence is often bound up with a need to apportion blame and men, in their defence, often pointed to their mothers as the figure that 'taught' them how to be men. I am not interested in entering into a debate over who is to 'blame' for men and women's violence; rather, I am interested in how certain types of violence warrant more attention than others.

with reference to the work of Pierre Bourdieu, key theorists concerned with processes of coercion and relations of domination have sought to distinguish power from the use of overt violence. Antonio Gramsci (1971) developed his study of hegemony (as distinct from domination) to understand the relations of power between elites and the working classes. In particular, he was interested in why the working classes appeared to accept their subordinate position. It was precisely the absence of violence or, more accurately, the apparent reluctance of the working classes to use violence to rebel against their disadvantage and to form alternative belief systems that was of interest to him. The role of the opposition in fostering an alternative political project was hugely influential in mobilising the Salvadoran population in the 1980s, yet many continued to work in support of the state. This is discussed in Chapter 2. In the post-war period, the emergence of youth gangs mimics the violent practices of hegemonic groups rather than fostering alternatives. While these may be a minority of youth, their engagement in violence is significant in terms of the pull of such forces. This indicates that hegemony cannot be static nor entirely uncontested.

Gramsci's development of the concept of hegemony goes beyond the material holding of power and emphasises that power relations have a strong ideological and symbolic component. Hegemony refers to a dynamic process by which groups create and sustain power, how 'normal' definitions and taken-for-granted expressions come to define reality, or at least people's sense of it. Hegemony constitutes a 'lived system of meanings and values – constitutive and constituting – which as they are experienced as practices appear as reciprocally confirming' (Williams, 1977: 110). It is the definitional power of hegemony to render patterns of domination normal and accepted commonsense that demands a critical evaluation. To borrow from James C. Scott (1990), those who aspire to hegemony must make an ideological case to maintain their privilege. People need to *believe* in power in order for it to be effective (Nordstrom, 2004: 75). Rather than assessing how power is distinct from overt violence, I am interested in how violence and power are productive of each other, particularly at the level of ideology and meaning.

Moser and McIlwaine (2004: 9) argue that: 'violence and power are inextricably related. Violence involves the exercise of power that is invariably used to legitimate the use of force for specific gains. Indeed, violence is often viewed as legitimate when exercised by the powerful and illegitimate when performed by the powerless.' There are two underlying assumptions for discussion here. First, people use violence to obtain or maintain power. The motivation behind these acts of violence is quite distinct. Second, the use of violence by subordinated groups is seen as less legitimate than its use by powerful groups. These two assumptions are at the core of much theorising on violence and power as touched upon above. A uniting thread is the issue of legitimacy. Implicit in any understanding of violence is the recognition that it is invariably mediated by an expressed or implicit dichotomy between legitimate/illegitimate, sanctioned or permissible actions (Galtung, 1990; Bourgois and Scheper-Hughes, 2004). This dichotomy underscores the broader process of judging violence: what is considered legitimate and what is deemed illegitimate? The process of judging violence, as I have argued above, is not incidental, though its power lies precisely in the fact that it seems just so. It is for this reason that any understanding of violence cannot be viewed as separate from the context of power relations in which it occurs. At stake here is whose voice is heard. The experience of domination and subordination produces very different accounts of social reality. Both violence and power are productive in that they forge a discursive space for meanings of violence to become fixed, albeit temporarily. Feminists have attempted to claim this space by foregrounding women's experiences of violence that are ignored in the dominant stories of violence. Power is not only important in the exercise of violence to force an individual or group to do something against their will, but it is also understood as key to resisting violence. The danger of simplistic linkages between powerlessness and violence attract precisely a currency of stereotypes about people who have least recourse to speaking for themselves.

Feminists have unpacked and challenged historic patterns of male power and domination. In order to do this, scholars and activists have focused on two fundamental interlinked questions that unite a broad spectrum of feminist concerns. First, they have challenged the organising principles and strategies of patriarchal power relations that naturalise the subordination of women. A challenge to patriarchy demands a critical evaluation of the social and political organisation of society and the institutions that facilitate gender inequalities. This involves an interrogation of power relations at all levels of social and political interaction and not just the public sphere. Second, the aim of feminism is the transformation of power relations, primarily, the recognition and realisation of the transformatory potential of women's collective action. This conceptualisation of power moves beyond practices of domination to assess creatively the possibilities for resistance. While this may be theoretically useful, an analysis of communities' responses to violence and women's reactions to male violence suggests that resistance takes on multiple forms and is not always productive. The effectiveness of the interaction between symbolic and overt forms of violence is that it limits the space for alternatives strategies to resist violence to develop. Citizens often resist with violence, or their coping strategies concentrate on avoidance and silence. Women often modify their behaviour or silently resist repeated abuse. These are explored in Chapters 3–5.

Michel Foucault's *History of Sexuality* proposes an 'analytics' of power that is both fluid and diffuse. He argues that power is present in all human relations and must be understood within the context in which it is operated. This involves analysing power 'from below' as productive as well as looking at its more negative effects. Relations of power, therefore, cannot exist outside the otherwise harmonious workings of human relations, but are central to them. Within this logic, power cannot be material, something that is acquired or seized. Instead, there is no central point to power, no fixed locus. 'Power is everywhere, not because it embraces everything but because it comes from everywhere' (Foucault, 1980: 93). I share the concern of some scholars who feel that if power and violence are deemed as 'everywhere', this detracts from the focus on its harmful material effects (for example, Hearn, 1998). I still, however, find this useful in undermining the homogenising tendencies of accounts of the relationship between oppressor and oppressed. There is no absolute division between the dominated and the dominating. Regarding power as fluid and present at all levels debunks myths of harmony and equality among subaltern groups (or indeed the powerful) and recognises issues of collusion, complicity and resistance. I return to this issue in later chapters. A Foucauldian analytics of power rejects simplistic or mono-causal explanations for the multiple ways in which violence is used and resisted. Instead, it demands a critical analysis of the strategies or specific techniques of power: 'the networks, the mechanisms, all those techniques by which a decision is accepted and by which that decision could not but be taken in the way it was' (Foucault, 1990).

The exercise of power is not random; rather it is produced and reproduced through certain disciplining and disciplinary strategies. One of the key disciplining mechanisms of power is through the production of knowledge. Knowledge by definition invokes ideas about what we know and what we believe. Feminist, post-colonial, subaltern studies scholars have all questioned the basis on which *what we know* has been produced, criticising the hegemonic tone of androcentric or Eurocentric processes of constructing knowledge (Said, 1978; Spivak, 1988; Mohanty, 1998; O'Hanlon, 2000a, 2000b). In particular, these approaches have been critical of the silencing effects of knowledges that privilege certain voices over others. Foucault argues that in order to evaluate the recursive relationship between power and knowledge, we need to be attuned to the strategies of discourse. 'Discourse has truth as its function, passing itself off as such and thus attaining specific powers' (Foucault, 1977, 1990: 112). Discourse is then more than just a way of speaking, but a disciplining strategy that informs what counts as knowledge, what is held as 'truth', and how individuals should behave in given locales (Whitehead and Barrett, 2001: 21). Foucault (1980: 100–101) cautions against imagining:

> a world of discourse separated by dominant discourse and excluded discourse, or between the dominant discourse and the dominated one . . .

we must make allowance for the complex and unstable process whereby discourse can be both an instrument and an effect of power, but also a hindrance and a stumbling bloc, a point of resistance and a starting point for an opposing strategy. Discourse transmits and produces power; it reinforces it, but also undermines and exposes it, renders it fragile and makes it possible to thwart it.

Therefore, the very existence of one form of discourse allows a challenge to it, or at least its possibility. An identification of the fluidity of power and its centrality to human relations opens up the potential for multiple forms of resistance. While it may be crucial to emphasise the conditions of possibility, it is perhaps equally useful to reiterate just how embedded such discourses can become. The effectiveness of resistance is not a given and although power may be everywhere, it still works to produce hierarchies that become sustained, in the Gramscian usage as 'commonsense'. In other words, it is the normalising strategies of power that are productive of unequal power relations over time. Its hidden or subtle operations within social and political institutions fix notions of hierarchy as given or indeed render them natural and in the common interest. Disrupting the accepted discourses of violence becomes a central strategy of resistance. The focus on the discursive element of violence is not to detract from its material effects; rather, it is to emphasise how something so plainly harmful can be legitimised. This is explored further in Chapter 5 where I explore responses to violence. In this way, power relations between men and women or different social groups appear fixed, though perhaps not static or unchanging. Despite strategies to silence alternatives, this can never be achieved in any absolute sense. Women have always resisted and challenged their subordination in varied and complex ways. James C. Scott (1985, 1990) analyses the varied ways in which the so-called 'weak' produce their own 'hidden transcripts' of resistance through speech, song and action. These may not be obvious or blatant strategies of resistance but they do represent an attempt to counteract the silencing strategies of domination. It is to the ways in which feminism has challenged hegemonic accounts of violence that the discussion now moves.

Gendered Hierarchies of Violence

Feminist academics and activists have argued that the wider political economy of violence devalues violence against women in comparison to other types. Indeed, one of the most consequential outcomes of feminist research and activism has been the recognition of violence in the home, or the private sphere, as a social problem and not merely, an unpleasant, if inevitable, extension of women's existence. Segal (1997: 234) states that the 'first job of feminists was to expose the myths' about violence. As I have stated previously, implicit in this challenge is the recognition that the development of knowledge about violence cannot be separated from the exercise of (male) power. It is not only urgent to expose the myths that surround violence, but it is also key to challenge how such myths have become so embedded in popular thought that they appear normalised. Recognising and deconstructing the potency of a gendered normalising logic within the social order is important to understanding how violence is perpetuated and reproduced. Much of the violence of the private realm is still minimised in comparison to its more public expressions. This is not to say that violence against women within the context of intimate partner relations is the same as other violence, but it is a call to analyse the linkages between different forms. Even more 'public' forms of violence against women seem to herald minimal attention. In their analysis of 'femicide' in Central America, Prieto-Carron et al. (2007: 26) argue that the murders of women cause 'no political stir and no stutter in the rhythm of the region's neo-liberal economy because, overwhelmingly, state authorities fail to investigate them, and the perpetrators go unpunished'. Questioning the strategies of power that determine response and legitimise aggression is of great consequence when looking at the gendered dynamics of violence. Individuals and groups who have been historically without voice are often confronted with high levels of violence in their lives. These same groups – women, children, the elderly and those marginalised from society – are also those who are least likely to have recourse to formal justice. Furthermore, as feminist research has highlighted, popular myths surrounding violence may even contribute to a minimisation, or, indeed, negation of the validity of their experiences (Dobash and Dobash, 1998). In many cases, alternatives to violence are not readily available and many of those women who do 'choose' to avoid violence are punished by societies that eulogise the family above women's individual and collective well-being (Bograd, 1988; Radford and Stanko, 1996).[11] In light of the previous discussion on power, it is, therefore, essential to examine *who* defines violence and *what* they recognise as violence.

I wish to explore this gendered process of recognising violence through two strategies of power that are central to sustaining ongoing acceptance and toleration of violence against women. First, I argue that the strategies of patriarchal power and, in particular, the separation of life into public and private spheres effectively insulates domestic abuse from public scrutiny. This not only denies women a voice and recognition of such violence, but it also limits the possibilities of justice. Second, I contend that gender roles

---

11   I use the term 'choose' with a certain irony. The notion of avoiding violence as a choice infers that this is a straightforward and linear process. This is clearly not the case.

within society and, in particular, the privileging of masculinities renders violence a normal, if unfortunate statement of what it means to be a man. I am not suggesting that such boundaries are fixed nor does this mean that all men use violence, but prevalent notions of masculinities do organise the tolerable limits of male behaviour. This is of particular consequence when analysing sexual violence.

Much of the discussion to date has centred upon the meaning of violence and in particular the disjuncture between an act of violence and its interpretation. I propose here that we need to unpack the analytics of violence precisely to foreground the disconnection between the recognition of violence and its material effects. Heaven Crawley (2000: 96) argues that there is 'nothing to differentiate the position of a man locked in a torture cell and a woman who is repeatedly abused within the confines of her own home ... [T]he same processes used to break the will of the prisoners are used by domestic aggressors to break the will of battered women'. Although similar degrees of physical and psychological force may be used, the social and legal interpretation of these two acts is quite distinct. The learned public morality of violence generally awards more significance to the case of the man in a cell than the woman in her own home (see also, MacKinnon, 1982; Stanko, 1990; Dobash and Dobash, 1998). One of the key ways in which patriarchal power works as an organising strategy is through the public/private divide. Challenging this dichotomisation of everyday life has been at the forefront of feminist struggles for decades. The 'personal is political' is a call to recognise that the two domains are 'inseparably connected', so much so that 'the tyrannies and servilities of one are the tyrannies and servilities of the other' (Jabri, 1996: 48).

By 'bounding' the public and private spheres, women have been historically confined to reproductive chores and their political voice has been ignored, as has their subjection to violence (Crawley, 2000). Such a division is not static nor rooted in a material reality, but is imagined (Owens, 2008). This has had implications on many levels of life, such as citizenship (Lister, 1997); human rights (Jelin, 1997), economic roles (Tiano, 1984), political participation (Pateman, 1987; Craske, 1999) and, of course, violence. The notion of 'private', however, has historically signified more than a physical space or relational dynamic; rather, it goes to the very core of understanding the reproduction of gender inequalities. The private is seen as pertaining to the family and reproduction. It has, therefore, been regarded as the site for much of women's activity. The private realm has been considered as central to the 'natural' order of things. In contrast, the public is understood as being 'socially determined' (Cubitt and Greenslade, 1997: 52). As such, the dynamics of the private realm are naturalised and taken for granted as 'given'. Key here is the hierarchy between the two.

Pateman (1987: 106) suggests that the private sphere has been the 'natural subordinate'. Conversely, the public sphere has been associated with being a male domain. It is the site of political struggle and production and, as such, has been awarded great significance in both policy and academic endeavours. The division has been so taken for granted in the past that the dynamics of private life were for a long time missing from mainstream analyses of social reality. As a vehicle for the organisation and representation of social and political life, the public/private dichotomy has become deeply embedded in ways of understanding the world. Behaviours and relationships vary from public to private and our way of seeing the world and defining it can be mediated by the distinction made between these two spheres. It is not that the distinction mirrors reality; rather, it is that it has shaped how we understand and naturalise the gendered oppression that characterises much of social reality, particularly, though by no means exclusively, at the level of popular epistemology.

The division of life into public and private works as a key organising strategy for recognising and awarding significance to violence. This division has effectively insulated the most common – private – forms of violence from sanction by propagating the notion that it is a private affair, a personal matter to resolve outside the public glare. 'Indeed, it often tends not to be viewed as violence at all; it is seen as a "personal", "private" or a "family matter", its goals and consequences are obscured and its use justified as chastisement or discipline' (Crawley, 2000: 92). Nowhere is this more evident as in popular justifications for not reporting incidents of violence in the domestic sphere, in order to 'keep the peace' (Kelly, 2000). By silencing women's experiences of violence, patriarchal structures are strengthened and their reproduction is secured. The silences that mark private and intimate relations are intensely political, reflecting and reinforcing gendered power relations. In this sense, silences both reflect a violent reality and form part of its construction.

The above distinction is indicative of a pattern of gendered norms, which give precedence to public realms of existence. These 'norms' ascribe greater significance to public forms of violence. This pattern is accentuated during times of war or political conflict, often when violence against women is seen as an issue of lesser importance, or an 'inevitable' outcome of war (Kelly, 2000). Unless an act is recognised and ascribed meaning as violence, it will not be defined as such. This has very real implications for how violence is addressed in policy terms. Historic masculinist epistemologies have privileged the public realms of existence and thus have missed the many types of violence that affect women and children. The non-definition of much of women's subjection to violence is a telling statement about male privilege. For example, in the context of the UK, Stanko (1990) explores how women overwhelmingly construct notions of fear and insecurity in the public realm – the threat of stranger violence – despite the fact that most women who experience violence do so at the hands of known men. In Chapter 4, similar tendencies are identified in the context of El Salvador. Where the victim and perpetrator know each other in an intimate or familial relationship, the act of violence is often minimised or in Bourdieu's terms 'misrecognised'. Underlying the meaning ascribed to violence is the relationship between the victim and perpetrator. Individuals and groups consciously and unconsciously grade violence according to what is perceived as more/less serious. A gendered hierarchy emerges, not of perceived harm, but of meaning. This process of gradation, from the initial act of violence to the reaction it provokes, passes through a prism of socially constructed ways of interpretation – or recognition codes (following Feldman) – to affect how different types of violence are perceived by society. Individual and group reaction within societies, different political contexts, age cohorts and social categories is not static, and it will and does change.

Kelly (2000) has stated that one of the most powerful findings of three decades of feminist research is that women are most likely to be assaulted by men known to them. This runs contrary to popular assumptions that continue to inform fear and danger. These are 'typically linked with violence committed by strangers in public places' (Stanko, 1988: 78). Stanko (1994: 102) emphasises that 'women are almost always harmed by ordinary men, who ... are not characterised as presenting a criminal threat to women ... "Criminals", at least those who attack women whose complaints are sometimes upheld in court, are portrayed as savage beasts, not as the guy next door'. This social fact 'starkly illustrates a profound difference in the structure of gender oppression compared to other structures of power; not only are women required to live alongside and respect their oppressors, they are expected to love and desire them' (Kelly, 2000: 52). Indeed, Kimmel (2000: 257) suggests that the home constitutes the 'single most dangerous place for women and children'. Such pervasiveness leads some to offer an ahistorical interpretation with violence against women in the aftermath of conflict viewed as a legacy of war or merely an expression of men's frustration. The recent focus on men and masculinities has produced allegations of 'men in crisis' whereby weakened male privilege within societies has been linked to an increase in the use of violence (for example, Gonzalez de la Rocha, 1994; Cornwall and White, 2000). This has been notable in post-conflict situations where a number of factors such as availability of arms, lack of employment opportunities and militarisation are cited as important factors that facilitate men's violence (Enloe, 2000; Morrell, 2001; Cock, 2001). According to Websdale and Chesney-Lind (1998: 55); it cannot be explained away as a deviant phenomenon that lies outside the otherwise 'harmonious relationships between men and women. Rather violence against women is endemic to the social condition of women, across both time and cultures.'

I propose that gendered violence, rather than a private matter, is a public secret. People know about it, but they do not talk about it. The continued 'unspeakability' of these crimes is suggestive of a socially acceptable negation and 'rationalisation' of certain types of (highly gendered) violence. Men and women are differentially located in relation to the naming and speaking of violence (Cavanagh, Dobash, Dobash and Lewis, 2001). If violence or, more accurately, certain expressions of violence remain unspoken, their meaning is denied. Silencing or refusing to speak about violence is an important strategy that restricts its meaning; its very existence is called into question. This is what makes gendered hierarchies of violence so enduring and so pernicious. As Jenny Edkins (2003) emphasises, that which is unspeakable becomes 'unsayable' in the language of the powerful. It is the powerful – predominantly men – who operate the 'acceptable' definitions of violence. Women's experiences are therefore 'reduced to unreality' (Cavanagh, Dobash, Dobash and Lewis, 2001: 702). The implications of this particular silence are twofold. The unsayability of violence provides an excuse to avoid listening to what is being said. It also reflects the view of survivors that what they have been through cannot be and should not be communicated (Edkins, 2003). In this way, shame and fear interact to refuse justice and acknowledgment.

It is simplistic, albeit common, to separate the analysis of public and private violence, yet it is in challenging these arbitrary divisions and in foregrounding the connections between them that feminist work on violence has much to contribute to broader debates. Drawing on these, I have argued throughout this chapter that violence must be understood within the discursive and material context in which it is exercised. It is important to look at the political connections between different types of violence. In her study of the politics of trauma and memory, Jenny Edkins (2003: 6–7) suggests that perhaps it is useful to draw out the parallels between the exploitation of women and survivors of war. She asks: 'what if, instead of linking family relations to a war, we compare the treatment of populations in wartime with the treatment of women in families? ... The modern state cannot be assumed to be a place of safety, any more than the patriarchal family can. Political abuse in one parallels sexual abuse in the other.' I wish to push Edkins's proposition. Political abuse may parallel sexual abuse in its mechanisms and tactics: both are often misrecognised and both are often denied. However, there is one key distinction that I wish to emphasise here. No matter how widespread and embedded violent political abuse may be, it is largely addressed as something outside the normal or acceptable range of political action. Thus, the widely held Clauswitzean notion that war is politics by other means or that political violence marks a rupture from the ordinary. Violence against women, on the other hand, is too often regarded as an unfortunate element of gender relations or, more generally, as a private matter. The recognition of sexual abuse as violence cannot be taken for granted.

Liz Kelly (1988a) contends that much of women's lives are marked by a 'continuum of sexual violence'. Instead of separating different forms of violence and abuse as discrete issues or events, the notion of 'continuum' highlights commonalities between them as forms of violence underpinning patriarchal power and control. These can range from sexist remarks, to physical violence, to sexual attack. Her notion of a continuum is not linear, nor is it based on levels of seriousness, but it emphasises that different acts of sexual violence share a common character. Kelly argues that there are no strict analytical categories in which men's violence can be placed, but that the notion of the continuum is important for identifying the a range of different types of sexualised violence. These may include 'commonsense' notions of violent attack by a stranger in public spaces, to marital rape to sexual harassment. In this way, violence against women becomes one of the key structures of creating and maintaining men's oppression of women in both symbolic and overt terms (Walby, 1990). Myths and stereotypes limit the range of male behaviour that is unacceptable to the most extreme, gross and public forms (Kelly, 1988a: 138). The notion of continuum is useful for conveying the multiple forms of violence against women, and the ways in which different types of male behaviour 'shade into one another' and are not necessarily classified within legal codes (Kelly, 1988a: 75).

As argued previously, only certain acts of violence within a given social order are classified as illegal: 'murder, assault, rape and robbery are the paradigmatic crimes of violence that hold a hegemonic position in legal discourse and public imagination' (Mc Laughlin, 2002: 285). Although rape may be illegal, it is worth noting at this point that popular understandings of 'rape' do not necessarily include rape as a 'paradigmatic crime of violence'. Robert Connell (1987: 107) argues that sexual violence is intricately woven into the production and reproduction of gender inequality. Rather than an example of deviance, he argues that rape 'is a form of person to person violence deeply embedded in power inequalities and ideologies of male supremacy. Far from being a deviation from the social order, it is in a significant sense an enforcement of it.' This conceptualization of rape challenges not only normative notions of violence but also demands an interrogation of the boundaries of 'normal' behaviour for men.

A recent study carried out in the UK foregrounds the distinction between men who murder and men who kill their partners. Men who murder are not generally seen as 'ordinary' men, but pathological killers or men whose violence can be explained by external factors, such as a troubled childhood, alcohol or substance abuse. Conversely, the study argues that men who kill their wives are commonly viewed as 'ordinary men' who 'snapped'. As such, they are not seen as a danger to society. This resonates with McWilliams's terminology of 'ordinary decent murders' and similar reactions in Latin America, suggesting that such attitudes are not confined geographically (IDHUCA, 2003). These assumptions ignore the fact that most murders of intimate partners are actually preceded by a history of violence. Therefore, the murder cannot be seen as a discrete act of violence: these men have acted *in* rather than *out of* character (see Dobash, Dobash and Cavanagh, 2004).[12] This work destabilises normative views on violence and masculinities, and calls for a radical reconceptualisation of men's violence.

A key theme of the critical research on men and masculinities is that violence is a characteristic central to the performance of masculinity, both as an expression of male power and a way of maintaining the patriarchal privilege (see, for example, Connell, 1987; Hanmer, 1990; Bowker, 1998; Hearn, 1998). It is simultaneously gendered and gendering:

> Men learn that violence is an accepted form of communication between men, and between women and men. This is so commonplace, so deeply woven into the fabric of daily life, that we accept violence as a matter of course – within families, between friends, between lovers, Most victims know their attackers, many know them intimately. (Kimmel, 2000: 254)

In the course of this research, several participants stated clearly that they did not believe that the crime of rape exists. Instead, they understood rape as an invention of sexually active/promiscuous women who wish to cover up their 'indiscretions'. During an informal conversation with one couple, the male partner persuasively argued that women have the ability to prevent rape. In the same discussion, his wife disclosed that both her mother and sister had been violently raped and that her sister's partner had abused his stepdaughter for many years. This violence was previously unspoken, which does not mean that people did not know about either the rapes or the abuse. It is thus that the public secrets of gendered violence operate.

The popular (mis)understanding of rape is not uncommon and, until recently, many Latin American countries held a provision in their legal code whereby the crime of rape could be mitigated by the aggressor marrying his victim (Chant with Craske, 2003). A woman's 'honour' (past sexual history) is still seen as admissible evidence in many contexts to determine whether

---

12   See also Dobash, Dobash and Cavanagh (2003) for a consideration of the methodology used.

a crime has been committed or not. Under conditions of gender inequality, recognising a crime is not just contestation over meaning. It is a contest in which men and women are competing from different positions of strength before key institutions such as family, judiciary and church. Catherine MacKinnon's (1982, 1983) challenging articles on the institutionalisation of the sexual subordination of women by men concluded that the idea of being raped by someone you know was both legally and popularly deemed to be 'less awful' than being raped by a stranger (1983: 649). This suggests that rape, from a women's point of view, is not prohibited but regulated. Her argument centres upon the premise that 'sexuality is the linchpin of gender inequality' and this demands an examination of the sexually normative limits of force (1982: 533). It is important, therefore, to explore the process by which 'narratives of denial' surrounding sexual violence emerge (Moffett, 2001).[13]

Violence against women is the most blatant expression of gendered inequality and is tied up with broader processes of discrimination. I propose that the questions asked by feminism go to the core of challenging violence in all its forms. They challenge the various ways in which violence is denied, legitimised and sanctioned, and move the focus of analysis from the 'other' to the immediate and intimate. Violence is a profoundly gendered process that is intimately linked to dominant ways of performing masculinities and femininities: 'the difficult thing to explain is not why gendered relations are so violent, but why violence is so gendered' (Moore, 1994: 154). The implicit gendering of social and political relations cuts across power relations based on class, ethnicity and age to minimise or 'deny' individual and collective experiences of violence. In this way, hierarchies of meaning emerge. To put it crudely, some types of violence matter more than others in normative accounts. The recognition of an act of aggression as violence cannot be taken for granted. Both meaning and response are moulded by processes of power relations that actively (and subtly) promote the symbolic codes and structures that discipline how violence is recognised, regulated and resisted. The more subtle these relations of inequality, the more difficult the challenge becomes to resist. This approach opens up the possibility for a critical analysis of the connections between different realms of violence and inequalities within social relations more generally.

---

13 Moffett's (2001) study of rape in South Africa argues that the widespread problem of rape is a widely understood 'personal problem' or an 'inevitable' risk for the female body. The conceptualisation of rape as such is a key example of the material effects of the debate about the meaning of violence.

Conclusion

This chapter has questioned how and what we know about violence. In particular, I have foregrounded the usefulness of the questions posed by feminist scholarship and activism in challenging violence. I have argued that meanings of violence are overwhelmingly constructed by popular assumptions, unequal power relations and in the immediate context of its material effects. This has three broad implications for theorising violence. First, the recognition of an act of violence is not a given process and I have argued for a theorisation of violence that is constitutive of both its overt and symbolic forms. It is for this reason that the interpretative process by which definitions are reached becomes equally important, if not more so, as the definition itself. Meanings and myths become enmeshed with the everyday realties of living with violence to shape the identities of the men and women whose life histories inform this research. Their narratives are based upon a range of social, cultural and political discourses that affect how individuals interpret and give meaning to the world around them.

Second, relations of power are productive of violence and produced by violence on both material and symbolical levels. This demands not only an analysis of the fluidity of power relations, but of the different ways in which actors use and receive violence. Power has epistemological as well as material effects. It is precisely how hegemonic forces discipline what we know about violence that I have been interested in pursuing here. Gendered norms are of particular consequence in shaping how individuals and groups interpret and live in society. In this sense, both power and knowledge are not only intimately linked, but active agents of each other. Hence, in the study of violence, it is essential to be alert to the conditions – or strategies of power – by and within which knowledge is constructed. The tremendous power of discourse is determinant to how individuals and societies interpret violence. The challenge that feminism has presented to the organisation of gendered power relations offers useful insights in how to move towards a theorisation of violence that reflects both difference and inequality. Obviously, violence is not is not confined to gender relations, because violence crosses a whole range of economic and social fault lines, which are themselves gendered.

This brings us to the third implication: subjugated knowledge about violence not only silences and normalises certain types of violence carried out by important groups; it refuses justice. Silence is, therefore, constitutive of violence and its reproduction. The use of interpersonal violence is more characteristic of women and children's oppression than that of other groups. Sexualised violence is differentially and more specifically targeted at women and girls (Kelly, 2000). Like other injustices embedded into any given social order, silence has important disciplinary power. Different types of silence are influenced by dominant notions of what constitutes violence and who uses violence. These underlie popular discourse on blame, guilt and justification. The types of violence imposed by patriarchal structures may not be obvious and, indeed, often go unrecognised or are regarded as 'normal'. The key rallying call for feminist movements throughout the world has been 'the personal is political'. This cry is more than rhetorical. It demands a critical interrogation of the connections between different political axes of oppression. It is precisely the challenge of addressing these connections between different stories of violence that are of interest in the chapters that follow. It is for this reason that I underline the necessity of a gendered theorisation of violence.

2

(Mis)recognising Violence in Latin America

A key challenge for research in Latin America has been to place contemporary criminality, youth violence and other forms of conflict and aggression both within their broader political economy and in relation to historical processes. Central to this aim is an appropriate balance between the analysis of contemporary forms of violence as different and evolving, while at the same time placing them in historic context. Uniting much of this emerging literature is a concern with how to understand the apparent contradictory processes of violence and democratisation. Notably, the shift in the parameters and tone of violence has informed a tendency in recent research to comment on patterns of 'new violence':

> Its 'newness' lies in its contrast with the norms and expectations derived from the democratisation process. Different forms of violence and conflict are subsumed under this notion, such as everyday criminal and street violence, riots, social cleansing, private account settling, police arbitrariness, paramilitary activities, or post-Cold War guerrilla activities. Hence, a variety of actors take to coercion and violence to pursue certain goals or simply to reproduce their own existence and way of life, or to pre-empt the usufruct by others of rights acquired through participation in the democratic process. (Kooning and Kruijt, 2003: 375)

While I am attracted by the analytical neatness of the concept of new violence to explain the different character of contemporary criminality and aggression, I am also wary of it on three counts. First, research on new violence rarely analyses its gendered dynamics and violence against women, for example, is marked by its persistence and not its newness. Second, a focus on non-state or non-elite armed actors as 'new' or the emergence of 'social' and 'criminal' violence as distinct from past political violence is not only undermined by a gendered analysis, but also by the empirical realities of the communities under study. The history of state-sponsored violence in El Salvador relied on the complicity, if not active collusion, of non-elite groups. Further, although the state and elite groups may no longer appear as central protagonists in overt violence, this should not detract from an analysis of the ongoing role of the state in promoting, or at least facilitating, symbolic and structural violence. This brings me to my final concern. The argument that 'its newness lies in contrast with the norms and expectations derived from the democratisation process' risks masking the very serious shortcomings of these processes.

Drawing on the critique advanced by Benson, Fischer and Thomas (2008), the notion of 'new' violence implies that it is not war and that the 'something better' that had been promised has been realised, at least to a degree. This is of particular relevance in the Central American context where 'norms and expectations' have been routinely ignored in favour of neoliberlising imperatives (Robinson, 2003). While I agree that violence can certainly be characterised as different from that of previous decades, I am concerned that a focus on its 'newness' risks erasing historic continuities in local and everyday stories of violence, especially their gendered dimensions. In particular, one of the most critical social effects of the civil war and its preceding years has been the extreme militarization of Salvadoran society and the accompanying high levels of interpersonal conflict.

Martín Baró (1990: 28) characterises El Salvador's war in three terms: *violence, polarisation* and *lies*. I draw from his analogy here to shape my analysis of historical developments in El Salvador, which I agree are typified by misinformation, polarisation and violence. The chapter begins by introducing some reflections on historic patterns of power in El Salvador and, in particular, the processes by which state terror developed. This period sowed the seeds of polarisation in El Salvador that continues to mark social and political relations. Second, I address the limits of El Salvador's peace, particularly in matters of political economy. The neoliberal peace that has been developed in El Salvador has not displaced historic logics of violence, inequality and polarisation. This has huge implications for how violence is regulated, understood and resisted in contemporary social relations. Finally, I explore some questions on how violence is measured in the region. I argue that not only are data collection mechanisms flawed, but they are open to political manipulation. This not only limits what we know about violence, but also contributes to widespread misinformation.

A Historic Political Economy of Brutality in El Salvador

Coffee is the 'explanatory thread' of Salvadoran history (Montobbio 1999: 30). More accurately, the shortage of land coupled with the ruthless ambition of a small group of families to maximise profit from coffee production help explain the scale of violence in El Salvador. After Independence from Spain in 1821, the *ejidos* (municipal commons) and common lands, which peasants had used for subsistence food production, were abolished in order to make way for the transfer of large areas of agricultural land to this small group of families to cultivate it for coffee and other export crops. Peasants were forced to rely on seasonal labour in coffee *fincas*, where wages were meagre and working conditions miserable (Dunkerley, 1982). The Agrarian Code of 1907 prohibited organisation among peasant workers and the National Guard was created in 1912 to oversee security on the coffee plantations (Pearce, 1986). The fall of coffee in the world market after 1929 sent coffee production into crisis—El Salvador's coffee exports fell from an estimated £8 million ($13 million) in 1928 to £2.4 million ($4 million) in 1932 (Pearce, 1986: 82). The response from landowners was to reduce workers' wages and food rations[1] Discontent grew among peasant groups and many allied themselves to the Communist Party, which had been formed in 1925. In the introduction, I outline how a tentative uprising led by indigenous and peasant groups in the western region in January 1932 was met by a 'reign of terror' during which as many as 30,000 people were killed (Dunkerley, 1982: 29).[2] Grenier (1999: 1) identifies this 'bloodbath' as the beginning of the modern Salvadoran state. The year 1932 is of great importance to understanding political developments in El Salvador in the latter half of the twentieth century because its events placed repression at the heart of Salvadoran political life and demonstrated the 'the extent to which the dominant powers in El Salvador are willing to use violence to "solve" social problems' (Grenier, 1999: 1). The collective memory of the brutality of *La Matanza* is seen as having been a key deterrent for political organisation in El Salvador for several decades following the actual event. For the peasants of El Salvador, the massacre of 1932 serves as 'a sobering illustration of the costs of insurrection that was unique to Central America' (Dunkerley, 1982: 29). Debates over 1932 remain at the heart of El Salvador's contested politics with both the left and the right competing for the 'official' version of events (see Lindo-Fuentes, Ching and Lara-Martinez, 2007).

Since 1932, Salvadoran society has gone through an extreme process of militarisation. Feminist scholarship has argued that the militarisation of societies impinges on men and women differently and it places value on particular forms of masculinity that value violence and misogyny (Enloe, 1993). Throughout Salvadoran history, violence has been linked to dominant notions

---

1   The daily wage for plantation workers fell from 30 to 15 *centavos* (Dunkerley, 1982: 22).
2   William Stanley (1996: 43) argues that the military knew in advance that the rising would take place so imprisoned many of the Communist Party leaders, leaving the insurgents without a clear military strategy. Therefore, the 'extent of the slaughter was dictated by political calculations rather than internal security' in order for the military to demonstrate its usefulness to the elite in squashing political dissent (1996: 53).

of masculinity. Alvarenga (1996: 124) highlights how corporal punishment was used by landowners to 'make men' out of their employees and rape was a widespread practice through which men took advantage of their 'property'. The raping of women cut across class boundaries but was rarely recognised as violence. Women, both in legal and symbolic terms, were treated as men's property and, within this deeply patriarchal logic, it was their right to 'enjoy' their property. Likewise, landowners felt a similar sense of ownership over their workers and demanded loyalty at all costs. This placed violence at the heart of (gendered) economic and social relations. Robert Holden (1996: 437) stresses that in Central America, the presence and persistence of state-sponsored violence has had a 'pivotal role' in shaping society. In El Salvador, this violence takes on particular forms that distinguish it from other processes in Latin America precisely because of the active engagement of intermediaries: peasants, neighbours and local sources of power. Violence worked through local networks, co-opting individuals and communities to blur the 'distinction between violence carried out by public officials and that by civilians' (Lauria-Santiago, 2005: 444).

State-sponsored *escoltas militares* (military guards), (ORDEN; National Guard and Democratic Nationalist Organisation), became the omnipresent face of violence for decades and worked to protect the economic interests of the landowning classes. ORDEN appeared in the early 1960s with no formal budget, no published statutes and no public accountability. It ensnared peasants within a particular coercive form of clientelism offering small favours to those who collaborated and punishing those who did not (Wood, 2003). Bearing in mind the crushing poverty of these groups and the tight control of landowners over their workers, many felt that they had no choice but to engage in this 'survivalist compliance' (Dunkerley, 1988: 368). At the local level, ORDEN provided an effective source of military intelligence with as many as 300,000 members. This is not only indicative of its widespread appeal, but of the rhizomorphic nature of the techniques of state power throughout society whereby violence is both constitutive of and reproduced through social relations. The fact that so many citizens were active agents in state repression in bodies such as ORDEN suggests that non-state violent actors are not new in the region and the particular patterns and depth of violence in El Salvador owe much to the widespread use of civilians (Lauria-Santiago, 2005).

In order to understand the level of penetration of state violence into civilian relations, William Stanley (1996) advances a convincing analysis of the organisation of the Salvadoran state from 1932 until 1979 as a 'protection racket' where the military served the economic interests of the elite in exchange for the control of the state. From a government perspective, supported by the United States, the perceived 'need' to defend against the possibility of a communist insurrection served to justify the murders of tens of thousands of civilians. Society was 'punished' in order to defend 'itself' against 'itself' (Torres-Rivas, 1999: 286). In this way, the fear of communism became a commonsense that drove repressive practices and all opposition was forbidden. According to the final report of the Salvadoran Truth Commission (1993), the state 'singled out as an enemy anyone who was not on the list of friends'. Patricia Alvarenga (1996: 62) argues that state terror(ism) became 'part of the everyday and also became fully integrated into a national culture, based on the resolution of social conflict in all realms of power relations'. Analyses of the family in Chapter 4 of this volume point to the historic centrality of violence to intimate relations, suggesting important linkages between public and private realms.

The notion of 'protection racket' also implies that society must 'pay' for its protection in some way, further reinforcing hierarchical relations between state and society (see Young, 2003). The debt garnered for state 'protection' was paid through the explicit collaboration or implicit support of large sections of the population. This bargain reached between the military and the oligarchy created the conditions of governance in which the use of violence was 'a currency of relations between state and non-state elites' (Stanley, 1996: 7). Important to this bargain were the vast numbers of poor men who filled the ranks of the military with many of these being forcibly conscripted.[3]

The training of peasants and working-class men to kill their neighbours and friends was noted in a homily by Monsignor Romero just before he was murdered when he called on soldiers to stop killing their 'peasant brothers'. For Daniel, an internee in the Salvadoran prison system who I interviewed in 2001–2002, this was all too accurate. Daniel was taken off a bus by soldiers at the age of seventeen and forced to serve in an elite force. His family came from an area where the FMLN had strong bases and his older brother was a member of the guerrilla. Although sympathetic to the leftist cause, his mother had taken him to the town of Zacatecoluca for economic reasons:

> Of course, if I thought about it I thought that it can't be possible that I am in this group and my brother is in the other. I don't know how many times we could have come up against each other in combat, we could have shot each other, he could have killed me or me him. My brother was in the mountains and he was with that group so that made me really confused. I was very confused . . . I think that because I had family there,

---

3   The Salvadoran army only conscripted men, while the FMLN had large numbers of women in their ranks. In some guerrilla areas, alcohol, fighting and domestic violence were banned, which led to a reduction in intrapersonal violence (Binford, 2002; Bourgois, 2001, 2002), though feminist writing on the FMLN suggests that conditions of discrimination against women did not disappear (Vásquez, Ibañez and Murguialday, 1996).

I felt more identified with the *Frente*. That is where my brother was. I also had seen things ... One time I was coming out of a guerrilla camp with my mother. We had decided to come down from the mountains into the village when we saw the army. The soldiers were going on a mission up there. We saw some bodies of innocent civilians just thrown there. They (army) had killed them and that has always confused me and I used to wonder if they had any humanity in their lives seeing the way they killed them, but that was one side as much as the other.

Daniel was not fighting for ideological reasons, but because that was what the military demanded of him. One of the participants in the self-help group who had also served in the army spoke at length about the brutal and brutalising systems of discipline he underwent:

What I thought was that they were just fighting. I didn't know why they were fighting. I didn't know where it all came from. What I did know was that I had to defend myself to survive. I had to kill in order to live. That's all I knew, because they don't explain anything. It's a dog's life and, as I say to many people, the war was terrible because we were killing each other and for some reason that I don't even know. (Teofilio, self help group)

In this context, where fear and terror regulate everyday life, young peasant men such as Teofilio were conscripted to defend elite interests for the good of the *patria* (fatherland). Central to Teofilio's military training was the value placed on violence:

They taught us that where we found him [the enemy], we had to eliminate him completely. We had to kill him. They made us develop a temper. I don't know how to say it, terrible, a steely resolve. If I was looking at you I was cursing you. You couldn't keep looking at me in the eye because I would easily dominate you. Those are the instructions that they give you. The training is really hard. You cry there. Men cry during the training because to make men fighters, they need a heavy hand, right, someone that won't feel pity because if you have a soft heart you are not a good soldier. That's what they teach you in the first months. Then when you get out and you meet civilians, they see you differently: your face, your character. Everything has changed. They completely transform you from the man before.

The indiscriminate and relentless use of terror against social organisations such as christian-based communities and trade unions closed down spaces for the articulation of non-violent opposition, deepening levels of polarisation and mistrust across society. Ongoing exclusion, the growing impossibility of the democratic project and continued state brutality proved decisive factors for the left to adopt violence as a political strategy in the late 1970s. Large numbers of men and women joined the FMLN and it was one of the first guerrilla organisations to have large numbers of women in active combat (Vásquez, Ibañez and Murguialday, 1996). The army targeted their torture of women in very sexualised ways. This normalised rape as an instrument of social control (Aron, Corne, Fursland and Zelwer, 1991). Torture, rape and violence against women became 'inevitable' to the project of state terror (Kelly, 2000). Pregnant women were also routinely tortured and their babies were taken from them. Women's bodies were mutilated by cutting off their breasts or ramming objects into their vaginas. The climate of widespread terror and suspicion also meant that all women were vulnerable. Evidence suggested that some women 'voluntarily' succumbed to individual soldiers' demands so as to avoid becoming the common property of a whole battalion (Aron, Corne, Fursland and Zelwer, 1991, citing Martín-Baró, 1989). Although terror has an explicit gender dimension, incidences of sexual violence were systematically ignored from the report of the Truth Commission (Tombs, 2006). This glaring omission from this internationally recognised document not only denies women a voice and recognition of their suffering, but highlights the very masculinist logic that informs 'official' histories of violence.

The techniques of power used by the state apparatus were multiple and varied and moved beyond direct and physical forms of violence to include actions such as surveillance, censorship, misinformation and propaganda. Chapter 3 outlines some of the ways in which this climate of fear affected community life in urban San Salvador. It also suggests that its legacy is still felt today. State-controlled death squads, operating in the 1970s and 1980s, were notorious not only for their brutality, but also for the very symbolic and public 'disposal' of their victims. Mutilated corpses, often displaying signs of sexual violence, were left strategically in public places as a warning to the local communities. These actions were as much about spreading fear and terror among the population as wiping out specific targets. Proof, due process and the rule of law were flouted openly by both security forces and extra judicial bodies. Gossip and rumour were dangerous since victims were judged not by evidence, but on the very fact that they had been accused at all. In this way, guilt by association, permanent threat and consequent fear became effective means of social control (Menjívar and Rodríguez, 2005).

The construction of repression as 'necessary' invites a deeper analysis of the relations between the Salvadoran state and civil society. Foregrounding citizen collusion (or 'survivalist compliance' to echo Dunkerley) not only has implications for how we study the history of political violence in El Salvador, but also affects how we approach its contemporary manifestations. Agents of state terror are commonly viewed as professional 'violence workers' specifically trained in the technologies of terror, but in El Salvador the institutionalisation of terror tactics through both formal and informal channels demands an analysis of the state that goes beyond its bureaucratic apparatus (Menjívar and Rodríguez, 2005). In this vein, Michael T. Clark (2001: 243–246) calls for an analysis of the state in Latin America as a 'pervasive social field constructed in and through discursive practice'. He contends that 'commonsense' concepts of the state as 'neatly bounded' and removed from society or as merely 'institutionalised government' reveal a 'misrecognition of the tip of the iceberg for the whole'. In other words, bounding our analyses of the state to its bureaucratic function ignores the ways in which the state works in and through social relations. It also allows us to see how violence becomes bureaucratised within state–societal relations. Clark makes a distinction between the state as 'the entire complex and contradictory field of social antagonism and power' and 'government' as the formal and visible institutions of governance. In light of the discussion above on ORDEN, thinking about the Salvadoran state as decentred and relational rejects any simplistic charge of antagonism between the state and civil society. This is not in an attempt to devalue the brutality of state forces, or to absolve government-controlled forces of responsibility for brutal crimes. Instead, the connected aims of such an approach are threefold. First, it points to the need for a more complex analysis of political violence beyond the simplistic formula of state versus society in order to address the collusion of civil society. Second, it requires a critical exploration of the appeal of the polarising logics that succeeded in engaging citizens to collaborate against neighbours and even family members. The (mis)recognition of threat and danger allowed the use of violent repression to be sanctioned by national political actors and supported by numerous elements within society. Third, viewing the organisation of the state as fluid and decentred (following a Foucauldian analytics of power as outlined in the previous chapter) opens up the discussion of multiple forms of resistance and survival in the face of such devastation. Our understandings of resistance cannot be restricted to the darker possibilities of civil society's collusion with state terror, nor the overt counter-violence of the FLMN, but we must also be attuned to the everyday hidden transcripts of survival and resistance within communities across El Salvador (see Wood, 2003).

While it is important not to overstate the linkages between the history of state terror and contemporary violence, it is also important not to understate the long-term effects of militarization. Many men did not leave violence behind with the signing of the peace accords, but have engaged in different acts of criminality and interpersonal violence. Daniel used his military contacts and the friendships he had made while in the army to enter a criminal gang after the war. His former sergeant provided access to both networks and weapons. Central to Daniel's militarised identity was to not be 'humiliated': 'I did not want to humiliate myself, you know, I wanted to show, I believed that I was brave.' As well as using violence for economic gain, Daniel's 'bravery' was founded upon demonstrating his hatred of women: 'I became a rapist, a murderer in that group.' The militarisation of men's lives is particularly gendered, reinforcing practices of hegemonic masculinity and domination. As discussed, placing value on violence and misogyny were central to the military project (see Enloe, 2004).

It is therefore reasonable to assume that the contemporary mass production and consumption of violence is directly related to the history of political violence. Torres-Rivas (2000: 55) argues:

> [the] ritualising of violence has many directions until it is, or makes itself, a daily presence in the public and private lives of normal people, of the terrorised citizen, who is only aware that he is alive but not of the causes of the death of others ... This climate also encourages other disassociate behaviours such as paid vengeance, taking justice into their own hands and delinquency, which has risen considerably.

Threat effectively became a valid means of control during the years of political conflict, with a marked deterioration in the quality of social relations. Mobilising fears is an historic strategy of social control. Its appeal lies in its simplicity: an identifiable group or enemy of 'good' citizens. It becomes important, therefore, to examine the continuities between how violence and fear are both managed and mutually constitutive: who was feared and who is feared.

Polarisation marks the terms of political debate on Salvadoran history and it continues to shape popular understandings of contemporary violence. The good are seen as the 'lovers of peace and order, opposed to the "bad Salvadorans", those who do not conform, who protest and rebel against the established order or worse still, terrorists' (ECA, 2006: 932). As in previous decades, this currency of stereotypes is not reliant on the concrete *facts* of violence, but on appealing to existing fears and various notions of the 'other'. Polarisation also raises questions as to the quality of 'peace' and 'order' and the price exacted on society for these. This is a different argument from saying that the forms of violence have not changed. Instead, it is demanding an interrogation of the ideological connections that continue to censor the recognition of an act as violence. In order to understand these, it is necessary to analyse the limits of peace in El Salvador.

El Salvador's 'Violent Peace'

> There is little peace and what there is, is of limited quality. (ECA, 2007: 197)

The importance of understanding the nature of peace in the region is fundamental to understanding how the many expressions of violence are enacted in the transition period. Here, we are confronted with a crucial 'paradox': peace building has succeeded in increasing violence and crime (Huezo-Mixco, 2000). In this sense, El Salvador is not unique in the region and efforts to achieve peaceful and more democratic societies throughout Latin America have been undermined by existing (and, in many cases, deepening) social cleavages. These cleavages, which Kooning and Kruijt (1999) call 'governance voids', provide key spaces for the propagation of violence: 'In spite of the demise of authoritarian rule–violence is seen as a *normal* option with which to pursue interests, attain power or resolve conflicts' (1999: 11). Normal here refers to both the frequency of violence as well as attitudes towards its use. Concha-Eastman (2001: 37) asserts that violence 'has recently acquired alarming proportions and dimensions in many countries'. Whether this is recent or not is debatable and I have outlined here that we should not sideline the central role of violence throughout the region's history. Chapter 3 explores further the notion of a process of normalisation of violence at a community level, while Chapter 4 suggests that some violence, namely its gendered expressions, are seen as more 'normal' than others.

Carlos Ramos (2000: 9) calls for an examination of the 'factors that trigger or facilitate violence' suggesting that in certain conditions, social groups or individuals appear to be more vulnerable to violence. It is therefore essential to address broader issues of political economy. The roots of El Salvador's civil conflict lay in its deeply unequal social and economic structures. With no political space available to them, opposition groups were 'dynamised by oppression and exploitation' to mobilise against El Salvador's blend of military and oligarchic rule (Dunkerley, 1988: 363). The 1992 peace accords are widely recognised as having put an end to the twelve-year war, although they have failed to build a new and more equal society (for example, Cruz and González, 1997; Pearce, 1998; Popkin, 2000; ECA, 2007). This failure is demonstrated by two key and interlinked processes under discussion here: continued political economy of inequality; ongoing problems of impunity and lack of transparency and confidence in state bodies (institutional weakness).

Political Economy

Kooning and Kruijt (2004) view new forms of violence as symptoms of failed states throughout the region. They do not suggest that this is uniform, but that across and within borders, patterns of violence vary, as does state effectiveness. The continued pervasiveness of violence in the region has been linked to weak notions of citizenship, underdevelopment and inequality. The notion of violence as a product of and contributing factor to underdevelopment is a common theme in recent literature on Latin America. This has mirrored wider trends throughout the region where both national and international organisations have placed issues of violence and security high on their policy agendas. Violence and criminality are increasingly viewed as development issues by multilateral agencies such as the World Bank (WB), the Inter-American Development Bank (IDB) and various branches of the UN, because high levels of criminal activity and insecurity are seen as hampering social and economic development.[4] In 1997, for example, it is estimated that violence cost El Salvador almost a quarter of its Gross Domestic Product (GDP). This is higher than the costs of Brazil, Colombia, Mexico, Peru and Venezuela (Londoño and Guerrerro, 1999).[5]

It is important to distinguish between the costs and the causes of violence when addressing issues of political economy. Philippe Bourgois (2001: 8) grounds 'everyday peacetime crimes' securely in matters of political economy, regarding them as a 'neoliberal version of peace time', in which violence fills the vacuum left by unemployment, underemployment and social disinvestment. The destruction of human and material resources during the war closed down opportunities for large parts of the workforce and this has been exacerbated by the exclusionary economic policies followed by the state since the cessation of conflict. Pedro, an internee in the prison, sums this up:

> Maybe the country failed because at the time of the demobilisation, there were no opportunities for work made available. The creation of jobs would have been the most essential thing to do to mobilise people and see where they could work. Many people were left [when the war was over] and when they had no money, they resorted to crime.

Violence is commonly linked to increased inequality and poverty and this is particularly acute among the poor themselves. Nonetheless, it is imperative to avoid simplistic linkages between violence and poverty precisely because of widespread attempts to criminalise the poor. The two poorest Departments of El Salvador, Chalatenango and Morazan, register the lowest homicide

---

4   The WB, the IDB and the UN have sponsored large-scale research on violence and criminality throughout the region. For example, Buvinic, Morrison and Shifter (1999), Moser and Shrader (1999), Moser and McIlwaine (2000a, 2000b) and UNODC (2007). Examples from El Salvador include Cruz et al. (1998) and Cruz, Trigueros Arguello and González (1999a). In El Salvador, the UNDP has a project entitled 'violence in a society in transition', which has been responsible for various publications, campaigns and advocacy initiatives with the media. This will be discussed further in Chapter 5.

5   The figures demonstrate that Brazil spent 10.5 per cent of its GDP on the direct and indirect costs of social violence; Mexico spent 12.3 per cent, Peru 5.1 per cent and Venezuela, 11.8 per cent. Only Colombia (in the midst of conflict) came close to El Salvador, spending 24.7 per cent.

rates. Furthermore, Zinecker (2007) highlights that Nicaragua presents much lower rates of violence than either El Salvador or Guatemala, yet its rates of poverty are comparatively worse. The post-war political economy certainly provides particular 'opportunities' for crime; it also restricts spaces that provide alternatives to violence. Although it is often the urban poor who are deemed responsible for high rates of crime, they are rarely the ones to benefit from it in any meaningful way. Ongoing levels of poverty attest to this.

Caroline Moser and Cathy McIlwaine (2004) stress that increased violence is not only a product of inequality, but actively erodes citizens' livelihood opportunities. A woman I interviewed in San Marcos in 2007 complained that increasing low-level extortion in her neighbourhood has meant that many people, particularly women who run small businesses from home, have had to close down their businesses: 'someone goes out to sell something and they have to pay to work' (Adela, San Marcos). For communities that already experience high levels of poverty, violence provides further obstacles to earning a living. In the case of women, who generally dominate informal sector activities, this has particularly harsh implications. Residents complained about the *renta* or 'tax' that *pandilleros* (gang members) demand from local businesses. Many local shops, bus companies and restaurants are required to pay a weekly subsidy to the gang. Interviews revealed that not all businesses are subject to this 'tax'; rather, it appears to be somewhat arbitrary. Likewise, although extortion is blamed on gang members, it engages a much broader constituency of local actors within neighbourhoods.

Aggressive neoliberal economic policies of the Central American governments in the early 1990s have proved incompatible with the goals of peace-building And a principal outcome of the transition period of the 1990s was the reorganisation of the Salvadoran state into the global economy. Rather than any meaningful redistributive policies in the post-war period, historic agrarian elites transferred their capital interests into finance while the economy was further opened up to transnational companies. A stated aim of this approach was to make El Salvador one big 'free trade zone' (Robinson, 2003). The flexibilisation of labour has undermined the organisation of workers and jobs created in the *maquila* (export processing plant) industry are largely filled by low-paid female workers who are expected to work in inhumane conditions (for example, Prieto and Quinteros, 2004). The feminisation of labour has coincided with the weakening of agrarian structures, and labour opportunities in the post-war period are scarce. Indeed, Robinson (2003: 101) argues that the 'accords preserved class rule of the Salvadoran elite and left the government, the state's institutionality, the economic system and the social order intact'. Evidence presented above highlights how certain demobilised groups (largely men) have become involved in organised crime, especially ex-army personnel who have formed criminal groups. These groups bring together both the skills acquired during armed conflict and relatively easy access to weaponry.[6] Others have joined the burgeoning private security industry.

El Salvador combines historic structures of violence together with widespread availability of arms and a dispossessed workforce 'skilled' in their use. High rates of violence and crime in El Salvador are not caused by guns, but they are facilitated by the easy availability of firearms. Lax laws and a high level of illegal firearms in circulation (dating from the war but also coming into the country since then) mean that, at a conservative estimate, there are some 400,000 to 450,000 arms in the hands of civilians, or two for every ten adults, only about 36 per cent of which are held legally (UNDP, 2003). It is also important to address broader social attitudes to gun ownership. Firearms are widely accepted as being 'necessary' for personal security and laws regulating gun ownership are extremely lax (Cruz and Beltrán, 2000: 54; see also UNDP, 2003). In a focus group discussion in the self-help group, men argued that having a weapon made them 'feel more manly' and that guns are central to a militarised male identities (Hume, 2004). One elected deputy (cited in Cruz and Beltrán, 2000: 4) 'would compare the case of guns to winter and the purchase of an umbrella: before the winter of criminality, everyone arms themselves'. This statement hardly represents a vote of confidence in state bodies and transfers onto citizens the duty to protect themselves (Amaya, 2006) One interviewee (Esteban, El Boulevar) explained why he holds a gun: 'For self-defence … for the protection of my family because everyone knows that, not with bad intentions … and not because of machismo, or anything like that, for protection, you protect yourself because the authorities do not.' His justification for carrying a gun is not only linked to fear of criminal victimisation, but also to the opinion that the authorities will not offer citizens, especially the poor, necessary protection (see also Hume, 2004).

Impunity and Institutional Weakness

The country's history of impunity has shaped the development of the rule of law in the post-war period. The ARENA party ruled the country from 1989

---

6 I presented the case of Daniel, an ex solider: now imprisoned for murder he became involved with a criminal gang through his army contacts: 'They introduced me to the man, but I already knew him. I think that he trusted me because, from the day I arrived, we began to smoke drugs and chat. He said to me: "I can help you get involved in something. You know that I can lend you that gun but I can also lend you any of these ones that you want." You see he had been a sub-sergeant and I was on leave [from the military] … I made friends with him [the sergeant] and, well, I think that he liked me because sometimes you just get on with people and he began to trust me. He told me that he could lend me guns to carry out crimes, that he could lend me the guns that I wanted. He had rifles, machine guns, pistols, revolvers and we went about together.'

until 2009 and successive governments have refused to acknowledge state responsibility in widespread human rights abuses and, indeed, arguably have obstructed the search for justice (IDHUCA, 2007). This refusal to offer even a minimum acknowledgement of past state repression stands in direct contradiction to the recommendations of the Truth Commission. The Salvadoran government declared a general amnesty to all those who had been accused of human rights abuses on 20 March 1993, five days after the publication of the Truth Commission's (1993) report. This set the tone for subsequent government policies of *Perdón y Olvido* (Forgive and Forget), which one author claims was a 'simple call to forget as mechanism of forgiveness' (ECA, 2007: 199). Mauricio Gaborit (2007) argues that this process is not just a matter of ignoring victims' stories, but it is about promoting an 'official' memory that effectively silences the collective memory of oppression.

A blatant example of this is the fact that the government has ignored the recommendation of the Truth Commission's (1993) report to erect a memorial to the victims of human rights abuses, yet there is a monument in San Salvador to the leading figure of the death squads (and founding member of the ARENA party), Roberto D'Aubuisson. This was paid for by public funds from the ARENA-controlled Antiguo Cuscatlan municipality.[7] A motion to name D'aubuisson '*Hijo meritismo de la nación*' (illustrious son of the nation) narrowly failed to get approval in the Legislative Assembly (IDHUCA 2007). Such symbolic acts reveal not only high levels of impunity, but the depth of contestation that continues to mark Salvadoran historical processes and its implication for contemporary relations. Partisan memorialisation and an official discourse that 'forgets' the victims of state atrocities has set a precedent for limited justice in the post-war era. It not only guarantees ongoing impunity for past abuses, but has opened the door for a 'compromised' and politicised judiciary whereby the administration of justice has eroded so far as to render it 'insignificant' (ECA, 2006: 934). The judicial system has not seen significant transformation since the peace accords and has been undermined by its lack of transparency and politicisation (IDHUCA, 2007, citing FUSADES, n.d.). Similar aspersions have been cast at the Procuraduría de Derechos Humanos (PDH; Human Rights Ombudsman), which has undergone several political

---

7 The monument was erected in a wealthy part of the capital between San Benito and Merliot. It is inscribed with D'Aubuisson's famous battle slogan 'Patria Sí, Comunismo No' (Fatherland yes, Communism no). Streets in the capital have also changed their name to commemorate him. This public acknowledgement of D'Aubuisson stands in contrast to the refusal of the state to erect an official memorial to the victims of the war. The memorial that was erected in the Cuscatlan park was done so by civil society organisations using their own funds (IDHUCA, 2007; Freedman, 2008). See also commentary in *Revista Envío*. [WWW document]. URL http://www.envio.org.ni/articulo/3717 [accessed 3 October 2008].

crises, attempts by the government to undermine its authority and vicious attacks by the media.

The National Civil Police (PNC), formed after the signing of the peace accords in 1992, has been considered one of the cornerstones of the peace process (Call, 2003). The new police force replaced the old security apparatus (the National Police, National Guard and the Treasury Police), which were considered responsible for some 85 per cent of the serious human rights violations that occurred between 1980 and 1992 (Truth Commission, 1993). The numbers of security agents were reduced drastically from 75,000 (including the army, the guerrilla, the civil defence and the old police forces) to 6000 (Stanley, 1996). Initially this severely reduced force enjoyed the support of the population, but this has been systematically eroded in recent years.[8] As well as being unable to address, in an effective manner, the wave of criminality in the post-war period, the credibility of the new institution has been detrimentally affected by a series of high-profile cases, implicating agents in criminal activities (Call, 2003). Corruption, the implication of officers in extra-judicial executions or 'social cleansing' squads, and increasing lack of respect for human rights have all served to undermine the institution's credibility as well as its ineffectiveness (ECA, 2007). Margaret Popkin (2000: 157) argues that El Salvador combines the 'disadvantages of a peace process that did not involve a change in government with a compromised judiciary'.

To a certain extent, this loss of confidence is reflected in the proliferation of private security companies to defend businesses and properties. No systematic study has been carried out into private security in El Salvador and it remains a highly unregulated area. In 2001, there were an estimated 70,000 private security agents compared to the PNC, which had an active force of approximately 20,000 officers (Melara, 2001). ECA (2006: 927) claimed that El Salvador spent 11 per cent of its GDP on private security. Since then, it is believed that the number of private security agents has risen further to as many as 92,000 while the number of police was around 17,660 in 2008 (interview with PNC, June 2008).[9] More worryingly, this lack of confidence

---

8   In 1995, 45.9 per cent of the population considered that the new police force was better that the old apparatus, 24.6 per cent felt it was the same and 21.3 per cent that it was worse. By 2000, 64 per cent of respondents believed that the PNC was losing the respect and support of the population, with 38.5 per cent agreeing that it was worse than the old regime and 26.3 per cent seeing it as the same (Aguilar Villamariona, Amaya Cobar and Martinez Ventura, 2001: 15–16). One of the key challenges of the FMLN government is to restore confidence in the police. A central strategy of the administration is to promote community policing and crime prevention policies (Interview: PNC, July 2009).

9   Interviews with various members and advisors to the PNC suggest that there is an active force of 17,660 police who have graduated from the Police Academy. In addition,

reinforces the prevalence of social attitudes and behaviour that legitimise and propagate the use of violence in *certain* circumstances and by *certain* individuals.

Extra-judicial murders and 'social cleansing' squads have reappeared on the public scene in recent years, although many local human rights groups fear that they never actually disappeared after the war (IDHUCA, 2007). Indeed, a key concern of the Truth Commission's report (1993) was the possibility that these forces could be reactivated in the future given their centrality to the state terror strategy and their strategic relationship to institutions of socio-economic power. At the end of 2002 and beginning of 2003, there were several incidences of decapitated corpses found in San Salvador reflecting tactics used by the death squads in the late 1970s and 1980s. These particular cases were largely dismembered corpses of young women that were found dumped in different locations across the capital and many displayed signs of having been raped. One notable case is the murder of Rosa N. whose body parts were found in different locations across San Salvador in December 2002. Her death was attributed to gang rivalries, but the trial crumbled due to lack of evidence. Amnesty International estimates that there were around twenty such murders of women between 2002 and mid 2004 (Rivas Martinez, 2005).

Recent studies and declarations from human rights organisations have pointed to the emergence of new generations of death squads and allegations have been made of official involvement in these initiatives (Aguilar and Miranda, 2006: 56). In 2007, two police officers in eastern El Salvador were arrested and accused of participating in 'social cleansing' groups. Interviews with members of the PNC insist that these officers were not acting on official orders, but that they were isolated cases. Human rights organisations are less convinced and one lawyer has suggested that they represent a type of 'perverse altruism' among elements of the police who felt that they were acting in the common good (interview with author, June 2008). One such group is the Mano Blanco operating in the San Miguel area with the stated aim of cleaning communities of gang-members and 'murder of *todo aquel tatuado*' (all who have tattoos). Mano Blanco is also the name given to a death squad responsible for the murder of thousands of peasants, workers and leftist sympathisers in the 1970s and 1980s, indicating important continuities in the mobilisation of certain polarised rhetoric and practices in the post-war period. Sources estimate that such bodies may be responsible for as many as 96 extrajudicial killings of young people (FESPAD, 2006). In August 2007,

---

there are a further 800 'extras' who have not graduated from the academy but are charged with looking after public figures. I was told that there are 70,000 registered private security agents and around 22,000 additional agents who are not registered.

citizens of the town of Chalchuapa in the western area received a flyer instructing them that they were under curfew: 'For your own good, we advise you not to be on the streets after 10 pm, because we are carrying out a cleansing campaign.' The flyer was signed only with the initials of a group calling itself 'EL', which many believe stand for the Spanish phrase *escuadron de limpieza*, or 'cleansing squad'. Even local authorities were ordered to stay off the streets becuase the group considered itself 'better equipped than the police' (Dalton, 2007).

Figures from 2003 indicate that 55 per cent of respondents would approve of the killing of a criminal who terrorises the community and 40.5 per cent would approve of lynching the criminal (UNDP, 2003: 142). In this context, order is recognised as more important than civil liberties and human rights in the face of high levels of criminality (Cruz, 2000: 518). Chapter 5 will explore community responses to violence and argues that such attitudes are indicative of a dearth of non-violent alternatives for resolving conflict within society, as well as the legacy of respect for authoritarian measures. Massive impunity and continued authoritarianism within the Salvadoran state mean that the development of alternatives to violence is limited. Citizens use and applaud violence to attack criminality and violence. Embedded polarisation nourishes this logic. 'It has meant that violence itself is ignored, justified and, sometimes, stimulated by those who see themselves as upstanding and exemplary citizens, against those they consider the scum of society' (Cruz and Beltrán, 2000: 5). Such attitudes are indicative of a certain 'complicity', or, at the very least, a conspiratorial silence regarding the use of social cleansing mechanisms, suggesting a tolerance, if not overt respect, for authoritarian measures. These attitudes mark a continuity in authoritarian practices that constitutes a grave obstacle to the quality of democracy in the region. Miranda (2000: 50) argues that a crucial effect of authoritarianism is that it is internalised on an individual level, thus making each Salvadoran an active agent in its reproduction: 'violence is one of the most striking characteristics of social relations between Salvadorans'. This is particularly noticeable among young men who dominate in both statistics for perpetrators of violence and its victims. Violence, in this situation, has become both something to fear and a tool with which to address problems. Mistrust and fear among citizens have nourished a situation of 'hypervigilence' where citizens have become both agents and prisoners of their own fear (UNDP, 2003). Such constructions of fear continue to be based upon a polarising logic of the 'other':

A world divided into 'black and white' or into allies and enemies (where the outside is not conceived of as part of a personal scheme of values), is nothing but a threat, a potential aggressor. In the face of this, it is necessary to prepare oneself with a logic of hyper vigilance and a defensive attitude against possible attack ... a fertile ground on which ideas and measures that support violence are sown. (UNDP, 2003: 21)

Although these attitudes may seem extreme and they certainly mark an endpoint in terms of responses to violence, they must be understood within the broader heavy-handed logic. State policies to combat crime continue to rely on fomenting a politics of fear and panic. Chapter 5 argues that crime policies are deeply polarising in both language and the substantive mechanisms of policy. Rather than focus on the structural causes of crime, it appears increasingly common to define the issue as one of social and moral decay, void of political causes or consequences (Snodgrass-Godoy, 2006). In this way, violence is conceptualised a moral or a social problem rather than a political and economic one. This not-so-subtle discourse changes the focus of political intervention, shifting the responsibility from the state to its citizens. It also displaces attention from other issues of weak governance, 'so that [citizens] will forget the extent of inequality and government mismanagement' (Chevigny, 2003: 91; see also Arana, 2005). Existing research is critical of issues of class-based stereotypes that result in the criminalisation of the poor generally and poor urban men in particular (for example, Goldstein, 2003; Snodgrass-Godoy, 2006; Hume, 2007c). Mobilising stereotypes in this way has potent pragmatism in the context of El Salvador and Latin America more generally. It also removes the need to problematise issues of gender, poverty and inequality. An historic characteristic of Salvadoran social relations is that the security of some groups has come at the expense of others. This is not based on evidence, but on stigmatising subordinated groups that have less recourse to speaking out for themselves and also to the channels of justice (BodyGendrot, 2001). It is to an analysis of data on contemporary violence that I now turn.

Measuring the Problem of Contemporary Violence

To speak of peace with an average of 11 murders a day is ironic. In this context it is not appropriate to speak of development, but of economic growth and then only from the interests of corporate capital. El Salvador ended a civil war, but it entered into another war, a type of war with itself, just as or more destructive than the previous one (ECA, 2006: 925).

The first chapter argued that our knowledge about violence is based more on myth than actual facts. One of the biggest challenges to research on violence is the accuracy of state registers and mechanisms for recording violence. Historical data are scarce for rates of violence and criminality in the region. Cruz and Beltrán (2000: 9), however, cite Pan American Health

Organisation (PAHO) figures from the 1960s and 1970s that indicate that El Salvador had a murder rate of around or greater than 30 per 100,000 inhabitants, compared to Colombia and Nicaragua's 22 and 25 per 100,000 inhabitants respectively. They consider such figures to be demonstrative of a historical problem of endemic violence in the country, since they are not only over and above contemporary world averages, but well over what is judged as extremely violent, that is, more than 10 murders per 100,000 inhabitants. Added to this, figures from the IUDOP/ACTIVA survey (1998) demonstrate that 80 per cent of adult respondents were subject to physical violence as children, highlighting that the problem of violence permeated both the public and domestic realms. Empirical data presented in this book support the notion that violence, in its many expressions, is a historic problem in El Salvador. Testimonies are permeated with incidences of brutality and force since birth (see Chapters 3 and 4). In this way, violence not only becomes normalised as an everyday occurrence, but becomes a lens through which everyday life is understood. Threat and violence had extreme repercussions on how society functioned, destroying not only material structures and weakening institutional capacities, but marking social attitudes, behaviours and norms. In previous decades, political violence overshadowed much of day-to-day existence, but it coexisted alongside other expressions of violence that were effectively rendered invisible and sidelined:

> In the 1980s, the phenomenon of 'violence' was expressed fundamentally by its political dimension, in the shape of an internal military conflict. Other forms of violence coexisted alongside the armed confrontation, but their manifestations and effects were diminished, overshadowed or confused with those of the war itself ... Social phenomena that incorporated patterns of violent behaviour, external to the conflict, were not included in the list of social and political preoccupations (Ramos, 2000: 8).

Although reporting mechanisms have arguably improved in recent years, El Salvador still does not have a credible register of criminal violence, with different state institutions providing contradictory records (see Table 1; see also; FESPAD, 2006). The quality of information is often dependent on the type of violence under scrutiny because of chronic problems of under-reporting and misclassification (Shrader, 2001). Registers on violence tend to be limited to physical effects because it is considered much more difficult to assess psychological or emotional impact (Arriagada and Godoy, 2000). Cruz, Trigueros Arguello and González (1999b) maintain that different state records can present contradictory views of the scale of violence and that certain areas (namely San Salvador) and certain crimes are better recorded than others. For example, figures from the Attorney General's Office (FGR)

Table 1. Murder Rate 1999–2007 According to Different State Registers

Year	Murder rate
1999	2270 (PNC)
	3845 (FGR)
	2544 (IML)
2000	2341 (PNC)
	3551 (FGR)
	2692 (IML)
2001	2210 (PNC)
	3590 (FGR)
	2374 (IML)
2002	2024 (PNC)
	2835 (FGR)
	2346 (IML)
2003	2172 (PNC)
	3536(FGR)
	2388 (IML)
2004	2768 (PNC)
	3897 (FGR)
	2933 (IML)
2005[10]	3778
2006	3928
2007	3491

Source: data accessed from Central American Observatory on Violence (OCAVI), 2009.

were considered more reliable for murder until 1998 and, since then, the quality of PNC records are seen as having improved significantly. Even then, however, actual figures are open to query, because different bodies may have their own criteria for the recording of intentional deaths. Table 1 demonstrates that the discrepancies between different state registers is not unsubstantial. Furthermore, murder rates per capita were based on 1992 census projections until 2007. Census figures for 2008 reveal that the population of El Salvador is considerably lower than the projections: 5,744,113 as opposed to the projected figures for 2006 of 6,980,279. If one were to analyse the 2007 murder rate of 3491 against the old population data, it would translate into 49.13 per 100,000 citizens. With new census data, this would jump to 60.78 murders per 100,000 in 2007 (FESPAD, 2008). These figures rank El Salvador as the most violent country in Latin America.

From an orthodox criminological approach, figures for murder are used as one of the most reliable reflections of the scale of the problem of violence because they are based on physical evidence and they measure an extreme endpoint of violent engagements that can be compared within and across

---

10 From 2005, a technical advisory group has presented unified homicide data registers.

Table 2.   Murder Rates Disaggregated by Sex 2004–2006

Year	Number of male murders	Percentage of total murders	Number of female murders	Percentage of total murders	Total
2004	2673	91	260	9	2933
2005	3422	90	390	10	3812
2006	3484	89	437	11	3921

Adapted from Central American Observatory on Violence.[11]

national boundaries and are therefore easily identifiable. Given the serious nature of such crimes, they tend to be recorded more carefully (Arriagada and Godoy, 2000). The use of homicide rates as a proxy demands caution on three fronts. First, in El Salvador, and other countries in the region, registers tend to be uneven and contradictory, as demonstrated in Table 1. Second, the dependence on homicide rates as a proxy for assessing levels of violence in society offers little scope for understanding underlying causes (Shrader, 2001). Third, a concentration on murder as the extreme endpoint of violence deflects attention from other non-lethal violence. While, as this book argues, violence is a pervasive force in everyday life for many Salvadorans, this is not uniform. Particular types of violence affect men and women differently and this is not only determined by gendered roles, but also by cultural and social norms that regulate levels of violence. Women, for example, may sustain regular low-intensity violence that does not result in death, whereas young people and, specifically, young men rank highest in homicide rates. On average 90 per cent of all homicides are of men (see Table 2). In 2004, 51.6 per cent of homicide victims were between the ages of 18 and 30; most of these were young men. The average homicide rate for young people was estimated at greater than 90 deaths per 100,000 inhabitants in 2004, while the cohort between 20 and 24 years was 114 per 100,000 (FESPAD, 2006: 23–24). The fact that it is men–and specifically poor young men–who are being killed is rarely singled out for attention. The gendered dynamics of such violence and the centrality of masculinity to murder seems so normalised that it does not appear to require explanation. Without understanding the critical relationship between masculinities and violence, both understandings and responses will remain limited.

Research carried out for Oxfam America in two municipalities of El Salvador indicated four interlinked problems in the measurement of violence, particularly at the local level (Hume, 2008b). First, the technical mechanisms for recording incidents are poor. Many local state bodies, including the PNC,

---

11   Figures are available at: [WWW document]. URL http://www.ocavi.com/docs_files/file_396.pdf (accessed 20 March 2008)

do not have access to appropriate information technology or the skills to maintain accurate databases. While manual recording is in itself not the problem, it does make the task of cross-checking and maintaining reliable databases more difficult. Second, the study indicated that data transfer mechanisms tended to aggregate basic data at a local level, thus losing important details for analysis. Another Oxfam America study (2007: 10) shows a particularly stark example of this, indicating that there is little disaggregated information on the sex of the victim in rape cases. In many cases, this was simply recorded as 'no information'. This dearth of detail hides important gender dynamics of certain types of violence, and it also contributes to misinformation on the scale of non-lethal violence. Third, although accessing public registers is slightly more straightforward today than even five years ago, it still remains a challenge to find local or disaggregated data.[12] Accessing basic data is difficult from outside state bodies, but even the sharing of information between bodies cannot be taken for granted. One civil servant spoke of 'institutional jealousy' with regard to the sharing of statistics. Her job was to set up a municipal observatory to monitor levels of violence and crime and to encourage greater liaison between agencies at a local level.[13] However, at the time of interview in October 2007, she had not succeeded in getting access to basic local data even after several months and multiple formal and informal requests. Finally, the study found that there remains a huge problem of underreporting of crimes, especially gendered violence and local conflicts. Lack of information about rights and processes, misinformation or indeed partisan politics at a local institutional level can have a deterrent effect on citizens reporting violence. I will return to this issue in greater detail in Chapter 5.

Allen Feldman (2003: 69–70) is critical of the 'actuarial logic' that predominates in analyses of violence. He suggests the 'enumeration debates' are merely abstract and fail to reflect the experiential dimension of violence, which is much more complex. Poor data undermine rather than enrich what we know about violence. The gendered dynamics of violence have not only been sidelined from public debates, but are rarely visible in aggregate crime statistics even for what are popularly considered gendered crimes, such as rape.

---

12 To a large degree, this has been facilated by organisations such as the UNDP, which has a programme dedicated to violence reduction and that offers up-to-date research on issues of crime and violence. Another recent initiative on a regional level is the Central American Observatory on violence, which contains state statistics for different types of crime See [WWW document]. URL http://www.ocavi.com (accessed 26 August 2009).

13 Such initiatives are being promoted throughout the country in order to maintain localised databases and design local-level prevention strategies. One of the stated aims of the new Funes administration is to focus more on preventative policies.

Oxfam America (2007: 9) highlights the lack of data concerning the causes of the murder of women. In 65.38 per cent of cases, the causes are unknown, while 2.45 per cent are attributed to domestic violence. It is interesting to note, however, that in 55 per cent of cases, the woman's corpse was found at home. Although this does not mean that all women who were killed at home were victims of domestic violence, it does contrast somewhat dramatically with the figure of 2.45 per cent being attributed to domestic violence. In this case, both the absence of reliable data and the attempts to derive causation obscure the hidden gendered dimension of much of the violence directed at women.

Often framed as 'femicide', the murder of women has received less attention in El Salvador than in other contexts, such as Ciudad Juarez and Guatemala, precisely because it remains numerically less significant than that of men. However, femicide is regarded as a growing problem and an issue for concern for local women's organisations who are increasingly calling attention to the particular 'misogyny' implied in the murders of women. Femicide is defined as the murder of a woman *because* she is a woman. It is often understood as an explicitly misogynistic backlash against women (Prieto-Carron et al., 2007). Rising murder rates since 2003 have also seen the proportional number of murders of women go up (see Table 2). These murders are attributed to a number of factors linked to gender discrimination, such as a male backlash against women's empowerment. Women's organisations have been highly critical of the ongoing impunity for a majority of these crimes. Prevailing social attitudes and prejudices are reflected in different social reactions to certain types of violence. The discussion of gendered hierarchies of violence revealed the differentiated levels of social acceptance for murder. Ongoing impunity in Latin America must also be seen in this context where certain types of violence are more tolerated than others.

By ignoring key dimensions of crime and violence, such as age and gender, policy intervention is limited (Shrader, 2001). Data on typically gendered violence, such as domestic and sexual abuse, are extremely difficult to quantify. Bar initiatives from the women's movement and the international community, no serious attempt has been made to date to analyse the extent of the problem in El Salvador (UNDP, 2000; Velado, 2001). The reliability of statistical information from Instituto Salvadoreño para el Desarrollo de la Mujer (ISDEMU; Salvadoran Institute for the Development of Women), the governmental body responsible for compiling information on gendered violence, has been criticised (UNDP, 2000).[14] Research suggests that more

---

14 A UNDP-sponsored study, carried out by Comité 25 de Noviembre, a network of non-governmental bodies, found that state bodies had serious problems in both their recording of information and implementing the necessary protocol to address the problem of

women are reporting abuse, largely as a result of feminist advocacy and international pressure. This will be discussed further in Chapters 4 and 5. International and national campaigns have succeeded in making the issue of violence against women visible, and some initiatives do exist to address the problem such as national campaigns or women's organisations that offer medical attention and advice to women survivors of violence. Nevertheless, such initiatives tend to be chronically under-resourced and merely constitute the tip of the iceberg in what is needed to tackle these issues.

The problem of gendered violence–specifically violence against women–in the region, therefore, remains largely under-studied and continues to be conceptualised in isolation from mainstream studies of violence. Moreover, the impact of such violence is still minimised in comparison to other expressions of violence in both official and popular discourse (Hume, 2004). Again, this is rooted in the under-reporting by victims, but it can also be linked to misrepresentation or non-recognition of this violence as criminal and violence more generally as gendered (see also UNDP, 2000). Women who experience intimate partner violence or sexual violence are not only less likely to denounce the aggressor, as he is likely to be known to them, but the legal system has been accused of demonstrating serious shortcomings in its capacity to address such issues (Velado, 2001: 57; Hernández Reyes and Solano, 2003; Macaulay, 2006). I contended in Chapter 1 that it would be erroneous to suggest that there is little public awareness of the problems of violence against women or 'gender violence', especially in the domestic realm. Nonetheless, its effects are minimised in comparison to other expressions of violence of a more 'public' nature by a tacit acceptance of its perceived normality. The glaring absence of discussions of the linkages between the 'public' and 'private' faces of violence should raise questions on how epistemologies of violence are being constructed. Whose perception of violence is made valid by such knowledge? How are historic silences and myths reinforced by the meagreness of the discussion of the subject of so called 'private' violences?[15] The widely held belief

---

gendered violence. The report is particularly critical of offices of the justice of the peace that deny responsibility for attending cases of 'intrafamily' violence. In addition, family courts are only open during office hours from Monday to Friday, leaving women with very little recourse to justice at other times (Hernández Reyes and Solano, 2003).

15 For example, Moser and Winton (2001) noted different approaches to the problem of violence and criminality in their consultations with the governments of Honduras and Nicaragua particularly with regard to these countries' Poverty Reduction Strategy Papers, where violence was highlighted as a crosscutting theme. The Nicaraguan government highlighted the need to understand the dynamics of violence in the home, as this is not only a major social problem, but the home is considered a site of socialisation where violence is learned. In contrast, the government of Honduras looked principally at the public dynamics of violence, which provides a very different

that the domestic realm is 'private' not only illustrates deeply entrenched patriarchal structures within society, but, more dangerously, that the rule of law all too often accommodates, rather than challenges, sex and gender discrimination (Acosta, 1999).

Unreliable data and popular myths not only affect the effectiveness of policy intervention, but also influence the noteworthiness of certain types of violence. Levels of visibility may lead to false perceptions on the severity or the incidence of some types of violence. In the early 2000s, for example, kidnapping appeared in a prominent place in the media and public debates. This was most likely linked to a series of high-profile cases. The authorities were quick to respond and kidnappings have been reduced drastically in recent years. It is perhaps no coincidence that this crime largely affects those sections of the population that enjoy most economic, political and social power. This is indicative of a broader pattern of uneven access to citizen security, which is often dependent on economic position (Arriagada and Godoy, 2000). This raises important questions about which or what kinds of citizens the debates on security contemplate. Chapter 3 cites an example from a focus group in El Boulevar where young women express their fear of being kidnapped. When they explain what they mean, they are referring to their fear of being abducted and sexually assaulted and not to being held for ransom, as the term 'kidnap' commonly implies. This draws attention to the labels applied to violence in the public imagination and how these hide or validate certain types of crime.

Statistical data are open to political manipulation and this is done in collusion with state institutions and the media that are responsible for telling the stories of violence. The media play a significant role in reflecting, shaping and even distorting public opinion and reinforcing fears of victimisation from a stigmatised 'other'. This is particularly noteworthy in the public attack on youth gangs or *maras*, which have emerged as the most public and most feared group of violence actors in the post-war period (Hume, 2007b, 2007c). Trigueros Martel (2006: 963) argues that the development of an 'official' discourse of gangs and 'public enemy number one' serves a dual purpose. On the one hand, it foments their stigmatisation through a division within society between 'us' and 'them'. On the other, it serves to legitimise the use of repression by the state in order to guarantee the 'security' of its citizens. This is not a new discourse as I maintain throughout this chapter. New 'wars' against gangs employ similar rhetoric to the crusades of previous decades against communism. In December 2005, President Tony Saca estimated that *maras*

---

analysis of the problem and, therefore, distinct policy approaches. Such issues will be discussed below, in reference to the pervasiveness of crime as a major source of preoccupation for citizens.

are responsible for 50 per cent of murders and 'disorder in the streets' (Saca, 2005). According to press reports, the PNC blame gangs for 60 per cent of all criminal activity, yet offers few sources of evidence as to how this estimate was reached (FESPAD, 2006: 22). However, based on available data, the Instituto de Medicina Legal (IML; State Forensic Unit) calculates that the causes of around 59 per cent of murders are unknown, 23.3 per cent are ascribed to 'common crime' and 13.4 per cent are gang-related murders. Most of the latter tend to be of rival *pandilleros* (cited in FESPAD, 2006: 22). Without accurate registers, realistic assessments of the problem are difficult and leave the way open for rumour and supposition. Chapter 5 argues that unreliable and politicised use of data informs short-sighted and limited policy interventions. In the context of Guatemala, Winton (2004: 85) notes that the high visibility of gangs and the associated fear have reached such levels that 'there seems little need for the perceived severity of the problem to be verified by actual data'. The paucity of hard evidence calls into question not only existing stereotypes of violence, but policies that have been developed based on flawed data.

It is therefore important to draw out the contradictions between public perception of crime, policy instruments to challenge it and the measurement of actual violence. Reaction to violence and fear of it is not always determined by levels of actual violence. One of the effects of the sensationalist treatment of crime is in a magnification of perceived insecurity. From 1998 to 2003 official rates for crime in El Salvador fell, yet the 'social impact' of crime was 'more powerful' (ECA, 2000: 494). This contradiction is illustrative of several key issues discussed in this book. To reiterate the point made above, the visibility of certain types of violent crime can exert great influence on public opinion and policy decisions. Awareness colours popular assumptions about threat and insecurity, which may not correspond to the real situation (Arriagada and Godoy, 2000). Popular understandings of violence, therefore, contribute to the wider problem of violence.

> Certain types of violence provoke less indignation than would be expected. One finds that there is more indignation about the rise in violent crime against property than toward the rise in crime against life committed mostly by young men from the poorest neighbourhoods. This lack of indignation may be the result of various factors: it may indicate the existence of a normalisation or acceptance of interpersonal violence when it is committed against those who are thought to be 'certain types of people', or in order to resolve certain types of arguments such as drug trafficking. (Cárdia, 2002: 153)

Given the problems outlined above of the weakness in measures of violence, this climate has particularly dangerous implications for both state and societal responses, not least of all the adoption of populist and repressive measures (see Chapter 5). In Chapter 1, I referred to the importance of analysing gendered hierarchies of violence in order to understand how the meaning of violence intersects with deeply embedded social, political and economic inequalities. In her study of Sao Paulo, Teresa Caldeira (2000: 19–20) suggests that the 'talk of crime' is 'contagious' and 'repetitive'. It organises certain understandings of crime that both reproduce and magnify actual problems. Narratives of crime 'elaborate prejudices and eliminate ambiguities'. I have argued previously that an important element of these closed narratives of crime is the removal of any reference to the crimes of the powerful. In order to achieve this, society needs a focus for its fears. 'Talk' of violence in the post-authoritarian era has become part of the vernacular of Latin American societies. Much of it is implicitly about certain types of crime by certain types of people. Although it may appear contradictory, despite this talk, there is little debate and little space to articulate alternative or divergent viewpoints. In the noise about violence and crime, certain versions dominate, leaving little room for alternative stories. Following a Foucauldian logic, these discourses are presented as authoritative and the material practices based on them are then used as an effective and immediate form of discipline and social control: the 'official discourse'.

Therefore, talk of crime serves as an organising strategy that reinforces the segregation of societies along historic exclusionary class lines. It should not be confused with measures of actual crime and violence. Ironically, this segregation is reliant on the compliance of the same groups it seeks to demonise, and support for heavy-handed measures is often strongest within the groups it most targets (Carranza, 2007). In this way, domination and symbolic violence work through local worlds 'via a misrecognition of power structures on the part of the dominated who collude in their own oppression' (Bourgois, 2001: 8). This facilitates the displacement of attention of structural forms of violence and shifts attention and responsibility to the poor and, specifically, poor men. These divisions are not restricted to a discursive ordering of society, but involve a 'literal' segregation of society (Foucault, 1977; Caldeira, 2000). Razor wire, walls and fences separate the spaces where decent law-abiding citizens live from 'no go' areas inhabited by the poor and 'criminalised' classes. Luxurious shopping malls and gated communities provide sanctuary for the upper middle classes and insulate them from the harsher realities of everyday life. Security based on such divisions, spatial and otherwise is, of course, illusory.

Marcuse (1997, cited in Bannister and Fyfe, 2001) asks: do walls provide security or create fear? This is an important question in contemporary Latin America. A new private economy of security has emerged in the region and the rationale for its success is provided by a fearful citizenry. The logic of threat provides the logic for protection and, in this way, citizens become dependent on a growing private enterprise that is rapidly replacing the public security function of the state. 'Security' therefore becomes yet another commodity in a political economy that divides those who have from those who do not. Rather than rendering the measurement of crime incidental, this context makes the need for reliable measures all the more urgent. Only by providing evidence, having access to reliable data, and challenging the silencing of alternative voices and debates can stereotypes be challenged.

Conclusion

The promotion of particular understandings of violence in El Salvador has huge implications for how citizens fear, survive and understand the world around them. This is a process that is based on class and gendered prejudices. It is both ontological and epistemological affecting how citizens coexist within a social group, and also shaping the ways in which notions of violence are constructed, internalised and reproduced. In short, it demands an interrogation of the hegemonic processes of how violence becomes possible: its ideological as well as material bases. In this chapter, I have addressed the historic ideologies based on a politics of threat and fear that continue to have repercussions in El Salvador's peace. I have argued that although the state may no longer be a central protagonist in overt violence, its role in promoting symbolic violence and naturalising unequal power relations should not be ignored in the post-authoritarian period. The very process by which violence is recognised is central to the maintenance of unequal power relations. The normalisation of violence among men is a worrying indicator of this trend. By foregrounding the centrality of gendered political economy to the reproduction of violence we can see the continuing influence of historic conflicts on contemporary interpretations of violence that invoke stereotypes based on class and gender.

In the introduction to the book, I cited a Salvadoran woman who believed that contemporary violence 'is worse because before if you did not get involved in politics, you did not get killed; now it is different: you could be at home and you could be killed there' (Cruz et al., 1998: 3, citing IUDOP, 1996: 240). The scale of historic repression in El Salvador questions the notion that previous violence only targeted political opponents, thus undermining perceptions of safety and security. What is missing in 'new violence' is the fictional assurances that insulate 'good' citizens who did not get involved in politics (or whose involvement was restricted to ignoring the excesses of the state) from being a potential victim. Thus, any study of terror must not be divorced from the contemplation of local ethnic, agrarian, ideological and personal conflicts (Lauria-Santiago, 2005). In such a situation, where so many factors combine to undermine social cohesion and equality, the causes and effects of violence become blurred, as their manifestations are embedded in social practices and codes of behaviour. Men's use of violence is a case in point. It is a complex, if not impossible, task to separate the causes of violence from its effects. Young men from poor communities may employ violence as an instrument for recognition or inclusion; however, the effect can be that society excludes them even further, thus creating a vicious circle, where violence indeed 'nourishes' and reproduces itself in other forms (Ramos, 2000). The boundaries between different types of violence–social, political and economic–become blurred, as does society's capacity to define them. As Arendt (1969: 80) cautions, although violence may 'pay' in the short term, the consequences for the longer term are devastating. She warns: '[t]he practice of violence, like all action, changes the world, [but the most probable change is to a more violent world'. The post-war context has created an environment in which sizeable numbers of citizens have turned to illegal activities and there has been a dramatic increase in criminality. State representatives and the media sensationalize the problem and grade violence according to hegemonic power interests, stigmatising certain groups, such as young men. The discussion has focused on highly visible forms of violence, reflecting both state discourses and popular understandings of violence. This serves to mask 'private' aspects such as domestic violence and other forms of violence against women. Such a backdrop will frame the analyses presented in subsequent chapters, which interrogate how citizens live with and resist high levels of violence on a daily basis.

3

'Terror as Usual': Uniting Past and Present Accounts of Violence

In the community, there are gangs, rapes. There are gang problems when others come here, drug pushing, gangs who beat up men. The gang mistreats people who visit, drugs, vices, lack of respect and gossip. Think about it, here, inside the community, there are gangs and they have problems with outsiders; sometimes their blood gets up and they hit people. Rape: they rape kids and they grab them and take them away. The sale of drugs and the same men from here know where they sell them. In those houses there, the bad treatment, the drugs that the men smoke, they become drug addicts. Vices: right here they sell alcohol, beer, everything. Lack of respect: lack respect for older people when they want to correct you and you know, 'that old bitch', as they say. Gossip that some in the community spread, what she says, 'look, you said this'. Sometimes someone tells you something and you don't keep it a secret, you go around telling everyone 'look, she told me that you are going out with someone else'. (Carmen, El Boulevar)

These words, spoken by a fourteen-year-old participant in a focus group in the school in El Boulevar, are a description of the different types of violence that a group of eight adolescent girls have identified in their community. The narrative not only reflects the high levels of violence in the community, but its many different expressions. It points to a life marked by 'terror as usual', where violence both frames and disrupts 'normal' everyday interaction (Taussig, 1989). The aim of this chapter is to explore the multiple types of violence that pervade the lives of the inhabitants of two low-income communities in Greater San Salvador. I trace the persistence of coping strategies, such as silence, that were developed during the war and continue to shape everyday life in the present. Based on empirical evidence, gathered in two communities, El Boulevar and La Vía, this chapter proposes patterns of everyday violence are formative. They not only shape and form identities, but can become embedded in patterns of social interaction between individuals and groups. This does not mean that all people are violent at all times, rather, as Kooning and Kruijit (1999) suggest, violence has become a *normal* option for many citizens. Normal here refers to both the frequency of violence and the fact that certain types of violence are so accepted within society that they can be explained and justified. Living and negotiating a context impregnated with high levels of violence has become part of the everyday routine for many Salvadorans. This process of normalisation is mediated by many factors, including the issues of political economy and the country's history, as outlined in Chapter 2. An analysis of the violence presented here should be understood against this backdrop of inequality and exclusion. Cultural norms and gendered roles shape not just *who* uses violence and *how* and *when* they might use it. They also inform both individual and wider social reactions. As I have underlined thus far, what is recognised as violence by some groups may not be considered violent by others. Such notions affect how violence is made visible and also influence how it is perceived, legitimised and tolerated in any given social context.

A uniting thread of this book has been the discussion of silences. I argue here that silences and non-lexical communication are as important to understanding the phenomenon of violence as the words that may be used to describe it. I agree with Taussig (1989) who makes a distinction between the production of silence and 'silencing'. Silencing, as I have argued, has been an overt political strategy of the state. It is a strategy that has produced multiple effects that continue to shape both epistemologies and ontologies of violence in the post-war scenario. Silences are threaded through the discussion presented in this chapter and subsequent chapters, where they are identified as a survival strategy, an expression of fear and a declaration of impotence. The chapter begins with a brief discussion of how violence has become embedded in everyday life and I introduce the two communities that inform my analysis. The chapter explores four central tenets of violence in El Salvador. I begin with a discussion of the framing of violence by those who live with it and must make sense of it. This is followed by an analysis of the brutalising forces of state terror and other forms of community conflict. The difficulty of separating different types of violence will be touched upon, as will the use of silences and communities' lack of resources with which to resolve conflict in a non-violent manner. Following this, there is discussion on the different impacts of violence on social groups. Finally, I conclude with a brief commentary on the highly visible problem of gangs in El Boulevar.

Introducing La Vía and El Boulevar

Most of this research was carried out in two communities on the outskirts of San Salvador that I call El Boulevar and La Vía. Both El Boulevar and La Vía are illegal settlements in the municipality of Soyapango, a satellite town of Greater San Salvador. Soyapango is considered the one of the most violent municipalities in El Salvador. Urbanisation in Soyapango has been sporadic and unplanned. Many of its inhabitants live in precarious conditions, with different levels of access to basic resources, such as electricity, water and sanitation. La Vía is one of the many communities located on the disused train tracks that cut across different parts of the city. The community grew initially as a result of population displacements during the war, although this trend has continued with arrival of economic migrants from different parts of the country. Although the land cannot be sold because it legally belongs to the national railway company, Ferrocarriles Nacionales de El Salvador (FENDESAL), many of the more recent arrivals have bought the few sheets of corrugated iron or *bahereque* [1] structures from previous inhabitants and a few have permanent dwellings made from brick or *adobe*.

El Boulevar is situated on one side of the main artery linking San Salvador to the eastern side of the country. It was set up for temporary shelter for people affected by the earthquake in 1965 and at the time of the research in 2001–2002, the community members were struggling to legalise their plots. This has been a long and arduous process. Some 90 families were also facing eviction in order to make room for a project to widen the main road that runs alongside the community. This process provided the backdrop to the research and tensions were running high among the population for people were, understandably, worried about their futures.

My introduction to both communities was facilitated by the Latin American Faculty for Social Sciences (FLACSO) who had a team of researchers looking at violence and social exclusion in both areas (see Savenije and Andrade-Eekhoff, 2003).[2] They provided introductions to the community *junta directiva* (management committee) that is elected by residents. From there, I arranged my own schedule with local residents and my research was independent of the FLACSO project. Initial impressions of both communities proved quite different. The community association in La Vía was extremely welcoming and agreed readily to assist me in my research. Within a short time of arriving in the community, I was, along with another local researcher, invited to attend a community fundraising event. The FLACSO researcher, Claudia,

---

1   *Bahereque* is a mixture of wood, mud and stones, used in popular constructions. Many of the buildings that fell in the 2001 earthquakes were made of *bahereque*, indicating that it is not secure.
2   The study carried out by FLACSO has been published by Wim Savenije and Katherine Andrade-Eekhoff (2003). It offers detailed survey material from both communities, as well as three other marginal communities in Greater San Salvador.

who was working in the same community, had summed up her experience in La Vía with the words of one inhabitant she interviewed: 'see, hear and shut up' (Silva Avalos, 2003). I, too, was immediately struck by the 'silences' I encountered on many levels. One community leader went to great lengths to assure me that the community had always been perfectly safe: 'Yes the community has always been safe; even though it has had its problems, it has always been safe; the community has always been really safe.' The presence of gang graffiti and anecdotes from other residents within the community suggested a different story. It later emerged in conversations with him that he had been the victim of repeated intimidation by neighbours. There was a long period of time when he was too afraid to leave his house. The young men who had been threatening him had since left the community and most residents felt that things had improved. Nonetheless, both communities on either side of La Vía have active gangs. Residents of La Vía often have to pass through these to enter and leave the community. Violence often spills over and leads to problems in La Vía. This is indicative of the need to assign narrow geographical boundaries to violence, but also the centrality of silence within narratives of violence. The protestations by residents that La Vía is safe despite evidence to the contrary also suggests that communities need to feel secure in their own spaces, however restricted these may be and however illusory or unstable notions of safety are. Living with high levels of violence require constant negotiations with danger and fear. In order to survive, people must create coping strategies on multiple levels.

My introduction to El Boulevar was markedly different. The management committee was very suspicious of me initially, because they had had some issues with a previous researcher in the community. They were much more wary of me than people in La Vía seemed to be and, although they expressed a willingness for the research to be done, they were very clear that they were my gatekeepers. It took months for me to establish trust with some residents and I went through a series of 'tests' in order to be accepted. One such example happened in the first weeks when I tried to organise a focus group with local men. I had talked about this idea with the management committee who felt it was a good idea to get to know people and explain what I was doing in the community. I decided to organise one for men and a separate one for women. One of the members of the committee helped me contact men in the community and invite them. On the day of the proposed group, I arrived at the community. After waiting for over an hour with the man who had helped me set up contacts, he told me that there was a football match so nobody would come. It is likely that I was naïve, but I found it difficult to understand why the committee member had let me go through the process of organising the focus group while knowing that it clashed with an important event for the men of the community. I persevered and the same man and his family became my closest friends in El Boulevar, though many months passed before I suggested organising another focus group. Instead, I attended community meetings and people got to know me that way.

This episode also raises questions about notions of participation and ownership of research processes and outcomes. As a feminist, I was eager for my research participants to have as much ownership of the research process as possible but I had not envisaged how the deep levels of mistrust and fear *among* communities would affect their willingness to participate in group events. Although people were willing to disclose information to me on the violence in the community on an individual basis, they were not ready to do this in a public forum. I had managed to establish rapport and trust with some of the residents. Nevertheless, this did not mean that they had the same rapport or trust with each other.

In stark contrast to the residents of La Vía, the violence of El Boulevar was almost palpable. This community is much larger than La Vía and has multiple entrances and passageways. It was covered in gang graffiti and *pandilleros* generally sat in a group at one of the entrances. The police only entered in large groups since the labyrinthine space meant that there were a lot of blind alleys and 'strangers' were vulnerable. Reminders of violence had a physical presence. I was warned in my first week there by Enrique:

> The least that they can do is rob you; it is the least they can do, leave you with nothing.
>
> MH: It's a question of luck then?
>
> Yes, it is a question of luck, because I tell you, this place is very, very, very threatening. It is one of the high risk communities in Soyapango; this community is one of the most dangerous in Soyapango.

The marked difference in these two introductions draw attention to two key ways of framing violence. In La Vía, violence was minimised and silenced despite evidence to the contrary. In El Boulevar, Enrique almost boasted about his community's violent reputation, although other residents were not quite so vocal. For him, the fact that his community was considered dangerous was worn like a badge of honour, though further conversations revealed that neighbours lived in terror. These different ways of addressing violence reflect an underlying ambiguity in popular understandings of violence that both sensationalise and minimise it. This process is not uniform within or across communities, but it is important to foreground the conflicting assessments of violence that are not necessarily informed by material realities. People speak about violence in different ways; they also refuse to speak about it. Michael

Taussig (1989: 8) speaks of a 'state of doubleness of social being' whereby citizens accept violence as normal, but are also shocked and panicked 'by an event, a rumour, a sight, something said, or not said'. This ever-present process of conflict between ambiguity and the need for certainty at the same time frames popular epistemologies of violence. The following discussion foregrounds some of the ambiguities, the silences and the stories of violence as a presence in everyday life.

Urbanisation and Legacies of Political Violence

The previous chapter argued that an analysis of violence cannot be reduced to a post-war phenomenon, but is firmly rooted in historic matters of political economy. A central hypothesis in much of the literature to emerge in recent years is that decades of political violence and more recent criminality actively erode social networks and undermine a sense of community. In a study of low-income communities in Guatemala and Colombia, Moser and McIlwaine (2004) highlight how pervasive violence weakens social capital (see also McIlwaine, 1998). In El Salvador, the war is generally seen as the key catalyst for such breakdown. Amaya Cóbar and Palmieri (2000) suggest that community structures in El Salvador, that had historically served to suppress or control violence, were broken down throughout the war. Thus, a vicious spiral is generated in which criminality and violence both contribute to and are facilitated by the atomisation and weakening of communities. According to UNDP (2003: 20):

> In the Salvadoran case, if the war meant the disintegration of many of these structures or networks that served to contain violence, the rise in criminality and social violence in the post-war period has contributed to an unravelling of the social fabric and an increase in citizens' alarm in the face of a environment which is considered hostile and violent, where the only possibility of having any certainty is through the use of force. It is here where the vicious circle is closed. Once the whole range of cultural baggage and normative behaviour has been internalised, people will not only have to behave according to the values and ways of the world that they were taught, but will be reproduced for the new generation.

While this is certainly a valid explanation, a closer analysis of community relations suggest that we should be cautious of presenting an overly idealised notion of community in pre-war years that fails to address historic conflicts that move beyond political violence. Empirical data presented in this chapter certainly support the idea that living through the war fragmented collective life in these communities, but it is important to emphasise that political violence was a major contributing factor to this atomisation, not the only factor. Everyday conflicts around resources, community politics and neighbourly arguments all combine to undermine community cohesion. This does not mean that quiet forms of solidarity no longer exist between neighbours; it does suggest that the space for these has been reduced.

Much contemporary violence is viewed as geographically distinct from previous decades in that it is primarily urban in character. This is not ignoring the violence of rural areas, but urban centres consistently demonstrate greater indices of crime, violence and perceptions of insecurity (see, for example, Kooning and Kruijt, 2007; Caldeira, 2000). While urban centres certainly demonstrate higher statistics of crime, research in rural areas of El Salvador suggests that rural areas show different dynamics of crime or 'banditry' linked to cattle rustling and economically motivated crimes. This is particularly the case near borders and in some coastal areas that attract organised crime (Hume, 2008b). Ramos (2000) foregrounds the unprecedented growth of Greater San Salvador, as a result of population displacements and migration during the war, as an important catalyst for contemporary violence in El Salvador. He argues that the dramatic and unplanned urbanisation put extra pressure on the already inadequate housing and service provision. Figures from 1992 to 1993 demonstrate that approximately 27 per cent of the total population of Greater San Salvador live in illegal settlements (Zschaebitz, 1999, cited in Savenije and Andrade Eekhoff, 2003: 65). Between 1950 and 1992, the population of Greater San Salvador grew by 420 per cent, with notable acceleration between 1971 and 1992. These processes were shaped by both political events and the industrialisation of San Salvador. Although much of the direct fighting during the war took place in rural areas, such as Chalatenango, Guazapa and Morazan, the inhabitants of these communities felt both the direct and indirect effects of the war and the years of oppression that preceded it.[3] Many of the interviewees originated from rural areas and came to the city to escape the war; others had come in search of work unable to make a living in the harsh conditions of rural areas.

The massive influx of population to San Salvador in the 1970s and 1980s was not welcomed by all residents. The arrival of 'strangers' spread unease among communities. In La Vía, Carlos, a resident who had been born there, commented:

> This place has certainly evolved, quite a lot. It was good. We are all, or most of us, are family ... on all the land that is here on this side. It was

---

3   Examples of studies of rural political violence in El Salvador include: Binford (1996), Pearce (1986) and Wood (2003).

lovely here, really peaceful, really peaceful. I remember that we used to wander about there. There, on that road, where those trailers are. That was a sugar cane field. On the other side there was a farm, where that residential area is. There were oranges, coconuts. Not today, they have built a neighbourhood. This part here was really peaceful. I remember that we used to play in the mine with all my cousins here and nothing happened. Now it is more dangerous because of all the people that have come here. In this part [where his family lives] it's okay, we are all united, but I remember that before it was really peaceful.

This idealisation of the past, as expressed in the above narrative, which Slim, Thompson et al. (1988) have termed 'persistent fake consciousness', creates a scenario where both good and bad can be exaggerated. It is important that analytical endeavours are not seduced by similar idealisations. Carlos's memory of a tranquil past was disrupted by the arrival of new people. Many of these were escaping political violence; others came seeking work, but because of the political climate, communities were afraid to trust them. This is a pattern that continues to mark contemporary relations. 'Newcomers', who can be residents of more than a decade, are both mistrusted and blamed for rising crime at the local level. This is a pattern not unique to La Vía or El Boulevar. For example, communities in San Marcos, another town on the outskirts of San Salvador, also blamed 'new' economic migrants who arrived in the municipality to look for work in the export processing plants for the rise of gang violence in their neighbourhoods (Hume, 2008a).

The explanation that violence is caused by 'new' people serves an important purpose in surviving ongoing violence and terror. It provides an organising narrative that insulates the narrator from any responsibility for the violence in his/her surroundings by placing it firmly as actions of various 'others'. Such a narrative serves a dual purpose. It creates a division between the supposedly 'decent' historic residents and untrustworthy newcomers. It also acts as a narrative to make fear manageable. Notions of the dangerous stranger inform classic ways to manage risk, but also perpetuate notions of fear. As I have argued previously, the particular commonsense of 'stranger danger' has been undermined by feminist research that has pointed to the centrality of violence within the family to the life experience of women and children (Hume, 2007b). Taking this feminist analysis to community violence is useful in that it points to the presence of threat and fear within immediate social relations, hence rejecting simplistic constructions of violence as 'other'. To stress this point further, the analysis of political violence in El Salvador also emphasises the pivotal role of local networks in rendering repressive tactics effective. A deeper exploration of historic relations in both El Boulevar and La Vía suggest that violent conflict is neither new nor isolated to conflicts between 'old' and 'new' residents. There is no neat starting point to conflict and violence. Furthermore, the idealisation of the past that is invoked here is rooted firmly in a public construction of violence. An examination of more private forms of violence in the next chapter will undermine this particular construction of the political economy of violence in El Salvador.

Testimonies presented here suggest that simmering conflicts within and between families pre-dates the war. 'In this sense, the problem is not new and was not created by the war. However, the war did contribute greatly to the institutionalisation of violence in the system of values and norms that regulate social behaviour' (Cruz and Beltrán, 2000: 40). I will trace some of the behaviours that have become institutionalised through decades of political violence and continue to inform survival strategies in the present climate.

The Politics of Violence: Silence and Fragmentation

Writing in 1983, in one of the bloodiest moments of the conflict, Martín-Baró (1983: 360) said, 'the war is the most totalising reality of life in contemporary El Savador'. Nobody escaped its effects although they may not have participated directly in the fighting. Residents from both communities speak about finding corpses around the locality during the war years. The repercussions of living and learning to survive in such an environment cannot be underestimated. Das and Kleinman (2000) suggest that in situations of extreme violence, individuals lose a sense of the *ordinary*, as they have to learn how to react or, rather, not react, to violent events. Empirical data suggest that, rather than losing a sense of the ordinary, the context shapes and transforms what is considered ordinary, increasing society's threshold for tolerating violence. In this section, I argue that non-reaction to terror and violence is a sustaining characteristic of survival in the communities under study. The use of silence as a survival strategy is far from new. It has been used in the face of political violence for centuries. Women have also kept silent in the face of domestic abuse, both as a strategy to 'keep the peace' and out of fear. These may not present ready alternatives to violence, nor do they encapsulate romanticised notions of what resistance might look like. However, I agree with Scheper-Hughes (1995: 415) who understands such behaviours as 'an evasive micro strategy of resistance'. This form of resistance, as the discussion here articulates, is not without its costs. Silence may afford a degree of protection on an individual level, but it contributes to wider structures of impunity and the disarticulation of community politics.

State terror was calculated to inculcate silence as a premeditated strategy in times of political turmoil. Silence, therefore, became a central way of coping with the everyday life of political strife for many. In La Vía, which saw an influx of inhabitants during the war years, residents ignored their new neighbours for fear of where their political allegiances lay:

> Yes, well, we were really afraid, because people told us that everyone who came were members of the guerrilla. So they told us and sometimes they let us know themselves that they had been in the guerrilla. So, seeing the situation we didn't say anything because we were afraid. Because before, during the war, god, threats were really, really ... hell. I mean the threats that they issued made you stop and think, because you didn't know where they came from, nor what kind of people they were. So we avoided them, we just let them live there. (Carlos, La Vía)

In El Boulevar, neighbours denounced each other, but also supported each other both in times of personal crisis and in the face of political violence. Many actively supported the FMLN despite the risk to their personal safety and the infiltration of informants in the community. Many participated directly as urban combatants (*commandos urbanos*), while other supported the guerrilla effort by providing shelter or distributing propaganda. María Dolores used to distribute leaflets after dark to her neighbours and, as a result, many of her neighbours stopped talking to her in public. Mistrust and fear both replaced and coexisted alongside historic social support networks. Interviewees narrated stories of terrible violence during and prior to the war years. Inhabitants were divided in their allegiance, supporting either government or left-wing forces:

> Here there were, there were people belonging to the death squads. My neighbour behind was a real butcher. He belonged to ... a sniper squad, which was one of the cruellest structures of the armed forces. Well, we had that neighbour there and didn't know what was going on, then the, the, a relation of his was the one who investigated the director of the *Unión de Pobladores de Tugorios* [UPT; Organisation of Marginal Communities] and the one that butchered him. They killed him up here. (Enrique, El Boulevar)

Individuals began, therefore, to adopt a code of silence and minding one's own business in order to avoid problems. Residents soon learned that silence was a strategic option in a climate where no one could be trusted. Individuals testified to feeling afraid of the *orejas* (informers): 'In those days, anyone who said anything, who heard anything and spoke about it, failed as well. You would find him with his ear cut off, cut off' (Meche, El Boulevar). Breaking the codes of silence risked anything from social ostracism, to physical mutilation and even death. Living like this has invariably affected communities in a negative way, contributing to their increased fragmentation. One woman from El Boulevar remembered that none of her neighbours would use the communal toilets at the same times as her, because they all suspected her of being in the guerrilla. A common theme that ran through many of the narratives from both communities was non-involvement in community dynamics, both past and present. Throughout El Salvador, high levels of brutality and the very visible disposal of victims proved effective teaching tools. They existed as highly visible threats to all citizens.

As well as an expression of fear and a strategy of survival, silence denied citizens political voice and undermined community networks. As discussed above, interviewees spoke at length about community conflicts and how they had witnessed several murders within or nearby the community. This was particularly acute in the early 1980s when government-sponsored death squads used the area around El Boulevar as a dumping ground for mutilated corpses. Throughout this time, the military ransacked and looted the community on several occasions. Enrique (El Boulevar) remembers this period as particularly turbulent:

> Well those were difficult times because we ... I mean, when there were the famous curfews, we couldn't go out. The community was invaded by soldiers and when they felt like it, they carried out raids, without warrants or anything. They came in and examined everything down to the last rag. They made us stand aside and they took what they liked. They also took advantage of the situation to destroy things. Then, still in the darkest part of the war, we had a shop and they attacked us one night. It was people from the air force who burgled it.

Such activities are indicative of the high levels of corruption within political bodies, contributing to an erosion of public confidence in agents of the state. State-sanctioned political violence became intermingled with criminality, resulting in corruption on many levels. This was ignored by agents of the state. Impunity has effects that transcend a refusal of justice. People felt impotent against such forces and the general context of mistrust was deepened. The repercussions of this are discussed in Chapter 5 with regard to different forms of 'community justice'. At this juncture, however, it is important to foreground the ways in which state violence worked through local communities. Formal community structures in El Boulevar, such as the management committee became monopolised by dominant political interests throughout the war years. In El Boulevar, members of ORDEN chose and changed the members of the directive at will and informed on their neighbours to the authorities: 'Here they were supposedly protecting the people, the community, but more than anything else, they were informers ... people didn't have a voice or a vote' (Enrique, El Boulevar). This co-opted structure not only failed to represent the community, but also actively worked to instil fear and mistrust among its inhabitants by silencing them. It has been difficult for the management committee in El Boulevar to regain the trust of residents. Their reputation was further tested by a series of thefts of community funds by its members. Enrique, a member of the committee, comments on the difficulties:

> Here all the members of the directive are thieves because they all steal. They are in the committee because they share the money from the water. When they finish collecting the money, people say 'sons of whores'; they are going there to see how much the water money is and to divide it up. That's what people say. (Enrique, El Boulevar)

This enduring legacy of corruption is indicative of the power of violence in informing popular perceptions of community bodies. On one level, the history of community organising along partisan interests illustrates the manipulation of community structures by dominant political interests to effectively silence community demands. El Boulevar was also mortgaged by a former mayor of San Salvador, Mario Valiente, which hampered processes to legalise the land.[4] The linking of party interest with particular groups within the community endures today, affecting the possibility and sustainability of community organising. On another level, the corruption within this local structure further eroded the possibility of a strong collective. This fuelled popular perceptions that continue to equate the management committee with corruption.

Nonetheless, there was a strong management committee in both communities at the time of the research and, although these may have been regarded with suspicion by some members, most residents cooperated and supported their work. In La Vía, the level of organisation was much stronger and many residents participated in various fund-raising and social activities. In El Boulevar, the FLACSO survey found that 30 per cent of the sample population evaluated the directive as 'very good' or 'good', with 41.7 per cent assessing its performance as 'regular' (Savenije and Adrade-Eekhoff, 2003). Both committees enjoyed good working relations with the local council and the council's outreach worker maintained regular contact with the communities.

Competition over scarce resources often underpins community conflicts. These communities are not exceptions. As I stated earlier, both communities are illegal and arguments over the legalisation of the land were particularly acute in El Boulevar at the time of the research. The fact that residents were

---

4   The debt on the land was paid by FMLN mayor Hector Silva in the early 2000s to facilitate the process of guaranteeing the legalisation of the plots.

still struggling to have some legal security four decades after the community had been settled is indicative of the deep insecurity that the inhabitants of marginal communities live with on a daily basis. It also points to the state's refusal to guarantee security of shelter. Rumours were rife about the management committee abusing of its role for its own gain. Partisan interests were also in danger of threatening the process, with both ARENA and the FMLN having their 'people' in the neighbourhood. Both 'sides' claimed that they had received death threats. Meetings were held in the town hall for fear of problems within the community where security could not be guaranteed. This was not an insignificant distance away and the location of the meetings here also meant that some people could not attend because they did not wish to leave their houses unoccupied. At one particularly tense meeting, one man who had supposedly issued the threats was taking photos of various residents. After the meeting ended, a member of the committee, Petrona, thumped the man in an attempt to get his camera from him. Despite both the mayor's office and the management committee's efforts to reassure residents, campaigns of misinformation proliferated. Rumour spread quickly, exacerbating mistrust and conflict, as well as increasing polarisation. The dynamics of this community mirror patterns of wider social relations. The erosion of social networks during the war has been perpetuated, even exacerbated, by the continued insecurity of the transition period. According to Torres-Rivas (1999: 294) 'to live in insecurity, with the sensation of a permanent threat, or close to pain and death, all contribute to the breakdown of basic solidarity'. Mistrust and fear have become so embedded in social relations that they constitute the principal components of a vicious cycle that continues to undermine collective well-being. Everyday life in the post-war period continues to be marked by fear and, indeed McIlwaine (1998: 663) suggests that pervasive fear 'is now one of the major barriers to the functioning of associational life and social capital'.

Although not the case for everyone, some people remained reluctant to talk about political issues in relation to the contemporary situation: 'You don't achieve anything by talking. By talking you put yourself at risk because political things are dangerous' (Meche, El Boulevar). Many continue to lower their voices and look around them when mentioning the war. This suggests that survival practices learned during the war are still present and useful today.[5] It is indicative of the lasting mark left by exposure to long-term political violence on social attitudes and behaviour. It appears that many

---

5   There have been few efforts to (re)build social trust since the signing of the peace accords. The fact that neither of these communities was a returned or specifically ex-combatant community has meant that they have not benefited from direct state and international development/peace building initiatives.

communities have not been able to recover the trust of their neighbours and silences learned in the war have become ordinary reactions. While instances of political violence have disappeared dramatically, silence remains an enduring legacy:

> I say to my kids that living is not just about living; you have to learn how to live. Learning how to live means only talking about good things, nothing dangerous. It is better not to talk about dangerous things because, in the first instance, you don't know who you are talking to and another thing is that you can't do anything. If you just speak for the sake of it, you might offend the other person and when they look for revenge, how do you defend yourself? That's how you have to know how to learn to live. (Meche, El Boulevar)

The destructive potential of speaking out had been corroborated all too painfully during the war years and silence remains an important survival strategy in contemporary times. Residents from both communities repeatedly talked about 'gossip' being a form of violence, particularly among women. In a focus group in the school in El Boulevar, one young women suggested that gossip was the source of fights between students: 'you speak of me, I break your face'. Gossip is not merely the source of much salacious information about people.[6] It also acts as a detonator for many physically and verbally violent reactions. Women have been accused of stoning their neighbours' houses, shouting insults, spreading rumours and even casting spells when disagreement occurs. Casting gossip as a purely female activity conforms to popular stereotypes but is short sighted, and fails to encompass the role of men and the broader range of behaviours that foster mistrust within communities. In this way, high levels of violence, with its associated fear and mistrust, create a vicious circle for the reproduction of violence. The weakness of social networks further reinforces existing fragmentation and public spaces for collective action become reduced (Cruz, 2000). Society is increasingly atomised and the collective capacity for containing violence is reduced.

A less explicitly gendered term that is used as a marker for levels of distrust and atomisation in the communities is *egoísmo*. This umbrella term covering a range of conflicts among neighbours translates literally as selfishness or

---

6   One of the men I interviewed in the prison also suggested that many inmates were serving their sentence because of 'gossip'. He linked this to false accusations and corruption. 'There are various men here who might be here because of gossip, it is unfair. As I said to you before, there are people who have the money so that poor people can be sentenced. That's what crime we're paying for here, poverty. Poverty is the biggest crime you pay for.'

individualism: 'Look there has always been individualism, envy and little solidarity' (Esteban, El Boulevar). *Egoísmo* can be understood as a catalyst for a range of conflict situations: robbery and corruption, jealousy, not participating in community events, and so on. Ana María talks about the history of conflicts between neighbours in La Vía:

> Here everyone was out for himself or herself. If you noticed that someone else had something, you were jealous. It was a problem; people were something else, or even between neighbours because someone threw rubbish on this side. Then the kids started and the mothers.
>
> MH: How did they fight? Shouting?
>
> They used to shout lots of things and sometimes the women fought. They scratched each other. It was awful.

Interview data from both communities indicate that many people suspected their neighbours had robbed them and some were aware of the identity of the robber. Fear and silence combine to create a context where individuals feel overwhelming impotence against the high levels of violence in their lives. The silence encountered throughout the research provides an indicator of the deep mistrust and disintegration of collective life. Margarita, a resident of La Vía, speaks of her experience following a robbery:

> Afterwards, I kind of found out [who had robbed her], but I didn't take any action, nor ask any questions, not even to them. But they [neighbours] told me things, but I never, I mean, I never said anything, not to them [suspects] nor to anyone else. I just observed and kept my mouth shut but it was scary at the time. I felt afraid for the two girls and especially as they were on their own. I have never liked leaving them on their own. I leave them now, but am always afraid.

Margarita has two daughters who spend all day at home. She is afraid to send them to school because she cannot drop them off and collect them herself and she feels that the short journey is too dangerous for them to make alone. Further, as her narrative suggests, people were reluctant to leave their houses empty for fear that someone from the same community would burgle them. This stands in stark contrast to the voiced understanding that appeared common among residents that local thieves and gang members would not harm neighbours or people from the local area:

> Say you were my aunt or even my cousin, then they can't do anything to you, because they will have seen you with us ... On the other hand, if someone comes in, say a postman, well then they just rob them. (Leonor, El Boulevar)

Nevertheless, such assurances are merely illusory and such an insecure situation has direct consequences on their ability to participate in outside activities, including education, paid labour and community events. According to the FLACSO survey, 51.8 per cent of respondents in La Vía and 69.8 per cent in El Boulevar testify to having to be inside the house early due to problems that occur inside the community (see Savenije and Andrade-Eekhoff, 2003). In La Vía, many residents change their route home to avoid gang members who hang around some disused railway carriages at the entrance to the community. One woman testified to taking the long route back to her house for fear of being robbed:

> The only place where I feel a little bit more scared is by those carriages there [she points to the carriages which are not far from her house], because there have been times when they are hidden there. I sense that I see someone behind the carriages when I am walking round there late. It has happened to me. A short while ago I was going to the market with my daughter. It was about 5.30 and I saw one or two men behind that carriage. We always take care so we went that way but when we were coming back, we looked for a different way. We go out that way but the other is safer.

As argued previously, Silva Avalos (2003) highlights that a general rule for survival in La Vía is 'see, hear and shut up'. In El Boulevar similar survival strategies function: 'Look, here people isolate themselves completely from all the criminal activity. Maybe someone takes something from in front of your nose and people won't say anything' (Esteban, El Boulevar). Silence and isolation from community dynamics have become survival strategy in the face of high levels of violence and criminal activity. While talking to Esteban one day in El Boulevar, he clearly stated the price that people must pay for speaking out:

> the uncertainty that you live with in this place, that fear that you live with, the insecurity of going out into the street because the criminals are there and they could ... you have to get on with it, the fear that you live with here, [people] are always afraid of sorts of things. Afraid that they are going to insult you ... that is why people shouldn't talk here. At one stage the thieves robbed here, and they left their loot in that house there. People did not say anything. They robbed the statue of the virgin from the church, loads of things and that was it, amen. If you say anything, you die in the street, know what I mean?

This multi-layered process of silence and silencing has serious and long-lasting ramifications for associational life. Trust that has eroded as a result of political violence has been further tested by continued community conflicts and a rise in criminal victimisation. Esteban states clearly here that if you speak, you die. According to his neighbour, 'I have always gone straight home from work. I don't like to be in the street if I don't need to be. I don't like making friends with people. It's not a good idea, you see' (Erlinda, El Boulevar). The fact that residents continue to live side by side with the very people that are responsible for violence both past and present presents huge challenges to community organisation. The familiarity and proximity of both the violence and its perpetrators has harmful effects on the quality of life for the residents, shaping their lives on a daily basis. This undermines any neat separations between 'them' and 'us'. Localised feelings of impotence and insecurity cannot be viewed in isolation from a wider political economy of insecurity and impunity. I will return to this issue in Chapter 5. At this juncture, it is important to analyse the ways in which violence affects groups in different ways.

Violence Discriminates

During the period of research in El Boulevar, Magdalena, a woman I knew well and saw almost every day, was robbed. She was in her 80s and her two-ringed gas cooker was stolen. Everyone seemed to know who had taken it, yet no one dared reproach him. Magdalena was in a particularly vulnerable position. Her cooker meant more than simply one of her few material possessions and, as such, was irreplaceable. To take it away from her effectively removed one of the last vestiges of her independence. She used her stove to make her coffee in the morning, living for the rest of the day on her neighbours' charity. Her neighbours looked out for Magdalena, giving her food and the odd bit of financial assistance. Their solidarity towards Magdalena was quiet and consistent. Despite the high levels of violence and mistrust, neighbours still look out for each other. In La Vía, water from the communal tap often flows in the middle of the night. Margarita and her neighbours keep watch for each other when they collect the water since being outside at this time is very dangerous and exposes the women to greater risk. The fact that they do not have access to basic resources such as water becomes a risk factor in terms of their possible exposure to violence and there have been reported cases of young women being raped when they fetch water. What these examples indicate is that violence does not affect all people in the same way. Poverty increases both the consequences of violence and risk of it. The effects of violence are not uniform and are not directly measurable against the action. In Magdalena's case, not only was the material loss of an old cooker significant given her extreme poverty, but the robbery attacked her sense of self, increasing her vulnerability and dependence on her neighbours. I asked one man why she did not report the robbery: 'She didn't want to report it, it's because [people] are afraid' (Pedro, El Boulevar).

The effect of the robbery on Magdalena highlights that episodes of violence generate different degrees of harm to different people. The poor are particularly vulnerable because they have few resources to insulate them against the effects of violence. Further, the fact that the women in La Vía, and many communities like it, do not have access to water except in the middle of the night means they are particularly vulnerable. In La Vía, residents suggested that the worst violence occurred after dark when gangs had shoot-outs and fights with their rivals.

> It was very frequent, but you were afraid, because of the fear you felt that you couldn't sleep easy. After about 7 or 8, you couldn't go out. You were afraid because sometimes they gathered in the path and they had a type of checkpoint [reten] or something like a curfew [toque de queda]. (Margarita, La Vía)

Issues of vulnerability are linked to issues of fear. The fear of different types of violence affects social groups in distinct ways. A group of girls in the school in El Boulevar, for example, indicated that the fear of rape was the type of violence that affected them most:

> Rape is also a problem, especially for girls because the mareros grab them and they 'hurt' them and then they don't take responsibility. (Esmeralda, fourteen years old, El Boulevar)

Interestingly, fear of sexual assault was followed by the fear of kidnapping, which is not normally a crime that one would associate with low-income neighbourhoods (see Figure 1). This not only reflects a preoccupation in the media at the time of the research with this high-profile crime, but also the labels used to hide particular forms of violence. One of the girls explained her understanding of kidnapping:

> A car comes up with blackened windows, they grab the girl and put her in the car and take her away. That's a kidnapping even though they don't ask for money but they go and rape her, they kill her and you never find out who killed her, who left her there. (Alicia, El Boulevar)

Here the term 'kidnapping' [secuestro] was used depite the fact that 'they don't ask for money'. Alicia explained that girls were sexually assaulted and sometimes killed. Young girls in this community live in fear of sexual attack from the mara because nobody dares 'refuse' a marero. Girls who join the

Fear that we will be sexually assaulted

Fear that we will be kidnapped

Fear of psychological abuse

Physical and moral abuse

Fear that we will be mugged

Fear of threats

Intra-family violence

Fear of being killed

Lack of communication with our parents

Figure 1. What Type of Violence Affects Us Most? (Girls).
Source: Participatory Workshop, group of eight girls, El Boulevar, 20 May 2002

gang are also vulnerable to sexual abuse and I discuss this further in the next chapter. Interviewees indicated that several families had fled the area because of conflicts with the gang. One particular family left because they were afraid for the safety of their adolescent daughter. The fear of rape expressed by these young girls highlights that different groups are more exposed to certain types of violence within the context of the community. Although a group of boys of the same age group did mention rape, this appeared after gangs, drugs and physical abuse within the household (see Figure 2).

Figures 1 and 2 demonstrate that these groups of adolescent boys and girls are differently affected by many types of violence even though they live in the same community. Young men are prime targets for gang violence and more likely to join gangs, whether this be motivated by a desire for 'respect' or protection. Young women also join gangs, but their numbers are less than young men. In El Boulevar, the local gang has been closely linked to drug dealing and use. It does not operate alone, but is said to have links with various families in the community who also sell drugs or are involved with extortion of local businesses.

Fear of violence is not uniform and it affects social groups in many distinct ways. Women testify to being most affected by bother [*intranquilidad*] in the house and in the street, suggesting that they have little access to a space free from violence in their lives (see Figure 3). The restriction of public spaces puts extra pressure on the home. Issues of violence against women will

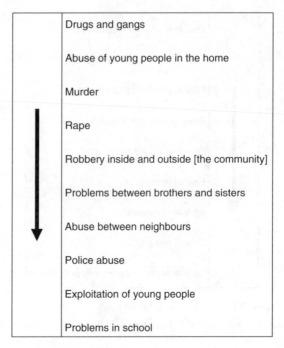

Figure 2.   What Type of Violence Affects Us Most? (Boys).
Source: Participatory Workshop, Group of seven adolescent boys, El Boulevar, 20 May 2002

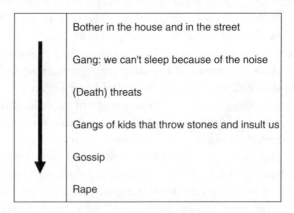

Figure 3.   What Type of Violence Affects us Most? (Women).
Source: Participatory Workshop, group of four women, El Boulevar, 2 June 2002

be discussed in more detail in the next chapter. Women also signal young people's violence as a problem for them, just as the young people signalled abuse by adults as a problem. This highlights that clear-cut distinctions between victims and perpetrators are problematic. Different social groups use violence to different ends and at different moments in their lives. Age, class and gender are three factors that will affect exposure to different types of violence and inform perceptions of fear. Likewise, different types of violence will affect individuals and groups according to their position within society. Not only does it affect people in different ways, but the discourse that organises violence legitimises certain types of discrimination. Young people from El Boulevar argue that they are all seen as gang members because of where they live and are treated badly because of their poverty:

> There is discrimination just because of where you live. It has happened to me too, because people think if you live here, they think you are a big rebel (*gran rebelde*), that you are a *marero*, that you're in the gangs, that you spend your time fighting, that you're against the teachers. They also discriminate against us because of where we live and it's not as nice as other places; they look down on you because of your poverty There are other places like Escalon [an upper-middle-class area]. If you go there, the people look at you as if you have dirt on your face just because we are poor people; it's as if we were something odd. Here in El Salvador there is a lot of poverty. (Jhony, El Boulevar)

Levels of discrimination like this may be more keenly articulated by young people, but they affect all members of society. Older residents spoke about using the addresses of family who do not live in El Boulevar on job applications to avoid being associated with the community. This is indicative of a broader social stigma attached to living there and to being poor. Their poverty increases their vulnerability to the effects of violence and discrimination. Individuals in these communities are agents in sustaining notions of 'other' to understand localised conflict; they are also 'othered' as poor people who live in communities marked by violence. One of the most visible markers of violence in the post-war era is the presence of youth gangs. It is to the issue of the gang in El Boulevar that I now turn.

Gangs: An Expression of the New El Salvador?

A series of focus groups in El Boulevar, which were held with adults and young people, began with an exercise entitled 'What I like about my community' and 'What I dislike'. A large majority of respondents indicated that they did not like the violence. Their answers mostly came under the heading of a criticism of gangs, although they did refer to other issues such as conflicts with neighbours and discrimination. Although this was common across all groups, young people were more willing to talk about violence than adults. This could indicate that the type of violence, that is, gang violence, adversely affects young people more than adults, for it is young people that make up the membership of gangs and are also targets of rival gangs. It could also indicate that the adults in the community have different worries, such as legalisation of the land. It does, however, resonate with an observation that young people are more likely to talk freely about violence than adults (Moser and McIlwaine, 2000a). Perhaps, they have not yet learned the rules of silence in order to survive, as advocated by the resident in El Boulevar cited above.

When adults in a focus group in El Boulevar were asked to reconstruct timelines of the community, all three sub-groups firmly marked the beginning of criminality (*delincuencia*) as being at the same time as the arrival of the *maras* in the early 1990s (see Figure 4). The presence of gangs in El Salvador has become synonymous with violence and delinquency. Donna DeCesare (1998: 29) constitutes *pandilleros* as having an image of:

> The new El Salvador, caught between a peasant past and the dislocations of the present, caught between the generation of romanticised rebel fighters and that of vilified young 'gangstas'. [Their] search for identity parallels El Salvador's search for a shared definition of justice, respect and participation.

Young people who join gangs cannot be seen in isolation from the society in which they have grown up. Many have internalised violence as a habitual form of dealing with conflict and establishing social relationships. The life-histories of Salvadoran youth provide an important reflection of the social context in which these post-war generations grew up. *Maras* are predominantly made up of young people (particularly, but not exclusively, young men) from low-income communities such as El Boulevar and La Vía. Young gang members can be understood as symptomatic of a changing 'political economy of brutality' both in terms of embodying broader issues of exclusion and of illuminating the contemporary 'ordering' of the problem (Rodgers, 2007). These young people may not have been directly involved in the war, but they have experienced its broader repercussions. Indeed, many join the gang to protect themselves against bullying by members of local *clikas* or other groups. These young people have first-hand experience of limited opportunities for education and employment. Indeed, many have been forced to make the journey to the United States and subsequently have been deported back to El Salvador where they implement gang practices learned on the streets of Los Angeles and Washington DC (DeCesare, 1998; Santacruz Giralt, 2005). In this situation, a minority of young people have learned to survive and assert their identity by reproducing violence (Cárdia, 2002). In the words of one gang member: 'you could say that

[+] Positive things in the community		[-] Negative things in the community
250 families arrive - basic services provided by the army	1965	
School built	1967	
Clinic built	1968	
Community centre	1973	
	1975	Some familes at the end of the main street are flooded every winter
	1992	Delinquency -*maras*
	1995	The community is mortgaged by the then mayor of San Salvador, Marío Valiente (ARENA)
The public lighting is restored	1999	
The road to the slaughterhouse is paved.	2000	
Signs are erected in the community.		
The flyover is built		
The mortgage is pardoned		
Rubbish bins are installed	2001	
	2001	Presumed kidnappers seek refuge in the community

Figure 4.   Community Timeline, Drawn Up by a Group of Seven Men in El Boulevar, 2 June 2003

their sport is killing, robbing, raping women, all sorts' (Vladimir, El Boulevar).

Communities live in constant fear of the *muchachos de la mara*, although many of the young people have grown up in these communities and their families still live there. When talking about the *mara*, interviewees continually lowered their voices and looked around, as they did when talking of political violence in previous decades. According to Lucinda, a participant in a focus group in El Boulevar:

> Well, in 1992, the *mara* appeared in the community and I am going to say it quietly because I am afraid [other participants laugh] ... no it is dangerous and I live alone.

Gang violence is highly public. The logic of their existence not only lies in protecting the *barrio*, but in asserting a collective identity. Gangs are highly visible; each *clika*[7] marks its territory with graffiti to delineate territorial boundaries and remembers the dead *homeboys*. Residents contest the gang's *raison d'etre*: that they exist to protect the *barrio*. In El Boulevar, the fear of the gang was palpable. Residents not only live in constant fear of reprisals from the rival *mara* in the form of shoot-outs in the community, but they also fear the gang members themselves. The *pandilleros* have been accused of a whole range of crimes, including: stealing, dealing drugs and rape. According to one resident:

> They say that they protect the community but they really protect themselves from the other *mara*, the 18. They protect the community from the 18 because they kill them here. But to say they protect the community is a lie, sure they themselves commit crimes here. They themselves steal from it. Here they'll rape anyone, and all that. (Enrique, El Boulevar)

The *mara* in El Boulevar terrorises the community. It is *todopoderoso* (the omnipotent force) and many residents feel impotent in the presence of such constant threat. In 2002, residents spoke about a 'war tax' that the *mareros* had charged, either demanding change from residents or charging small businesses protection money: 'there are some *mareros* who sometimes ask for a peso and if you don't give it to them, they want to hit you' (Elena, El Boulevar). In 2002, Alfonso already (La Vía) recognises the increasing violence of the gang:

> It used to be a bit different, but the same as well. They weren't as severe as they are now. You only look at them and they want to beat you up. No, they were friendlier. They looked after the neighbourhood. Now even your own neighbours want to beat you up.

---

7   There are two main gangs, the Mara 18 (ns-18) and Mara Salvatrucha (ns-13). The latter is present in El Boulevar and around La Vía. Each gang is organised into community groups, or *clikas*.

Youth gangs are an evolving force and their involvement in localised extortion has become increasingly sophisticated in recent years. 'War tax' on a small scale has evolved into *renta* on a much bigger, and more organised scale. Aguilar and Miranda (2006) point to a change in the internal norms and values of gangs since the introduction of tough anti-gang legislation, the *Mano Dura*, in 2003. Since then, *maras* have become increasingly criminalised and better organised. Most notably, they are involved in extortion in the transport sector. The narrative that introduced this book told the story of a bus driver who had been killed in San Marcos because he refused to pay. Instead of being motivated to join the gangs for friendship and a sense of belonging, young people are now attracted by the lure of alcohol, drugs and economic gain. Nonetheless, an interview with a police officer in 2007 suggested that the gang is not the only actor responsible for extortion, but that it is now a widely used common practice in certain communities where many families use it as a way to generate an income. Blaming the gang is not always an accurate assessment of local dynamics.

In El Boulevar, there was an overwhelming sense that the community felt powerless against the *mara*. Residents also indicated that several families had to flee because of conflicts with the gang. Esteban explains:

> We haven't left because we don't have the faces of animals, not because of those who want to take control of the community, they want everyone to leave; they want everyone to get out. That would be good for them, to have the area free, to feel powerful. People leave all the time. Over there [he points across the passage where he lives], there are two houses and the people don't want them. They don't come near them because they have a 'war tax': one hundred *colones* to give them to the crooks (*maleantes*) who are [in prison]. One of them is called Curly. [The gang] rules and they use the hundred *colones* to get 'Curly' out.

People complained about the *mareros* and were afraid of them, yet most people had children, nieces, nephews or friends directly involved. Alfonso, a young man in La Vía, had repeated problems with both major gangs because his brother had been a member of the the group. Since the brother left the gang without 'permission', Nara Salvatrucha (MS-13) they have come after him and his family. On one occasion, they attacked his elderly grandmother.[8] He also faces aggression from the MS–18 because a member of his family is a

---

8   Their family story is complex. Alfonso said that his grandmother used to allow the gang members to use her house, but that they fell out with her. At the time of interview, she had been missing for several years and the family suspected gang involvement in her disappearance. His brother, who had been in the MS had become a Christian, got married and left San Salvador.

member (albeit no longer active) of the MS–13. Alfonso speaks of his hatred for gangs. He resents the fact that he is hampered in his ability to earn a living and that he feels insecure because of gang threats. He cannot go to certain areas because of what might happen to him:

> I used to sell bread in Ilopango but I had to stop because the *mara* was watching me instead of my brother . . . they knew I was his brother and they realised that I was old enough [*que ya aguantaba*], as they say, I could now handle a hammering [*una taleguiada*].

> MH: what do you mean?

> That instead of my brother joining the gang again, they wanted to have me. I was going to have to pay for his mistakes. So when I realised that, I couldn't sell bread any more. It was a real blow for the bakery because I used to sell lots of bread, about three sacks of flour worth and the bakery went bust. I also had a rough time because I couldn't leave the house and the *mareros* came to get me here . . . I hate the *mareros*. They have beaten me and stolen my bicycle. If a *marero* speaks to me, I don't answer him nicely. I don't like it when people go on about the gang, the gang here, there gang there . . . when the gang has come near me, I don't run, I stand up to them . . . I am not afraid of them because I think that they are not from a different world. They feel a thump the same way I do so I shouldn't be afraid, nor should I have to be afraid of them. They are the same, made of the same flesh. Just because they are covered in tattoos doesn't mean that I should be afraid or because they try to scare you. It's not like that. Maybe I am a bit twisted [*torcido*] about it but every time I see them, they have a go at me. A little while ago, about a year and a half ago, they came to get me one night. There wasn't one or two of them but there were a few. They came in a pick-up. I realised they were coming to get me, to take me away. My brother couldn't be in the gang so I was going to be in it.

Luckily the gang did not find Alfonso on this occasion. Instead, they hit his girlfriend: 'I found her bleeding several times.' I talk about his reaction to this in the next chapter. The hatred of gangs is not uniform, however; others make use of gangs to deal with certain problems and, more particularly, as arbiters in local conflicts or as low-paid contract killers [*sicarios*]. This has created a contradictory situation, where people hate or live in fear of the gang as a collective yet, at the same time, defend them as individuals and even use their 'services' when necessary. Ways of understanding the world and making sense of it are turned upside down. One woman whose son was a gang member stated that he is a part of her. No matter what he did, he was still her son:

When it comes to the crunch, as they say, we jump up and defend them ... so what are we doing? Of course if we let them beat each other up, till they killed each other. I wonder who would go out on the street to see if he is going to be OK, he gets better but the, then we the family help him, that's the problem. (Paty, El Boulevar)

Paty blamed herself for her son joining the gang. She had been a FMLN combatant in the war and her son's father was killed. Her son told me that the army also killed her baby. After her second husband died, she had a breakdown, which is when her son became a *pandillero*:

I know that I have three kids, but of these kids, only one of them went wrong [*se descompusó*]. It was because of my illness ... when my husband died, I went mad. I went to the psychiatric hospital and when I got out, my son was already in the gang. I wanted to rescue him but I couldn't. But you know one thing, he will always be my son, even if he is in a gang and I cannot deny it here and I can't turn my back on him. (Paty, El Boulevar)

Such dynamics are indicative of the centrality of violence to the everyday lives of the research participants. They are also testament of the complexities that go to the core of understanding this highly negative force. Violence is at the heart of everyday relations. The emotions, messiness, pain and rationalisation that characterise everyday life shape the multiple and often contradictory meanings that are ascribed to violence. Relations in the communities appear to be characterised by both solidarity and conflict. Women and men speak of deep-rooted conflict, yet also of deep mistrust of their neighbours. On one level, the communities have become fragmented and the histories of violence appear to have contributed to a disintegration of collective life. This was confirmed by a group of women in El Boulevar who stated: 'Because of the badness [gangs], charity has ended', linking the disintegration of support networks with the increase of criminality in the community and, specifically, the formation of the *mara*. They suggest that neighbours no longer help each other and there are no more celebrations and social events in the community because of the everyday terror that restricts their lives. In El Boulevar, the clinic has had to be closed down because of high levels of insecurity. On the other hand, individuals claimed a deep sense of loyalty to their communities. Residents attested to enjoying strong support networks within their communities, which are vital at times of crisis, such as family illness or bereavement. There were many cases of men and women supporting each other in times of need. Magdalena, for example, relied entirely on her neighbours' kindness in order to survive. Students from the school in El Boulevar spoke about feeling discriminated against because of where they were from yet many interviewees from that community spoke with pride about *mi comunidad*. In particular, in focus groups with adults and children alike, they singled out unity and good neighbours as things they liked about living in El Boulevar. Such are the contradictions inherent in violence. Realities are shaped and redefined by the violence present in everyday life. The next chapter will analyse this dynamic further, paying attention to the gendered meanings of violence.

Conclusion

Violence has become, as Bruno Moro (2000) suggests, a *central thread* of social relations in El Salvador. The stories presented here have uncovered the historic presence of violence in the lives of research participants. To understand violence in this context, therefore, is to attempt to comprehend evolving everyday realities of communities, how they are spoken and how they are silenced. The exploration of individual histories and the context in which they have been enacted exposes common threads that enhance and nuance existing epistemologies of violence. I have argued that violence responds to, and is shaped by, changing political and social processes. There is no neat starting point to violence, nor can we easily separate its different strands. Community conflicts preceded the war and have continued since 1992. The experience of the war in reinforcing and undermining community cohesion should not be underestimated, but it should be located within a critical exploration of both historic and contemporary processes of inequality. Likewise, continued conflicts over resources should be situated within their broader political economy of exclusion, and not merely understood as localised community squabbles. Living with and using violence may, in some instances, have become a routine option, but it is only when we listen to historically subjugated voices that we can begin to understand how such a process can occur.

Important to this process is the ongoing dominance of silence. Silence is both a reaction to and a strategy of violence. Testimonies reveal that speaking out is dangerous and remaining silent generates a whole range of problems on individual and community levels. This chapter has demonstrated that violence has touched the lives of all the people that were interviewed in its manifold expressions, to contrasting degrees and at different social and political moments. Violence is not uniform within or across social groups; its effects are multiple and it discriminates. Violence is immediate to everyday life, undermining the anaesthetising potential of a discourse based on constructions of 'us' and 'them'. This moves a discussion of violence beyond strict binary notions of perpetrators and victims into questions of accountability, complicity and responsibility. The following chapter analyses the private realms of existence and how the use of and exposure to violence is intimately intertwined with dominant gender constructs.

4

Gendered Hierarchies of Violence

Men are machista so they think that no one should disrespect them. They lift us, they throw us about, they hit us and it's all down to their machismo. (Hilda, focus group, Ahuachapan, 2007)

Feminists have argued for a study of violence that takes into account the gaps between the ways in which violence is 'lived', understood and theorised (Morgan and Thapar Björkert, 2006; Hume, 2007c). One of the guiding principles of this research has been to uncover the silences and gaps that limit society's capacity to recognise or to know violence. In a context of extreme aggression the capacity to recognise and resist violence is intimately tied up with the exercise of power. In particular, empirical evidence from El Salvador has exposed the immediacy of violence to everyday life, undermining fictional assurances implicit in the public accounts of violence that rely on the fear of various categorisations of 'others'. Notable to the debates about violence in the region is the unsaid, or what is considered 'unspeakable'. I have engaged critically with debates from key theorists to argue that the effectiveness of power lies in its representation as normal and natural. The less 'overt' and more taken for granted a system of domination is, the harder it is to resist and the less likely it is to provoke overt reactions. Some of the most notable silences are those surrounding the linkages between gender relations and different forms of violence. In this way, speaking out and breaking silence becomes a principal strategy of challenging violence.

This chapter uncovers multiple forms of violence within gender relations that appear precisely as taken-for-granted or routine elements of what it means to be a woman or a man. Bourdieu (2001: 8) argues that the 'division between the sexes appears to be "in the order of things", as people sometimes say to refer to what is normal, natural, to the point of being inevitable'. The commonsense perception is that such an order is not only constitutive of the gaps between how violence is 'lived' and understood, but also limits strategies for recognising and resisting common forms of violence. Such strategies are explored in greater detail in the next chapter. A central argument of this chapter is that the use and perception of violence is intimately linked to dominant gender constructions, notably those that ascribe appropriate behaviours for men and women. Gendered power relations are imbued with tremendous symbolic power that serves an explanatory or legitimising function for certain types of violence. Violence against certain groups in El Salvador is 'excused' through the pervasiveness of symbolic structures of power that regulate appropriate behaviour for men and women. This chapter will expand the analysis presented in Chapter 3 of violence as a pervasive force in everyday life to include an examination of violence in the private spaces of everyday lives. The discussion reveals that the intimate and familial relations of the interviewees are impregnated with violence on many levels. Furthermore, historic patterns of gendered discourse not only render such violence 'private', but also minimise its significance in both public and subjective accounts of violence.

The chapter begins with a brief discussion of 'private violence'. The division of everyday life into public and private serves as an ordering discourse with which to legitimise, explain and ignore violence against women. Several key themes that emerge from life-history interviews and focus group discussions are examined: the minimisation of private violence and linked normalisation of violence against women in intimate relations; the perceived functionality of violence against children; and the inevitability or naturalisation of men's sexual aggression. These issues affect not only popular understandings, but also contribute to the reproduction of certain types of violence. I am interested in exploring the potency of hierarchies of violence based on gender and age that limit both interpretations of violence and the possibilities available to resist it. Hegemonic accounts of male sexuality and the pervasiveness of *machismo* serve to excuse men's violence and enforce strict codes of behaviour on women.

Encountering Public and Private Violence

Throughout this research, men referred to women's violence and its role in reproducing *machismo*. The process of interpreting violence is closely bound up with a need to apportion blame, yet it is necessary to move beyond a narrow analysis of individual responsibility to analyse the structures that give meaning to violence. The challenge is to dissect the larger systems of oppression and exploitation that allow violence to be an acceptable and routine element of everyday social and political interaction. Men, in defence of their own actions, often pointed to their mothers as the figure that 'taught' them how to be men. During an informal conversation with a group of men in El Boulevar, the men stated that violence against men was more of a problem than violence against women in the community: 'Here, the women are terrible' (*aquí las mujeres son tremendas*), they laughed. Although a flippant remark, the sentiment implicit in the statement deserves some discussion. Violence against men in the public sphere is indeed a major problem, particularly against young men who dominate in statistics of both perpetrators and victims. The gender dimensions of such crimes are rarely noted, yet the use and experience of violence appears bound up with dominant notions of what it means to be a man. Further, pointing the finger at women is not incidental. It suggests a tendency among certain groups to blame others in order to deflect attention from their own use of violence. It is also suggestive of broader attitudes that trivialise the problem of violence against women. Cavanagh, Dobash, Dobash and Lewis (2001: 695) speak of the 'exculpatory and expiatory discourses' that dominate men's narratives of violence. Central to such narratives is the twofold objective of 'mitigating and obfuscating culpability while at the same time seeking forgiveness and absolution'. A criticism made by feminist research on violence is that men impose their own definitions of violence in order to neutralise or minimise women's experience of abuse. Importantly, this also has the effects of controlling the ways in which such abuse is interpreted (for example, Kelly, 1988a).

The separation of everyday life into public and private is enduring in mainstream (read masculinist) epistemologies of violence, which continue to ignore violent dynamics of the private realm in favour of promoting normative notions of the home as a safe space or family relations as harmonious. This is often particularly acute at times of stress or indeed in the context of high levels of public insecurity when the notion of the home as a refuge garners more relevance. The privileging of the public sphere is common to analyses of violence. Debates around issues of risk and danger, stereotypes of perpetrators and victims; guilt and blame are informed by an almost exclusive public reading of violence. To dichotomise the study of violence into strict public and private spheres is to ignore the very important connections between the different realms of social existence in which violence is enacted: from the international arena and the state level to the level of the community and family relations (for example, Jacobson, Jacobs and Marchbank, 2000). The continued subordination of private realms of existence reinforces myths that serve to reproduce certain socially accepted behaviour, reproducing not only persistent inequalities within the social order, but the violence that accompanies them. Behaviours and relationships vary across public and private spaces, and our way of speaking about the world is mediated by the distinction made between these two mutually dependent spheres. The distinction does not mirror reality, but it has shaped how we understand and naturalise gendered oppression. It is the relational dynamics underpinning the violence that dictate its social meaning and not the realm in which it occurs. In these case-study communities, the symbolic power of the physical space of the private realm remains huge. Notions of privacy and silences are connected to deep fears that permeate different realms of social existence. The powerful symbolism of the private world is reinforced by high levels of violence in other realms.

In general terms, men (and women) who were interviewed agreed that violence against women was widespread in their neighbourhoods. 'It is rare the home that is not affected' (Enrique, El Boulevar). Most of the women with whom I spoke testified to having been subjected to violence at the hands of their partners. This was summed up, rather poignantly, by one elderly woman in a focus group in La Vía, who informed me, 'I no longer have the problem of a husband. He's dead'. This sentiment was shared by other women who I interviewed, who also no longer had the 'husband problem'. The routinisation of violence can become so entrenched in everyday relations that it is almost expected as an inevitable and culturally sanctioned element of growing up or being a woman. As one woman emphasised: 'It is the simple fact of being a woman.' The degree of violence to which women are subjected, however, is not universal. For some, it was part of systematic physical and psychological abuse at the hands of partners, whereas others mentioned specific episodes of physical violence. According to Eteban (El Boulevar), who distinguished between *maltrato* (abuse) and a *golpe* (slap):

> This can happen when, maybe the couple don't know each other very well, at the beginning of a relationship perhaps and maybe the partner is jealous or something. Sometimes discomfort results in a slap.
>
> MH: and is that justified?
>
> Yes, that's justified because it is just a slap because of the problem, it is not continuous.

He justified hitting a woman through provocation and made a distinction between repeated abuse. His partner of over twenty years, María Dolores, spoke of several episodes of violence throughout their relationship. The fact that the instances of physical violence were isolated events lessened their severity in her eyes. Violence in the relationship was minimal in comparison to her relationship with a previous partner. In contrast, Esteban was seen as a good man who only used physical violence on occasion. Her threshold for tolerating violence was high, given that she had been subject to repeated violence from an early age. She had also learned to accept and minimise violence against herself: it could be and had been worse. Her response was to modify her behaviour in order to avoid provocation. She had learned not to 'answer back', and to 'behave'. Silence had become a key strategy for María Dolores to avoid provocation: 'So it's better if I shut up, and then I don't let him humiliate me like that.' The fact that María

Dolores minimised the violence against her reveals important issues in the continued disjuncture between women's lived experience of violence, how it is understood and how it is theorised. The routine measures that women take to protect themselves against men's potential violence are 'almost automatic' (Kelly, 1988a: 32). This points to a certain naturalisation of men's aggression and it also shifts the 'behavioural responsibility' to the woman, who is charged with protecting herself (Richardson and May, 1999).[1] Failing to adequately 'protect' themselves against male violence shifts issues of responsibility to women. This is a process that marks relations between men and women, but is also bolstered by interconnected power relations that produce and sustain gendered hierarchies.

Men invoke a range of strategies to justify and excuse their behaviour. Although some of the male research participants spoke of the physical and psychological violence they had used, this was often minimised by language–'problems at home'–or they sought to explain their behaviour through the influence of drugs, alcohol or provocation. It is not uncommon for violence against women to be associated directly with the consumption of alcohol and many men and women in the communities blame alcoholism for violence against women and children. The self-help group addressed the problem of alcohol addiction alongside men's violence, but the facilitator was careful to refute the notion that alcohol caused the violence. It is important to unpack issues of blame from issues of cause. By naming alcohol as the root problem, attention is diverted from the violence itself. It also ignores the fact that many men use violence without the 'mitigating' effects of alcohol or drugs (Cavanagh, Dobash, Dobash and Lewis, 2001).

In the men's group, all of the men were convicted under what Salvadoran law terms 'intra-family violence'. The law against intra-family violence in El Salvador was passed in December 1996. The new Penal Code (1998) sanctions (Codigo Penal Republica de El Salvador, 2001), for the first time in Salvadoran history, intra-family violence as a crime (Article 200).[2] This broad definition includes violence against women, children and irresponsible paternity, namely the failure to provide financial contribution for children. The definition has been criticised by feminists and human rights organisations, as it hides the fact that women suffer disproportionately because of violence at

---

1 Richardson and May's (1999) discussion is on violence–or so called 'hate crimes'–against the Lesbian, Gay, Bisexual and Transsexual (LGBT) community. I find the analysis analogous with some of the attitudes towards violence against women particularly around issues of victim blaming and behavioural responsibility.

2 Women's legal status in society has improved with the implementation of new laws and the signing of international agreements, such as the Belem do Pará Convention (1994), which seeks to eliminate all forms of violence against women.

the hands of men in the domestic realm. Moreover, the authorities responsible for enforcing the law, such as the PNC and family judges, have been criticised for their ineffectiveness and, in some cases for siding with the aggressor (IDHUCA, 2003; see also Hernández Reyes and Solano, 2003).

Only two men in the five years that the self-help programme had been in existence (at the time of research) have come voluntarily. The rest have been required to attend as part of their parole. Indeed, one man in the focus group informed us one day that 'it is her fault that I am here', suggesting that either he claimed no responsibility for the violence, or did not regard it as an offence. Another man who attended the group from the local prison where he was serving a life sentence for murdering his wife, told the group how he had 'lost it' when he had suspected his wife of cheating on him. His incorrect 'justification' highlights the powerfully gendered legitimising discourse behind certain forms of violence. If this man portrayed his wife as unfaithful, he could achieve some sort of empathy with a wider constituency. It also hints at the notion that some types of violence can be justified by provocation; in this case, the women's alleged infidelity explains his violent reaction. Another told the group how his friends had encouraged him to sort out the problems with his wife, whereas yet another was advised to hit her harder. This indicates that peer group reaction is not universal and not all men advocate the use of violence. On one occasion the local judge came to talk to them and advised them: 'Before it was normal to hit your wife. Not any more because the laws have changed.' Perhaps my reading of what the judge said is overly literal–only the laws have changed, not the normal act of hitting one's wife–but it did strike me as a telling statement of how gender relations are played out. The law may have changed, but domestic violence remains a pervasive force in the lives of men and women. Indeed, IDHUCA (2003) is critical of the role of some judges who pay more attention to the violence that children suffer over women. The collusion of the state happens on a number of levels. Police minimise or refuse to attend cases of domestic violence, women are often misadvised by state agencies about how to report incidences of violence and which agency is responsible. Women in San Marcos and Ahuachapan suggested there is a common tendency for institutions to pass the buck. The complex legal process not only confuses women but tires them out and dissuades them from seeking justice (Hume, 2008b).

One 76-year-old woman in El Boulevar had lived with two very violent partners. In the first case, her family were aware of the degree of abuse that she suffered, but refused to intervene 'because I was his wife', despite the fact that he once beat her unconscious with a piece of wood. They did intervene when he tried to hit her younger siblings because he had no 'right' to beat them. She did leave him when the abuse became too much to bear and neighbours offered her protection when the state refused. Women's fear of reporting violence is nourished by wider patterns of aggression. One male respondent highlighted that men in his community not only intimidated women into silence with further violence, but also threatened them with engaging the local gang.

> MH: And do the police never arrive?
>
> Sometimes but they take longer to take him away than the woman does to get him out again.
>
> MH: She gets him out?
>
> Yes, because he says to her, you get me out or I will tell the gangs, you know, that's the threat. She prefers to get him out. So yes, there is lots of violence, lots and lots of intra-family violence here. (Enrique, El Boulevar)

The above example highlights that individual men can use the threat of wider social violence to ensure their patriarchal privilege. One woman explained that on the one occasion she had reported her husband, the police had criticised her for leaving her children alone to go out and make the phone call to them from a public telephone. Despite important changes in the legislation, women are still expected to maintain a strict silence with regard to men's use of violence. In a focus group in San Marcos, women suggested that they face a double threat (Hume, 2008b). Police invoke notions of the ideal type family to dissuade women from reporting the 'father of your children' and men punish the women for speaking out:

> You call the police but all the police do is say, 'So Missus, your husband hit you then? but he's your husband, the father of your children, are you going to leave your kids without a father? No? OK then, forgive him and let him in.'
>
> MH: is that what the police say?
>
> Yes, and the husband says 'why did you put the cops on me?' and beats her up again. That's the reality; he hits us and we can't do anything about it.

This narrative also exposes levels of institutional collusion with men and how this actively limits the options available to women. A group of women from La Vía highlighted that they would not intervene in cases of domestic violence for fear of what might happen to them. 'We are afraid to call the police because they might see you and thump you.' Indeed, one woman was beaten by her partner for being 'nosy' (*metida*) when she intervened to protect her sister whose husband was hitting her with a hammer on the street:

Every day he came home drunk. Everything annoyed him even the tortillas wrapped up in a cloth ... He used to grab my sister's clothes and throw them into the sink. He used to chase her out of the house with a belt. God, how my sister has suffered and she is still with him. Well, one day he came along with a hammer and when he went in he hit my sister with the hammer here [she points to her head] and he kept hitting her hard with the hammer and she had a big bump here. Those hammers are heavy, pure iron, and then he came here and I said to him. I said the bad word, 'don't you hit my sister like that because you are not her father or her mother'. I said, 'you're not her mother who gave birth to her, nor her father who engendered her so you have no right to hit her like that'. So he [her brother-in-law] insulted me and he [her partner] asked what it was all about. 'I don't know', I told him [her partner]. As [the brother-in-law] was drunk, he said 'It's with her because she is nosy. I have problems here with my wife and she is sticking her nose in.' So he [her partner] came along and hit Don Mateo twice and then gave me a hard time because I got involved ... 'Stop sticking your nose in where it doesn't belong.' 'It does concern me because she is my sister and who are you to be saying anything to me, you're not my father.' I didn't go out, not even to the toilet ... I had to go in a bucket and then dispose of it at night so that people wouldn't see me all bruised. (María Dolores, El Boulevar)

Women's experiences are often invalidated by wider society and they are chastised for violating this 'patriarchal privacy'. In the above case, a woman was 'punished' by her own husband for trying to defend her sister. Notions of privacy here refer clearly to the power relations between men and women as the incident took place on the street, which is considered a 'public' place. From an early age, women have been subject to the authority of their fathers and mothers. The childhood of many interviewees–both men and women–was often marked by violence. For many women, violence is still a routine component of their most intimate relations. Some women expect it and many have not known any other reality. People not only learn to use violence, they also learn to accept and tolerate it. The silence that obscures much of the violence within the private realm is intertwined with dominant discourses awarding importance to the patriarchal family to create a situation where women's experiences are minimised and invalidated by society. Violence, in this case, has become naturalised and, to a certain extent, rationalised. There exists a tacit acceptance of men's aggression, especially within the structure of the family. Such a scenario effectively denies women and children the right to have rights and assures continued impunity for many of the crimes of the private realm. Women's position in society is structurally weaker than that of men and their opportunities for defining violence more limited. This has particular impact on their capacity to defend themselves effectively against violence. This does not mean they do not generate strategies to resist and survive men's violence. Kelly (2000) reminds us that an emphasis on the 'agency' of the perpetrator effectively ignores such activities. I will return to this issue in the next chapter.

María Dolores's narrative above also makes reference to the fact that the man had no right to hit his wife because he was not her father 'who engendered her' or her mother 'who gave birth to her'. Implicit in this is that parents have the 'right' to use violence against their children. This was a common theme in the research and it is to the issue of violence against children that I now turn.

Violence across Generations

Most of the interview narratives reveal very brutal episodes of violence in the lives of the research participants. Women and men alike talked of the *cinchazos* (beating with a belt) and *leñazos* (beating with a piece of wood), machete sleeves and other instruments that were used to 'correct' and 'punish'. María Dolores, like many of the women in the communities, had learned to negotiate high levels of violence from an early age.

> Señora María arrived, I told her, she asked them to let me fill it, I told her, I asked them for a pitcher of water but they [older women who were washing at the well] didn't want to give it to me. I couldn't fill it ... I was afraid that she would hit me hard, I put the jug on the table and I tried to run out, but I couldn't run and she was coming towards me. I couldn't run because the house only had one door, you see. She wouldn't let me leave. I went under the oven where we made the fire, under where the wood is kept and I stayed there. As I had put the jug in the middle, all the water spilled out. You know for that, she hit me even harder and me under the oven. She grabbed a bundle of wood and bang, bang. 'no *mamá*, no *mamá*, no *mamá*, no *mamá*'. I was all over the place and she was hitting me and hitting me and when she realised she had broken this hand and my foot with her beating, thwack. '*Mamá*, I can't stand it any more, *Mamá*, I can't stand it any more' because one of these bones had slipped out here.
>
> MH: Do you mean that she had broken your arm?
>
> Yes, yes, this bone here and she wouldn't stop hitting me, she thought I was making it up and she kept hitting me. Well, I crawled out as best I could and when she realised that I couldn't stand up she stopped hitting me.

In the above narrative, María Dolores speaks of how her mother broke her arm because she was angry with her for taking a long time to collect water from the well. She acknowledges that the level of force used by her mother was excessive and quotes the healer who attended her and admonished her mother:

> You should learn to punish children. Children aren't punished like animals, you should have got the belt and hit her two or three times, not flatten them.

Such advice was not seen as extreme; indeed, it was perceived to calm the excesses of the mother's punishment. This is illustrative of the existence of hierarchies of violence, where those individuals that have more power not only consider that they are legitimate in their use of violence, but that this is normalised into notions of what it means to be a good parent. Savenije and Andrade-Eekhoff (2003: 145) link these relations of power to notions of property: 'Intimate relations are often confused with property relations. The meaning of phrases, "she is my wife" or "these are my kids" undergo an essential change in meaning.' When I asked men and women how they punished their children, the reply was usually by hitting them *con el cincho* (with a belt) or with a rope. In one woman's case, the violence was so excessive from her alcoholic father that the whole family would sleep in the fields to avoid it. The same woman stated that she has continued to use corporal punishment against her own children. This does not suggest that the use of violence is an inevitable product of having grown up in a context where violence was employed with great regularity; rather, it indicates that violence has been and continues to be used as a normal and effective tool for discipline. Its value is that it appears to get results, even if this is only in the short term. Strict boundaries between perpetrators and victims are blurred and the use of violence continues across generations and time. Issues of responsibility and the questioning of strict binary oppositions between perpetrator and victim take on a particular relevance if we are to analyse how. Maria Dolores's narrative continues:

> MH: Do you think it's okay that she hit you like that?
>
> I don't think so because you can't hit your child like that, can you? With a piece of wood, sure you could almost kill him. Well, I haven't told you about one time when my son began to gamble. The first time I saw him gambling there in front of the house and I said to him 'come on home' and I hit him here [points to hand] but I hit him like that [makes a slapping gesture].
>
> MH: with your hand?

Yes but I told him 'if I see you again, I will burn your hands so that you won't do it again'. About two years later maybe, I saw him gambling again, that time he was playing dice. So that time I saw him with coins 'hey, change that ten colon bill for me as I don't have money to pay for something' I said to him 'and you go straight home now, go' and he came obediently. 'Do you remember that I told you that I was going to burn your hands?' I said, 'well I am going to burn them so that you see that I keep my word, so that you listen and remember'. Well, I got a small candle, one of the smallest and I lit it and I said you have to hold it here [under his hand] until it burns out and put the other one here [under other hand]. Thank God he doesn't bear a grudge and he did it ... I had my son on his knees there with the candle burning. He was in the third year of his *bachillerato*, and he put a handkerchief on each finger, imagine, imagine that.

MH: and why did you do it?

I did that to him, in my mind I did it as an experience so that he would not gamble, because in my mind, I said that I did not want him to have vices. I don't want a drunk for a son, nor do I want a gambler. They cause too much heartache. 'Look son' I said to him, 'my granny told me that a brother of hers was killed because he had won a lot of money and, since he no longer wanted to play, they killed him'.

MH: and was there no other way to 'correct' him?

Sure, sure but to keep my word for what I had told him I would do to him. I did it because I told him, 'the next time, I will burn your hands'. When I burnt them I told him that if I saw him playing again, I would cut off half a finger, 'but I don't want you becoming a gambler'. When he went [to the USA], he didn't even smoke. Now they tell me that he even drinks. There's no one to control him you see, only God.

The notion that the use of violence was a valid, and even admirable, element of good parenting was a theme that ran through many of the men's and women's accounts of violence. For María Dolores, the above episode was also a matter of keeping her word; as well as disciplining her son her pride was at stake. This is not an argument that violence breeds violence, or that exposure to violence as a child leads to a propensity to use physical force as an adult. Rather, it points to the particular rules or 'commonsense' that regulate towards whom and how violence is used. Social and cultural myths that give value to violence–such as the use of violence as an expression of a male gendered identity or authoritarian practices to maintain a sense of order in the face of high levels of criminality–aggravate this situation. Violence is formative and society reacts accordingly (Feldman, 1991).Violence appears to have a functional and even central role in familial relations. Goldstein (2003) notes similar practices in Brazil, where punishment is rooted in the harsh ethos of survival in low-income communities. Notions of 'tough love' are seen as necessary to teach children how to survive the harshness of reality. One man in El Boulevar talked about how his father castigated him in a very 'brutal manner', but that such a punishment worked: it kept him on the straight and narrow:

> My father, he got me on my knees and once he left me marked with the belt for being naughty. When I went to school, I liked taking coins and so I took the money out of the drawer where he had the money from the pharmacy, bundles of money. And I handed it round the boys in my class. Someone told my mother that I was handing out money to all the kids in the school and that's how they found me out. And that's why my father punished me. I remember it well, he made me bend down and hit me with a belt, so hard that it made me wince and thank God, I never did it again. If he had given me a light punishment, do you think that I wouldn't be robbing, or I would have been killed already or in prison, condemned to death? (Esteban, El Boulevar)

The above account suggests that there is certain logic to the violence exercised against the son by the father. The son himself perceives that it was for his own good, which is a perception shared by many of the interviewees. A good parent, and especially a good father, is respected for using the heavy hand or *Mano Dura*. *Mano Dura* is a common theme of narratives of violence in El Salvador, in both public and private realms. Rather than being seen as excessive, *Mano Dura* commands respect. In the prison, all of the men I interviewed talked at length about fatherhood. They linked their responsibility to their offspring to using the *Mano Dura* with their sons, because gangs and other youths had been leading them astray since they (the fathers) had been in prison. Daniel (29 years old), who has no children, spoke about the lack of a father figure in his life. He had grown up with his mother and sisters. He saw a lack of discipline, which he linked to his absent father, as a major reason for his drug abuse, which he blamed for his violent behaviour and involvement in criminality. Implicit in these assumptions is that violence is used to prevent something worse. Interview narratives suggest that men have more 'right' to use violence than women, as their gender identity prescribes the use of force. Women, on the other hand, as mothers may discipline their children with violence because it is 'for their own good'. Such notions of 'right' were not only based on the legality of such acts, for violence against women and children is now illegal, but were also supported by social and cultural norms that make it acceptable for individuals to use violence against others in certain contexts. Cultural constructs of acceptable behaviour regulate how violence is defined and even what is recognised as violent. This is discussed in greater detail in the following section with reference to the connections between sexuality and violence.

Men, Women and Sexuality

Galtung (1990: 291) argues that language is one element of culture 'that can be used to legitimize violence in its direct or structural form'. Language is intimately linked with other powerful discourses on *appropriate* behaviours for men and women. It gives meaning to a gendered reality, offering a sense of 'order, naturalness and timelessness' (Whitehead and Barrett, 2001: 12). This 'illusion of order' invariably shapes popular reaction to violence against women. Popular language concerning women's sexuality is laced with prejudice and moral judgement. There is immense social value ascribed to young women's virginity. When a young woman had sex for the first time, especially if it took place outside marriage, participants in this research claimed that, '*está arruinda*' (she is ruined) or '*ella fracasó*' (she has failed). The stigma was placed clearly with the woman, she was no longer 'as God brought her into the world', that is, a virgin. Men's role in sexual activity was described in much less judgmental terms. Examples from testimonies range from 'he made her his woman' to the victorious 'he conquered her' (*la conquistó*) and 'I will be her owner' (*yo voy a ser el dueño de ella*). In the last case, the woman becomes–literally–the man's object. He is her owner, stripping her of all agency and rights. Moreover, one woman described an attempted rape while she was still a virgin: 'he wanted to make me a woman', a phrase that removed all traces of violence from the action. In their study of gendered socialisation in El Salvador, Gaborit and Santori (2002a: 9) suggest that women, whose bodies are less valued than men's, are further devalued when they begin to have sexual relations: 'A body born with little value acquires even less when she is no longer a virgin, and, curiously, when she has succumbed to masculine outbursts.'

Gaborit and Santori (2002b: 7) suggest that there are three principal mechanisms that construct and regulate female gender identity in El Salvador: shame, submission and victim identity:

> These three important mechanisms work together to ensure the supremacy of masculinity ... These social mechanisms operate as rules of conduct, in other words, as daily disciplinary measures supported by ideological justifications, sometimes explicit and sometimes rationalised implicitly through a series of myths or stories that are contained in local 'wisdom' and popular sayings.

It is interesting, therefore, to explore how local 'wisdom' and popular knowledge of gendered sexuality shape the social expectations of men and women. There is almost a sense of inevitability among women that men will conform to dominant constructions of *machismo*. As mentioned above, mothers speak of using violence as a tool to prevent their sons from taking part in traditional male activities, such as drinking or gambling. Many women resign themselves to men's promiscuity and, in some cases, their violence. Men's behaviour, therefore, cannot be analysed in isolation from its effect on women. More dangerous, however, is the implicit inference that women have the responsibility (and duty) to protect themselves from sexual advances. 'Men's sexual desire appears like an uncontrollable force that can stem from aggression; for this reason women must act modestly so as not to open up this source of danger for them' (Vásquez, Ibañez and Murguialday, 1996: 145). The practice of victim blaming has invariably shaped women's own sexual behaviours and also their reaction to men. According to one man, it is a mother's responsibility to protect her daughters from men:

> Look it is logical. There have always, always, been bad people, always. Even history mentions it. And sometimes the very fathers have raped their daughters. So, in order to avoid this horrible chain of events, mothers, perhaps instinctively, try to isolate their daughters more, their little girls. The man ultimately is a man. That's my way of seeing things anyway. Either men are rogues or not, but mothers always try to take care of their daughters. (Esteban El Boulevar)

Many women develop a range of survival strategies to avoid 'tempting' men. 'Men's sexuality is uncontrollable and it is up to [women] to stop it by behaving "decently", not provoking men' 'One example includes covering young girls' genitalia for, while it is common to see young boys naked, girls' nudity is frowned upon' (Gaborit and Santori, 2002a). These notions continue to have currency among younger generations, highlighting the prevailing norm of the 'sexual double standard'. One boy in the school comments:

> In the whole country there have been a lot of rapes ... even of men, even men are raped and they look at women all provocative because women even wear mini skirts and you can see almost everything and that tempts the man and he goes and fucks her (*la va a amontonar*) and worse if he is drunk or on drugs, he grabs her more.

Another woman remembered how her mother set a series of traps to stop her biological father from entering the family home to resume his relationship with her mother (including chicken wire and bolting the door). He did not live with the family and the mother was recently widowed from her husband (the woman was born from a relationship with this man prior to the mother's marriage). The sense was that now that her mother was without the protection of a husband, she was available for other men whether she wanted to or not. The man was so persistent that, in the end, the family slept in a neighbour's house. Such notions are also linked to women's sexuality. One 76-year-old woman from El Boulevar stated: 'I love being single because it is only then that you have control over your own body.' This statement suggests that many women still do not feel that they have autonomy over their own bodies. Indeed, many interviewees became pregnant in their early teens without having any real knowledge of what was happening to them. This was the experience of Isabel from La Vía:

> When I fell pregnant with my daughter, I didn't know. Before you didn't hear any talk about [sexual education]. None of that was spoken about. So my mother sent me to a woman's house [to work]. The woman said to her, 'Niña Rocio, send that girl to me because she doesn't feel like eating, she doesn't want to eat and she looks pale. I have no idea what's happening to her.' It was only then that my mother realised I was pregnant, that I was going to have my daughter. Then I had my baby; the father denied her from the moment I realised, when I was four months pregnant. He denied her; he said that it wasn't him. He has only recognised her recently, now that she is grown up and can defend herself.

In this context, women often take sole responsibility for the care of children, financial and otherwise, even when there is a man present. This unsettles some accounts of women's dependence on men as a reason for their remaining in violent partnerships. Figures from 1998 demonstrate that 24.6 per cent of fifteen- to nineteen-year-old women have had at least one pregnancy and sexual education still remains a 'taboo' in El Salvador, blocked by Conservative elements within the Catholic Church (de Innocenti and Innocenti, 2002: 27). Indeed, access to formal education for the women I interviewed over 40 was minimal. One woman's father refused to send her and her sister to school, because they would only learn to write 'letters to her boyfriend'.

Women's lack of autonomy in relation to their sexuality nourishes and is nourished by wider social perceptions of sexual violence. In Chapter 1, I mention a lengthy discussion with a couple in El Boulevar when the man argued that he did not believe that rape existed, but rather that women have the responsibility of preventing it. The transfer of responsibility to women is a common theme in popular understandings of male violence. This minimisation of the violence contained in certain sexual activities was reflected in the opinions expressed by several men and women in this research. A particularly brutal example concerns young women who want to enter a gang. They are offered two options: *golpes* (beating) or *el trencito*, which means having sexual relations with male members of the *clika*. Men are only offered one option: *golpes*.[3] According to Vladimir, a member of the MS-13 gang in El Boulevar, the women who enter into the gang through sexual intercourse are not 'worth' much as they do not feel pain in comparison to the girls who are beaten:

> Thirteen men, but you can't even imagine, you have to give it to them from behind, in the mouth and in front at the same time, For me, that's fucked, I mean, you give them a choice. Some women say better beat me up and others, stupid bitches, who say better do what you want with me and maybe the women who do what they want are the ones that are of no use and the ones who have been beaten up are the ones who stand up in the gang . . .

> MH: Why?

> Because, what pain has a woman felt who has been fucked by thirteen men compared to her who has been beaten?

Despite the brutal description of the process of gang rape, she fails to recognise the trauma the victim may suffer.[4] There is almost an inference that women enjoy such violent sexual episodes. Interviews with women gang members in 2004 suggest that they are not allowed to talk about such practice. When I asked one woman who had been in the Mara 18, she asked me how I had heard about that. She suggested that the women were 'stupid bitches' who underwent this option. On asking other women, they all said that they responded either by saying they did not about this practice in their gang or that they were not allowed to speak about it. This points to a code of silence regarding intra-gang violence. Women gang members face double vulnerability: from the wider society and also from their fellow *homies*. Another resident of El Boulevar, Erlinda, subscribes to the dominant notion that it is a woman's responsibility to defend herself against sexual attack. She herself had been the victim of attempted rape on several occasions. The fact that she was able to defend herself had coloured her opinion on sexual violence:

---

3   According to Aguilar (2007: 881), changes in the internal structures of gangs since the introduction of the *Mano Dura* anti-gang measures now require aspiring members to kill rival members: 16 per cent of those surveyed said that to get into the gang, one had to kill.

4   Similar processes have been identified in other contexts. For example, Bourgois (2002) notes that rape is an element of everyday violence among crack dealers in East Harlem, while O'Sullivan (1998) indicates that the practice of gang rape is not uncommon among male fraternities in the United States.

There was always someone who wanted nothing more from me than to do me harm. No, they only tried to force me, you know, but never ... Maybe because of this I don't really believe in rape, because there are things that you don't want, if a woman doesn't want it, she us very capable of defending herself.

However, despite her doubts, levels of sexual violence, both in the domestic realm and wider society, are considered extremely high.[5] In El Boulevar, young women live in fear of sexual attack by gang members. According to a girl in the focus group: 'Rape, mostly of girls because the gang members get us, well they grab the girls, cause her harm and then they don't take responsibility.' Indeed, one woman suggested that her father was a good man, since he never abused them sexually.

He was such an honest man with us. That much I remember. One night, who knows how, he came into my room and when he felt my little body, that it wasn't my mother's, he rushed out ... well, in that sense, my father was such a decent man. (Meche, El Boulevar)

The suggestion in this narrative was that her father was somehow an exception to the rule and, indeed, she later found out that the father of three of her children sexually abused her eldest daughter: 'Of all the bad things he did to me [she cries], the one that hurt me most ... is that he took advantage of my daughter, he took advantage of her.' There has been little research done on the prevalence of sexual abuse within families in El Salvador. A study carried out by the Universidad Tecnológica (UTEC) on 714 students demonstrates that 38 per cent of respondents had been sexually abused as children. The figures highlight that 40 per cent of men and 36 per cent of women were subject to varying degrees of abuse during childhood, which is a significantly higher percentage than found in other countries where similar studies were carried out (UTEC, 2001: 110).[6] Two of the men I interviewed in prison were convicted of abusing their daughters. Both men denied the abuse and in separate interviews the two men suggested that they had been the victim of a strategy by the ex-wives to get rid of them so that they could get together with other men. Gabriel explains: 'she wanted to get together with

---

5   Figures from the FGR indicate that 3339 cases of sexual violence were reported in 2001, 3396 in 2000 and 3102 in 1999 (interview with PNC advisor, May 2005). It must be noted that these figures are likely only to be the tip of the iceberg.

6   The authors point out that this higher incidence is not a result of using a wider definition of sexual abuse than other studies. Indeed, they point out that their definition is, in fact, somewhat narrow in that it excludes exhibitionism and only includes experiences of sexual contact.

another man; maybe she was betraying me before but you know how it is, maybe you don't want to accept things . . . finally she achieved her objective to separate from me, maybe by bringing me here [to prison]'.

Sexual abuse was not necessarily hidden, nor was it necessarily conducted in secret. María Dolores had been abused by an elderly relative at the age of ten or eleven. Her mother knew about the abuse, and Maria Dolores believes that her mother had actually arranged it with the cousin for some financial recompense.

> You won't believe it; she had made deals with the old man because he had bought me the cloth, the gold chain and the earrings with the pink stones. He bought all the girls he wanted like that.
>
> MH: and was that common in the countryside in those days?
>
> Yes, that old man broke-in young girls

Whilst there has not been any research into this practice, anecdotal evidence provided by women from different parts of the country indicated that, while not common practice, they did know of similar cases. Another woman in El Boulevar narrated an episode where her mother-in-law tried to prostitute her to some men and she narrowly escaped being raped by running into the fields. The focus groups in the school and individual interviews also pointed to high levels of sexual abuse in the home. One interviewee's niece has been abused by her stepfather for many years. The girl's mother and other relatives knew about the abuse and, whilst they did not condone this man's actions, they felt powerless to intervene. This also suggests the continued power of the symbolism of the private sphere. Indeed, in the three years that I worked with a women's organisation in different parts of El Salvador, we came across many instances of women who had been abused by their fathers and stepfathers. In some cases, the mothers and the rest of the family blamed the girl for the abuse, as it was perceived that she had somehow provoked the attack.

Most of the women who participated in the research shared the view that men were unable to control their sexual behaviour. According to Welsh (2001: 20): 'young men are taught that their masculinity is measured in great part by their sexual prowess. The concept of women as sexual objects is constantly reinforced by male relatives and friends and by mass media representations of women.' This relational dynamic not only affects men's perception of women, but also shapes the ontology of women's sexuality. Indeed, it appears commonplace for women to accept–or, at the very least, tolerate–their husbands having relationships with other women: 'Men never have only one woman' said one woman in a focus group in La Vía. Two women whose partners were having affairs with neighbours claimed that they did not mind the infidelity because it was to be expected from men, but that they found it humiliating that the affair was taking place so close to home. Interesting here is not so much whether the women minded their partner's infidelity, rather the fact that they had resigned themselves to it. The perceived inevitability of men's infidelity, in the eyes of these women, bears testament to the power imbued in dominant gendered roles. Like many of their neighbours, they have stayed in relationships despite the knowledge that their partners have sexual relations with other women. Many different types of men's behaviour remain unquestioned because of the social value ascribed to gendered roles. In the case of women, however, infidelity is unacceptable and, indeed, merits sanction. As one woman informed me, 'When you get married they say that no man has a right to mistreat a woman, except in cases of infidelity', binding the accepted use of violence with the policing of women's sexuality. Indeed, a recent survey found that 32.7 per cent of men in El Salvador believe: 'A man can punish a woman if she is unfaithful to him.' Half of adult men interviewed accept that women's infidelity is more serious than that of men (Orellana and Arana, 2003: 88). This 'sexual double standard' places value on women's chastity on the one hand and the importance of men's virility on the other (Chant with Craske, 2003: 141). This has huge implications for how society recognises, regulates and responds to sexual behaviour. Constructs of masculinities are intimately linked to the performance of men's sexuality, which also shapes how men use and legitimate the use of violence. The following section will explore linkages between male gender identity and the use and experience of violence.

Men, Machismo and Violence

There are other issues that underlie the perceived right to use violence that beg discussion. These are intimately linked to the construction of male gender identities. One key notion of this type of violence is to 'control' children's behaviour. The above examples infer that, without the violence used to keep them in check, it was impossible for these young men to resist the temptation of stealing or gambling. Connell (1987) proposes that dominant notions of masculinity–'hegemonic masculinity'–laud the use of violence by men as an expression of dominance and power. In the context of Latin America, one of the most dominant expressions of masculinity is considered to be 'machismo' (Gutmann, 2003). Although not unique to Latin America, machismo has become an ubiquitous force in analyses of masculinities within the region (see, for example, Martín-Baró, 1983; Melhuus and Stølen, 1996; Gutmann, 1996; Welsh, 2001). Martín-Baró (1983: 166) distinguishes four central characteristics pertaining to machismo. First, he suggests that there is a 'strong tendency towards and value ascribed to genital activity'; second, a propensity towards bodily aggression; third, 'a systematic nonchalant attitude' ('*valeverguismo*') or indifferent attitude towards everything that is not related to his image of 'macho'; and finally, what he terms '*guadalupismo*', the cult of the virgin Mary, which refers to men's extremely close relationship with their mothers. Machismo is reinforced by individuals and structures within society, such as the Church, the family and the education system (see Welsh, 2001). Notions of machismo not only ascribe value to men's violence, but also help to maintain the enduring myths that support and normalise violence.

In this vein, Teofilio linked the violence that he was subjected to by his father to notions of machismo, suggesting how both the perpetration of violence and the subjection to it are intimately bound with dominant constructions of what it is to be a man:

> I remember when I was a child, well I worked really hard. My father, well, he treated me like a man, with that machismo that most fathers in the country treat you. Like, when I did something bad, he whipped me until my back was in shreds.

To be treated as a macho, this man had to undergo intense violence. He learned from a young age that his role as a man was to be castigated in this way. He considers that his subjection to violence was worse than that of his brothers because his skin is darker, thus binding gendered violence with racist prejudices. Don Beto recounted how his mother burnt his hands under the *comal* (griddle) because his stepfather had taken a *centavo* and his mother, mistakenly, thought her son had stolen it:

> He took the coin that my mum had and he went for a shave. He didn't tell my mother and because of that *centavo*, she put my hands under the *comal* till they were covered in blisters. She burnt me for a *centavo*. She hit me about twelve times with a piece of wood, she didn't hit me with a piece of cloth, but with whatever she found. I have scars, my shin is broken from beatings with wood, here on my back I have two other scars from wood which became infected. I used to ask her why she was like that and she would say 'cry you son of a bitch, cry'. But I couldn't cry, I couldn't. She wanted me to scream, but I couldn't cry. I was biting my tongue with each slap that she gave me.
>
> MH: And why did you feel that you couldn't express . . .?
>
> I couldn't cry because I felt a lump here in my throat and that lump made me feel as if I couldn't scream or shed tears . . . no, I couldn't do it.

MH: And could you not do it because you learned that boys were not supposed to express emotion?

I didn't learn it, I was taught. If you scream, I will kill you, she used to say. So I had to cry on the inside, not on the outside but on the inside. That's it.

MH: How did that affect you, having to cry on the inside. How did you feel?

I felt worse because I swallowed my feelings, I swallowed the pain and the beatings. I let nothing out.

As a boy, it was unacceptable for him to cry, despite the severity of the violence. Men are taught at an early age, as this interviewee highlights, that they should not express emotion. They should 'be firm'. The old adage of 'boys don't cry' is central to what Salvadoran society expects from men. Both men and women actively participate in this highly gendered socialisation process. Expressing emotion is regarded as expressing weakness, which 'real' men are actively discouraged from doing. A survey carried out in El Salvador in 2003 demonstrates that 61.3 per cent of interviewees agree: 'Women represent love and weakness while men, intelligence and strength' (Orellana and Arana, 2003: 89). According to Welsh (2001: 18), writing on Nicaragua, '[t]ears, fears and weakness are prohibited and punished with accusations of being a *cochón*–a sissy or poofter'. The men that participated in this research were subjected to violence from an early age and most continued to use it to exert their authority as men. Violence, for them, continued to be a normal element of their male gendered identity.

Violence, drinking and womanising have become so bound up with dominant constructs of masculinity that they are seen as natural. Within this pervasive logic, individual men cannot be held responsible for conforming to socially prescribed roles (Greig, 2000); it is to be expected. This was a theme that ran through many narratives and appears key to understanding both how women perceive men and, indeed, how some men perceive themselves. This model of hegemonic masculinity denies men agency, choice and the possibility to be different. This does not mean that all men conform to this model, rather that it is indicative of the acceptable boundaries of male behaviour. Many men who participated in the research do not voice responsibility for their actions, and, indeed, many women do not appear to expect it of them. Issues of violence and economic irresponsibility are buried under layers of justified and socially accepted discourse.[7]

---

7   All the women I interviewed have engaged in productive activities and, even when they have a male partner, their contribution to the household economy is vital.

In an exercise with the self-help group of men convicted of domestic violence, the participants established that being a man is intimately bound up with the use of violence. Respondents testified to feeling more manly by threatening and beating women, never giving in (*no se deja*), being brave, having sexual relations with many women, leaving women pregnant, having lots of children, feeling more important than other men and being proud. Some men said that carrying weapons made them feel more like a man.[8] If a woman bosses a man about, he is a 'culero' (focus group, 24 January 2002).[9] Furthermore, Vladimir, a member of MS-13 in El Boulevar, also used this term for those gang members who are not good fighters: 'There are guys who are in the gang but they have never killed and they haven't even stabbed anyone. Maybe that's why we call them *culeros*.' Such notions conform to dominant notions of 'hegemonic masculinity'. Those who deviate from this model are not regarded as 'real' men and their sexuality is questioned. Homophobia is widespread and the demonising of homosexuality is learned at an early age. There have been a series of high profile attacks on gay men and transvestites over the last decade in El Salvador.[10] Dominant discourses about the 'deservedness' of violence against certain 'types' of people closes down the

---

Decades of feminist research have highlighted the importance of women's economic contribution to the household, although this is still masked by popular gendered stereotypes promoting the idea of the male breadwinner (Boserup, 1970, Elson et al., 1991; Craske, 1999). Such evidence unearths important considerations about gendered economic roles within the household and disputes notions that women are forced to stay in difficult partnerships because of economic dependency, such as suggested by Ehlers (1991) in her study of a Guatemalan community. It also questions recent debates about masculinities in crisis and an upsurge in violence, which assume that men have historically been breadwinners and are plunged into crisis when their role is changed (for example, Chant, 2000).

8   See Cock (2001) for an analysis of the centrality of guns to male gender identity in South Africa. See also UNDP (2003) for a study of firearms in El Salvador.

9   Derogatory term for gay.

10 According to the 2001 Report from Human Rights Watch: 'Gay men, lesbians, and transgender people have been subjected to a campaign of terror, violence, and murder in El Salvador over the last several years. Governmental indifference to these offenses was compounded by state agents' active participation in violence. A person who identified himself as a member of the special Presidential Battalion used his weapon to threaten a transgender person who was participating in Lesbian and Gay Pride Day celebrations in the Constitution Plaza in San Salvador. Asociación "Entre Amigos" Executive Director William Hernández repeatedly received death threats. The Salvadorean police acknowledged that Hernández and "Entre Amigos" qualified for protection due to the repeated attacks and threats to which they had been subjected. Nevertheless, the then chief of the National Civil Police at first refused to appoint any officers to provide protection because officers who "do not share the sexual tastes" of those they should protect would feel uncomfortable doing their work. Hernández was placed under special police protection following an international campaign.' (See Human Rights Watch, 2001).

possibilities of justice and sustains the toleration of violence against particular groups (Richardson and May, 1999). In one focus group in the school in El Boulevar, this was highlighted when students mentioned homosexuality as a type of violence. Such notions inform widespread perceptions on how gender relations are enacted or, specifically, on the use of violence as a legitimate element of this 'machista' gendered identity.

Alfonso, an eighteen-year-old man who grew up with his grandmother, accepted his experiences of violence, seeing them as 'normal'. His grandmother beat him regularly and used to insult him and his siblings by likening them to their mother–she was a dog and so were they. On one occasion, she electrocuted him with the light cable: 'Our grandmothers always treat you badly, but it wasn't either too nice or too complicated, it was more or less normal . . . Yes, she was a bit cruel but, even still, I can't not love her. I will always love her but I can tell you, she was something else.' Violence, in this man's life, was commonplace. He met with threats and beatings on a daily basis on his bread round. He had been systematically targeted by local gangs, and used to fight on a regular basis with his brothers. Now living with his partner, he spoke about using violence against her. 'Look, I, at the beginning, I didn't do any of that, hitting her but now, after, since about a year ago, I like, not that I like, but that I liked to hit her.' Interestingly, in the same interview he also spoke about gang members who had come into his house looking for him on several occasions and had beaten his partner. This made him feel bad because she was not a man, yet at the same time, she was the woman who he openly admitted to beating: 'it makes me feel bad because, maybe if she were a man I wouldn't feel bad because a man can take it [*aguanta*].' This glaring discrepancy raises huge questions about the accepted use of force, by whom and towards whom. Does the fact that she is a woman and *his* partner give him the right to beat her that others do not have? This question goes to the core of understanding the continued pervasiveness of violence against women. At stake here is not only the issue of force or aggression, but who can use violence legitimately, when they can use it and against whom. It highlights how the gendered relational dynamics of violence affect the different meanings ascribed to the act of violence.

Violence against women is one of the clearest expressions of gender inequality and its continuance is shaped by discourses that minimise its significance. In the case above, the violence used by the gang is awarded a different meaning from the violence the young man himself uses against his partner. Violence against women has become a routine element of expressing male gendered identity. The interviewee narratives expose hierarchies of victimisation patterns on both gendered and generational grounds. Violence against women is understood within the context of gendered power relations that gives some individuals–namely men–the right to beat others–namely women–and this is reinforced by the naturalization of gendered hierarchies within the social order. A gender order that prescribes 'appropriate' behaviour for men and women serves both to construct and reproduce notions of 'acceptable' violence. Women's experience of violence at the hands of their intimate partners is viewed as a 'private' or 'family' matter. One of the most damaging consequences of the acceptance of certain expressions of violence is that they are left unquestioned and, thus, rendered invisible. In order to understand this process, we must analyze how gender roles and identities are enacted and, specifically, how existing gendered norms serve to naturalize certain types of violence.

Conclusion

The extreme violence contained in these narratives contrasts with prevalent myths about the sanctity of the family. A premise of this book is that violence harms, yet society does not understand all violence as harmful. Indeed, it even justifies or accepts certain types of violence. A key question of this research concerns what individuals and groups recognise as violence in their lives. The social meaning that is ascribed to violence leads to a variety of reactions that affect how people assess violence. The process of recognition is not only dependent on the harm of an act of violence, but it is directed by hegemonic myths within society that inform our reactions. This chapter has argued that we need to analyse the gendered relational dynamic of violence. I have argued that there exist layers of socially approved gendered discourse that minimise and even rationalise violence. Social reaction to violence is not uniform. Nonetheless, there are discernible patterns, many of which are shaped by fear, mistrust and gender inequalities that allow hierarchies of violence to emerge. The myths and 'powerful fictions' that underpin popular epistemologies of violence are fundamental to understanding the power relations that produce and justify violent behaviours. Many of these myths are based upon the legitimacy of certain types of violence over others. A key framework of analysis has been the division of life into public and private spheres. More specifically, I have examined the ways in which a privileging of public realms of existence in both popular and public debate minimises and invalidates violence in the private sphere.

The public/private dichotomy endures as a central prism through which men and women make sense of the world. It is neither an accurate nor a fixed description of reality, but it does promote important ideologies that regulate power relations between men and women. As such, it is essential to be alert to how this distinction can naturalise and even legitimise certain types of violent behaviour. As a conceptual tool, public/private is both useful and dangerous. It is useful in that it permits a more nuanced view of how people see their everyday reality, but dangerous in that this construction is based on and reinforces a masculinist illusion of a social order. This has meant that the inequalities of the private realm continue to be ignored, despite important feminist challenges. The task here is to examine how meanings of violence are constructed. The process of ascribing meaning or recognising an act of violence is intimately linked to social and cultural processes that not only create, but validate, knowledge. Such processes affect the explanation and justification of certain types of violence. It becomes, therefore, crucial to analyse how such 'events' have been assigned meaning in the narratives of the participants in this research and how certain types of violence continue to be seen as more normal and, therefore, more acceptable than others in contemporary life.

This book argues that these 'master narratives' are profoundly shaped by dominant gender constructions, which continue to regulate the meanings and significance assigned to violence. The life-histories of men and women presented here suggest that individuals learn certain norms and values associated with the use of violence within familial relations. This is not an argument that violence necessarily breeds violence, or that exposure to violence as a child leads to a propensity to use violence as an adult. Rather it is pointing to the particular rules or 'commonsense' that regulate towards whom and how violence is used. People learn to tolerate and reproduce violence from an early age. Violence is formative and society reacts accordingly. This makes the task of resisting violence all the more challenging. The next chapter will therefore examine social and political responses to violence in El Salvador, including attempts by the women's movements to address issues of gender abuse.

5

'Kill Them, Attack Them at the Roots and Kill Them All': Examining Responses to Violence

When Wim Savenije of FLASCO asked what should be done with youth gangs in El Boulevar, Enrique replied 'Kill them, attack them at the roots and kill them all'. Although his answer is extreme, it is not an isolated response to violence in El Salvador. Such opinions do not reflect merely random ways of reacting, but are purposeful, dynamic and functional (Cavanagh, Dobash, Dobash and Lewis, 2001). Understanding how a society responds, or fails to respond, to different types of violence is a vital component of any policy that aims to reduce violence in an effective manner. Social reactions to violence are affected not only by individual subjectivity, but also by dominant cultural and social norms that shape normative behaviour. Examining responses to violence opens up the possibility of reviewing the interaction between the micro and macro politics of violence. In particular, it addresses the place of colonising strategies of power in shaping subaltern reactions to violence. In the case of men, social reaction to violence can be modified by the belief that violence is a central element of their gender identity. In the wider community, reactionary violence is legitimised by the presence of threat. This affects how we live in the world, but it also shapes the ways in which we come to understand and ascribe meaning to lived experience.

In this chapter, I address key responses to violence in El Salvador on state, community and civil society levels. I argue that a critical analysis of dominant modes of response to violence offers important resources for understanding the problem. Reactions must always be understood in the context of how the problem of violence is defined and within a critique of power relations that discipline both knowledge and practice. Building on guiding arguments presented in previous chapters, simplistic definitions generate partial and short-sighted policies. The review of responses presented here does not pretend to be exhaustive since new initiatives are emerging and the very nature of violence is reconfigured by responses to it. The interrelation between the performance of violence and reactions to it produce a moral and a political economy that restrict alternatives to violence. Three interlinked tendencies characterise responses: fear, inconsistency and repression. Dominant state intervention against crime is often reliant on the promotion of a politics of fear that has been discussed in previous chapters with reference to historic violence. Contemporary reactions fail to displace historic logics based on repression, polarisation and misinformation.

Rather than employ reliable data, the state management of violence has continued to rely on myth and ambiguous notions of potential threat. In El Salvador, as in much of the region, state responses have tended to focus on the repression of criminal actors rather than the prevention of crime. Such approaches ignore historic issues of uneven development, growing inequality and exclusion that are linked to high levels of violence. One of the key issues for concern that has emerged in both policy debates and community-level research is the issue of youth gangs – arguably, one of the most misunderstood expressions of violence in the contemporary era. The present chapter offers a detailed analysis of the politics of fear that surrounds gangs.

I address four interrelated themes. First, I explore the main government responses to the growing problem of violence and the continued logic of repression that inform these. Second, I examine community reactions to violence and, in particular, I address how citizens forge their own forms of 'justice'. Third, I consider alternatives to violence promoted by both citizens and organised civil society. Finally, I look to the practical alternatives provided by a feminist analysis of violence. Before embarking on this exercise, I introduce some reflections on fear.

A 'New' Politics of Fear in El Salvador's Peace

Studies in new and emerging democracies across the region have pointed to 'societies of fear', populated by 'citizens of fear' for whom ongoing apprehension over violence has become 'a way of life' for many (Green, 1994; Kooning and Kruijt, 1999; Rotker, 2002). Fear has a notably divisive effect on populations, buying into popular stereotypes and panic about certain people and places. Notions of 'safe' and 'unsafe' spaces and fearsome 'folk devils' both inform and misinform the politics of fear. Within popular imagination, fear is understood almost exclusively as pertaining to public realms of existence (Pain, 2001). In policy terms, similar distinctions are made. In the Salvadoran Legislative Assembly, there is a clear demarcation between public security and issues of 'intra-family' violence. The former comes under the remit of the Comisión de Seguridad Pública y Combate a la Narcoactividad (Commission for Public Security and Prevention of Drug-related Crime), while intra-family violence is seen as a problem for the Comisón de la Mujer y la Niñez (Commission for Women and Children).

The relegation of the problem of violence in the home to the sidelines of the security debate indicates an enduring privileging of public expressions of violence on the national political agenda. Nonetheless, this focus on public violence has ignored and invalidated the terror that many people, particularly women and children, live with on a daily basis within the 'refuge' of the private sphere. In many respects, this failure to analyse violence from a gendered perspective has led to a normalisation of such fear and violence, to such a degree that even those who are subject to it barely recognise it as valid. Participation is restricted, therefore, to the 'defence of the private given that the public is seen as lost' (Cruz, 2000: 617). Fear of the public realm, therefore, has negative repercussions on associational life, as discussed in Chapter 3 above. Implicit in this concept is the notion that the private is a safe space. The concept of the home as a refuge has been undermined by women's and children's experience of violence explored in the last chapter.

Fear was a recurring theme during interviews, whether expressly articulated or 'euphemised'. Much has been written on the somatisation of fear and many women, in particular, complained of headaches and problems with their nerves (Scheper-Hughes, 1992; Green, 1994, 1995). Both adults and young people in El Boulevar said that living with fear is a direct and negative effect of violence. When asked how violence affected them, young people named fear as a principle problem: 'we live with fear'; 'it affects us psychologically'; 'we are afraid that someone will hurt us or our families'; 'we are afraid of revenge'; 'we see so much damage, we are afraid of acting in the same way'; 'we are afraid of speaking'; 'we are afraid of leaving the house'. The experience of fear is highly gendered and transcends both public and private domains. Chapter 3 argued that young boys were frustrated at not having the freedom to go out of their houses because of gangs in the community. They also indicated that they were afraid of 'reprisals' from rival gangs. For young women, their principle fear was of sexual violence. They mentioned that they were afraid to leave the house for 'fear of rape by the *mara*'. Young women with children also said that they were afraid of repeating the abuse that their mothers had inflicted on them, pointing to patterns of violence and fear in the home. They also stated that they were afraid of getting married or getting together with someone and making the mistakes of their parents.

Fear may be subjective and emotional, but this does not detract from the need for a critical analysis of the ways in which it is shaped by social norms and political interests. For the young people in El Boulvar, fear is very much a part of their everyday social interactions in public and private. Patterns of violence are intricately interwoven into both the ontology and epistemology of fear. Violence does not just 'happen', it is defined, interpreted and legislated: who and what we fear is constitutive of who we are. Notwithstanding, who and what we fear is often contradicted by the realities of violence. It is based as much on myth and stereotype as actual patterns of aggression and it is rare that people articulate their fear of family members or indeed friends and neighbours in the same way that they might of 'strangers'. Caldeira (2000: 32) argues that categories of the criminal generate knowledge, but also misrecognition: 'without which the violence would not be tolerable to the very people engaging in it'. Rather than ordering or containing violence, the discourse of 'crime' may serve to foment fear. A critical engagement with how fear is managed, resisted and stimulated is therefore warranted. In the light of the discussion of violence against women and children in the previous chapter, it also asks what fears are silenced and denied. One of the ways in which violence gains currency is by conflating fear with respect. This was particularly noticeable in accounts of violence against children and women explored in the previous chapter, when force was used to teach them to 'respect' their parents or male partners. It was also mentioned by young people who joined a gang in search of 'respect' from their peers and wider society.

Interview data and literature on violence suggest that crime and, in particular, youth gangs appear particularly threatening in contemporary El Salvador. Chapters 2 and 3 explored the atomisation of communities and the increasing sense of vulnerability in the face of arbitrary criminal victimisation. The polarisation of society, therefore, is both a cause and a consequence of the symbolic power imbued in a fear of the 'other'. Without discounting the very real sense of terror that communities are faced with, I suggest that the mobilisation of public fears contains a political instrumentality. Referring to Chile, Lechner (1992: 27) suggests that a fixation on crime allows individuals to trace their fears to a 'concrete origin ... when the danger is confined to a visible, clearly identifiable cause that has been officially stamped as "evil", the fear can be brought under control'. The fear of crime becomes, therefore, a way of expressing other silenced fears. Fear is then both a product of and a premise for authoritarianism because it reinforces a sense of personal and collective impotency against the waves of violence and crime. Without collective alternatives, society is fragmented and 'thence is born the fear of difference and the suspicion and even hatred of the other' (Lechner, 1992: 29). Fear of the 'other', and its various embodiments, continues to feed a vicious circle of mistrust, polarisation and repression in contemporary El Salvador. In popular discourse, fearful 'folk devils' are employed to make sense of the world, to create an illusion of order even if this is not objectively manageable. Key to this book is to question who benefits from this 'illusion'. The danger of this climate of fear is that debate on the causes of crime and on urgent political priorities is pushed to one side in favour of uniting against 'evil'. I wish to draw out this argument by examining the principal government responses to crime and violence. In particular, I explore the anti-gang strategy that has been central to government rhetoric and practice since 2003.

Gangs, *Mano Dura*, Violence and the Absence of Alternatives

In 2007, the Minister for Security and Justice, René Figueroa, argued, 'a country should not be judged and condemned for the number of deaths, for the number of murders; a country should be judged for its coherent measures [to] prevent and suppress criminality'. He was challenged on this statement by opposition parties. Members of Parliament for both the FMLN and Cambio Democrático commented precisely that the National Assembly did not have knowledge of any National Public Security Policy, unless the minister was referring to a 'computer presentation'.[1] This episode is of more interest than merely exposing yet another spat between opposing political groups in El Salvador. No unified or consistent public policy to deal with public security exists and, despite very high-profile isolated governmental efforts to combat crime, there is little transparency as to how these initiatives were formulated or whose interests they represent. New strategies seem to spring up amidst media fanfare and then disappear, indicating not only the lack of strategic planning, but also long-term policy vision. The difficulty of accessing crime data has discussed earlier. Without such evidence, it also becomes impossible to measure the impact of new initiatives in any objective or transparent way. This section will therefore explore different government reactions to criminality and violence in the 2000s. I argue that, if anything, the Salvadoran government's response to growing levels of violence has been characterised by incoherency and a focus on repression. The most consistent policy response to high levels of violence in recent years has been to target gangs through repressive and reactionary policing. *Maras* may be the most 'emblematic' expression of violence in the post war period, but they are also its most 'misunderstood' and politicised expression of post-war violence (Hume, 2007b).

A key strategy of the *Mano Dura* or 'Heavy Hand' plan was the development of military anti-gang units, Grupos Territoriales Antipandilleros (GTAs), which brought together police and military operatives. The reintroduction of the military into matters of public security directly contravenes the spirit of the 1992 peace accords that sought precisely to remove the military from matters of public security. It also contravenes the

---

1   See the article published by El Salvador's digital newspaper, El Faro.net that cites both Figueroa and the response by opposition Members of Parliament. Hector Dada (CD) makes the important distinction between a PowerPoint presentation and a national policy (Baires Quezada, 2007).

country's constitution (Amaya, 2006).[2] In the first year, the state deployed 39 groups in 39 municipalities that were deemed to have a serious gang presence. Almost 20,000 young people were arrested in the first year of its operation, but the cracks soon began to show. Despite – or indeed because of – mass arrests, less than 5 per cent of those detained were charged. A lack of evidence meant the charges could not be processed. Under the plan, the police did not need a warrant, nor were they required to follow due process so they detained large numbers of urban youth in an arbitrary manner. The measures were strongly criticised by members of the human rights community and were deemed unconstitutional by judges (FESPAD, 2004).

On taking office in 2004, one of the first actions of the incoming president, Tony Saca, was to upgrade the existing *Mano Dura* into *Super Mano Dura*, further emphasising its repressive intent (Aguilar, 2007). The revised policy contained a three-pronged approach: the *puño de hierro* (iron fist) policing component; and the prevention and rehabilitation elements, *Mano Extendida* (Extended Hand) and *Mano Amiga* (Friendly Hand). In practice, it continued to operate much in the same way as the previous plan. Many thousands more were detained under these measures, and the police were given more powers of arrest. Under *Super Mano Dura*, 30 per cent of detainees were charged and allegations of police abuse rose dramatically (Cruz and Carranza, 2006). Attempts to address the deficiencies in prevention and rehabilitation were discussed through a series of consultative meetings with members of the policy community and civil society, although these have remained at a largely 'rhetorical' level (Wolf, 2008). The inaction and lack of concrete policy to come from these meetings have discredited this space as an effective arena for policy formulation. Prevention and rehabilitation have been, to a large degree, sidelined and have translated into minimal and isolated initiatives, carried out by the Consejo Nacional de Seguridad Pública (CNSP; National Public Security Council). The Council, which had originally been set up as an office to advise the government on matters of public security, has become more of a service provider since 2002 (Amaya, 2006). It promotes initiatives such as a tattoo removal service, a 'farm' for 'rehabilitated' gang members and limited training in manual skills such as baking, dressmaking or mechanics. The projects are almost exclusively heavily reliant on international funding with the Salvadoran government concentrating its resources on repressive measures. While these may be useful and necessary initiatives, they remain a minimal component of the overall governmental strategy.[3] Moreover,

---

2 *Mano Dura* was not the first time that joint police and military task forces were deployed since initiatives had sprung up since the late 1990s (see Amaya, 2006).
3 The PNC had developed community policing models in the late 1990s/early 2000s, inspired by similar models in other countries, but these were pushed aside under *Mano*

the reliance on external funding raises issues about sustainability and also questions the government's commitment to preventative strategies.

In sum, the *Mano Dura* response represented the systematic failure of government crime strategies since the signing of the peace accords in 1992 (ECA, 2003). Amaya (2006: 145) argues that the state management of security has 'traditionally responded to political interest or to media perceptions rather than to concrete societal needs'. Security policy is fomented by the broader climate of panic and promotes the use of repressive policies – in this case, towards youth. Such policies are ideologically grounded and serve to deflect attention from other issues of weak governance, 'so that [the populace] will forget the extent of inequality and government mismanagement' (Chevigny, 2003: 91). As a strategy of governance, *Mano Dura* is both constitutive of, and a response to, the heightening of citizens' fears. As such, heavy-handedness receives support from both above and below, with both the government and citizenry buying into populist prescriptions of *Mano Durismo*.

In the early 1990s, public opinion data show that citizens felt that socio-economic issues were major problems underlying rising crime figures. By the 2000s and in response to public debates, they were calling for more authoritarian responses (Amaya, 2006: 137). Thus, within the new democratic context, fearful constructions of youth, poverty and violence combine to sustain an authoritarian and exclusionary politics. The continued weakness of Salvadoran state institutions have not only meant that the state is ill equipped to deal with violence, but that politicised policy-making has prevailed in the context of democratic reform. These challenges are not exclusive to El Salvador and 'tough on crime' measures characterised by 'punitive populism' appeal to a broader public, which helps explain their pull.[4] According to Chevigny (2003: 79), this 'is just the sort of populism that elites have been looking for'.

Punitive populism is identifiable by the potency of its rhetoric and language, as well as by the actual rationale that underpins policies (Roberts, 2004). The promotion of this hegemonic politics proved particularly fruitful as an electoral strategy for the ARENA party, who successfully used *Mano Dura* to mobilise support during the 2004 presidential elections. Eighty-eight per cent of the respondents in an opinion poll conducted shortly after the launch of the policy in July 2003 expressed support for the measure; support

---

Dura. Interviews with PNC officers in July 2009 suggested that officers were hopeful that the force would invest in the community policing model once more. Amaya (2006) argued that local policing initiatives are often frustrated because they do not fit with national institutional plans.

4 See Chevigny (2003) on the United States, Mexico and Argentina, Ahnen (2007) on Brazil or Roberts (2004) on the UK.

for ARENA in opinion polls also increased dramatically. In May 2003, ARENA was lagging behind the FMLN with 23.9 per cent support, compared with the leftist party's 40.6 per cent. By October, the parties' fortunes had reversed, with ARENA receiving 41.1 per cent in contrast to the 22.3 per cent support for the FMLN. A key factor in this change has been identified as the broad appeal of the *Mano Dura* initiative (Artiga González, 2004). The success of this approach was based on a particular emotive rhetoric, reliant on the construction of youth gangs as a common enemy of good citizens. Ex-President Francisco Flores intimated that the anti-gang law was a matter of state pride, and the state must display its strength in the face of gang violence. In his public address to launch *Mano Dura*, he stated:

> There are more armed gang members than police and military units combined; they are, therefore, a menace to all Salvadorans ... Criminal gangs have descended into dangerous levels of moral degradation and barbarism. We have all known cases of decapitations, mutilations, satanic acts and dismembering committed against minors, old people and defenceless women. It is time we freed ourselves from this plague (Flores, 2003).

The *Mano Dura* approach is 'seductive' in its simplicity and the measures have received widespread and heavy support from the population (Snodgrass-Godoy, 2004). Three years after its introduction, a majority of citizens continued to express support for the policy despite rising murder rates and a consensus that the policy had been ineffective (IUDOP, 2006).[5] Designed as a temporary measure, the *Mano Dura* rhetoric has decreased in recent years, though interviews with civil society activists in 2007 and 2008 suggest the practice has remained the same. In the short term, *Mano Dura* has shaped the reconfiguration of youth gangs into more effective criminalised units. Previously identified as localised groups who defended their barrio, gang members have responded to the climate of repression by becoming better organised and more clandestine. The imprisonment of gang leaders has strengthened, not hampered, internal organisational structures and many continue to give orders from prison. The physical appearance of individual gang members has also changed. They are no longer encouraged to have tattoos on visible parts of their bodies; they have modified the dress code and restrict their use of sign language in public places. Aguilar and Miranda

---

5   By the end of 2006 about 40 per cent agreed and 26 per cent disagreed with the policy, though 32.6 per cent affirmed that it had not reduced gang violence while another 31 per cent of respondents considered it had only reduced violence a little (IUDOP, 2006: 3).

Table 3. Causes of Murder in El Salvador, 2003–2006

Cause/year	2003	2004	2005	2006
Common crime	57.4	33.7	23.3	18.3
Gangs	8	9.9	13.4	11.8
Unknown	28.9	48.4	59	67
Other	5.7	8	4.3	2.9

Source: Aguilar (2007: 885).

(2006) note a change in the norms and values of gangs. The historic pull of friendship and a sense of belonging have been replaced by alcohol, drugs and economic gain as important organising principles. The violence used by gangs is also more sophisticated and more lethal, with many young people now having to prove their eligibility to join by killing members of rival gangs (Aguilar, 2007). Before, entrance rituals included being beaten by members of the *clika*, or women had the option to choose gang rape (as discussed in the previous chapter).

Important to understanding the dramatic rise in crime in recent years is that the focus on *maras* has also forged a space for other forms of organised crime and social cleansing groups to emerge and consolidate. Jeanette Aguilar (2007: 878) argues that the *Mano Dura* approach has not just been ineffective, but it has been 'counterproductive'. Since its introduction 'the country has been submerged in a crisis of security that does not have precedent in the post-war period'. The focus on gangs to the exclusion of other forms of violence has exacerbated the existing situation of impunity, rather than confronted it. Murder rates rose by 78.1 per cent between 2002 and 2006 (Aguilar, 2007: 887). Extremely brutal forms of murder have also becomes more commonplace with more corpses being found that display signs of torture or having been dismembered. Figures from forensic medicine (the Instituto de Medicina Legal), demonstrate that the numbers of murders attributed to gangs demonstrate a slight rise since 2003, peaking in 2005. This is not nearly as dramatic as those attributed to 'unknown causes' (see Table 3). This directly contradicts information given to the press in a presidential address in December 2005 by Tony Saca, who estimated that gangs are responsible for 50 per cent of murders and 'disorder in the streets' (Saca, 2005). Press reports have agreed, and attributed 60 per cent of all criminal activity to them, yet offer few sources of evidence as to how this estimate was reached (FESPAD, 2006: 22). It is important to note here the collusion between sections of the media and elements of government who put forward a campaign of misinformation that was used to justify the policy approach.

Neither youth gangs nor society's response to them have emerged in a political vacuum. I suggested in the introduction to this chapter that contemporary responses to violence could be characterised by lies, violence and polarisation (also see Chapter 2). To analyse youth gangs in isolation from their social and political construction is to ignore a key element of the problem. Authoritarianism and violence have been key features of Salvadoran political culture since Independence, and multi-layered exclusion both facilitates and exacerbates the appeal that gangs present for young people. Notions of fear and risk are socially constructed and updated according to the historical period, as are 'modes of response' (Reguillo, 2002: 192). In this sense, collective gangs have come to represent the 'ideological conductor' of citizens' fears in the new El Salvador (Hall, Critcher, Jefferson, Clarke and Roberts, 1978). In the rhetoric of the authorities in El Salvador, gangs have replaced the 'communist threat' as the great danger to society: 'Judging by the [government] rhetoric ... with the disappearance of those groups who were considered a danger to society in the past – the communists – the identification of a new stereotype of threat has become necessary and the chosen ones have been young people' (Cruz, 1999: 269).

The process by which certain groups become 'othered' is not incidental, but reflective of a political instrumentality that is used as a mechanism for social discipline:

> It is a strategy of depoliticisation that does not require repressive means, except to exemplify the absence of alternatives. It suffices to induce a sense of personal and collective inability to have any effective influence over the public realm. Then the only alternative is to take refuge in the private realms in the hope (albeit in vain) of finding minimal security in intimacy (Lechner, 1992: 31).

Mechanisms to understand social and political processes, which have been shaped by exposure to decades of state brutality, continue to reflect deep polarisation in the understanding of violence. Both feminists and critical criminologists have been critical of an 'androcentric' or dualistic ideology that bifurcates social reality, such as good/bad, public/private, victim/perpetrator (Yllo, 1988: 39; see also, Harding, 1987; Stanko, 1990; Pain, 2003). I would like to stretch this particular critique of violence to address how contemporary constructions of violence in El Salvador not only limit policy response, but also shape the micro politics of fear and violence. Green (1994) cites a study carried out during El Salvador's civil war that demonstrates that children understood the best way to achieve peace was to 'eliminate the enemy ... through violent means'. There was no elaboration of the category 'enemy', which could be defined as either the Salvadoran state or the FMLN guerrillas. Important to the management of fear in this context was the existence of an 'enemy'. In the politics of violence in El Salvador, 'fearist discourses' have been consistently associated with the development of 'criminologies of the other' (Shirlow and Pain, 2003). Both the talk of violence among citizens and governmental rhetoric – past and present – provide a mutually constitutive narrative for the politics of fear. Much in the same way as previous decades, the existence of threat (however imagined) renders citizens vulnerable. The state is vested with the authority and legitimacy to pursue whatever means it deems necessary in order to fulfil its protective mandate. The existence of threat facilitates the canvassing of support among the citizenry who, through apathy, fear and support, collude with a repressive state.

It is therefore important to separate public opinion in supporting such rhetoric from public participation in the formulation of public policy (Amaya, 2006). It would appear that a politics of fear is both symptomatic of and informs policy response. This was evidenced in 2001 when the incumbent, Francisco Flores, and his Minister for Public Security both opposed reforms to the gun laws under the rationale that citizens had the right to guns for protection against criminals. Flores's support for (certain) citizens' right to bear arms is not only a statement of incompetence, in that the head of state is advocating that citizens bear arms, but it reveals a logic in governmental responses to violence that shut down alternatives to the use of force. The social panic surrounding current levels of criminality in El Salvador creates a situation where many condone, if not openly advocate, the use of violence and the restriction of democratic practices. This was discussed in the opening section of this chapter in relation to Enrique's prescription for dealing with gangs in his community. On multiple levels, violence is not only the problem, it has been the answer (see also, Amaya Cóbar and Palmieri, 2000).

Both the broader problem of violence and the responses to it operate to restrict democratic governance and the promotion of non-violent alternatives at multiple levels, from the community to the state to the international arena. An updated politics of terror heightens citizens' perceptions of insecurity and is still reliant on the narrative of a common enemy. Since '9/11', the discourse of terrorist 'threat' that informs a politics of fear has dominated a global political agenda (Ferudi, 2006; O'Driscoll, 2008).[6] The actual definition of

---

6   It is no coincidence that the term 'terrorist' is also still used to refer to the FMLN. Indeed, in the course of an interview in 2004, a senior criminologist in the PNC spoke of identifiable links between youth gangs and the FMLN. He said that senior members of the party went to the high security prison in Zacatecoluca to visit alleged gang leaders. When pressed as to which gang, he became evasive. In subsequent interviews with other serving police officers, I asked about this and they all said there was no substance whatsoever to such claims.

terror is at best confusing, particularly viewed from the perspective of Latin America. It is interesting to note how notions of 'potential terrorist threat' have been adopted within the regional discourse on security. US involvement in promoting this security agenda has been significant. In 2004, the FBI set up a special task force to combat gang activity in the region, using El Salvador as its centre of operations, and an agreement has been signed with the Suffolk police force in Long Island (FESPAD, 2006: 1).

Debates on the threat of terrorism led to accusations of links between Al Qaeda operatives and the Mara Salvatrucha (MS). Honduran security minister Oscar Alvarez alleged that Al Qaeda operatives had been recruiting Central American gang members to carry out regional attacks (Alvarez, 2004). Although such claims were later rubbished, El Salvador's President Saca did not wish to rule out the possibility that, 'gang members are involved in terrorist acts. With more reason, the Plan *Super Mano Dura* will work to capture all those people who are capable of committing terrorist acts'?. The role of the media, as well as political rhetoric, in the creation of this panic has been important. Pictures of detained young people and sensationalist headlines accompanied the strategies. This corresponded with the existing tendency within the mainstream media to link gangs to most expressions of crime and violence, but became increasingly marked since the introduction of *Mano Dura* in 2003 (WOLA, 2006). As argued above, such links rely on the creation of a particular image of gangs, rather than being based on evidence. As Zilberg (2007: 48) notes, 'the implicit has been made explicit, if only through rumour and innuendo'.

Ambiguity is important to the politics of fear, as is the creation of false certainties under the broad conceptualisation of threat. In 2006, El Salvador promulgated an anti-terrorism law though no specific definition of what is understood by 'terrorism' was included:

> The purpose of the law is to prevent and punish crimes that 'by their form of execution, or means and methods employed, evidence the intention to provoke a state of alarm, fear or terror in the population, by putting in imminent danger or affecting peoples' life or physical or mental integrity, or their valuable material goods, or the democratic system or security of the State, or international peace ... Article 6 of the law prescribes a prison sentence of 25 to 30 years for people who participate in "taking or occupying, in whole or in part" a city, town, public or private building, or a variety of other locations, through the use of weapons, explosives or "similar articles," when these acts "affect ... the normal development of the functions or activities" of the inhabitants or other users of the location. Again, this provision criminalizes a variety of actions that do not fall within any reasonable definition of terrorism. (Human Rights Watch [HRW], 2007)

Human Rights groups have been vocal in their criticism of the law, precisely because of its ambiguity (Amnesty International, 2007). Amaya (2006: 142) states that one of the effects of this legislation has been to 'banalise the category of terrorism and its self-serving uses'. As a consequence, the term 'terrorism' justified 'arrests in cases as dissimilar as juvenile gangs caught with homemade explosives in their possession and ... unionised government workers involved in violent labour protests with the argument that, legally, these constitute acts of terrorism. However, such actions can be interpreted as a manipulation of labels to invent enemies who did not exist before' (Amaya, 2006: 142). Two notable cases stand out. In July 2007, plans to decentralise water were met with protest by a range of civil society actors. Thirteen civilians were arrested and charged with 'acts of terrorism' which meant a potential sentence of up to 60 years in prison. International human rights organisations were critical of the 'misuse' of anti-terror legislation to criminalise legitimate social protest. A similar confrontation with street sellers in the centre of El Salvador provoked violent clashes between protestors and the police. Several traders were arrested and also charged with acts of terrorism. In both cases, the terrorism charges were dropped after several months, and the protestors faced the lesser charge of civil disobedience. These two events form part of a larger pattern of social unrest and authoritarian response and are indicative of a tendency to criminalise social protest (Ramos and Loya, 2008).

Although the prescription of repressive policies may be not be an uncommon reaction to high levels of violence, it has broader implications for civil society in El Salvador, given the historic context where violence and repression have been prioritised and legitimised as tools of governance. The repressive tone reinforces mistrust and polarisation, particularly between those perceived as 'upstanding citizens' and those perceived as 'criminals'. It closes down spaces for debate and political action. Furthermore, it is constitutive of a wider legacy of polarisation in which the logic of the state as an agent of repression – updated to a democratic context – has not been displaced (Hume, 2007b). In the past, high levels of state repression resulted in the generation of an alternative political project (albeit one that was predominantly, though not exclusively, articulated through violence). The contemporary situation is different in that radical political alternatives to the status quo have not found coherence. Neither the political left, nor organised civil society, have been successful in forging collective ways of dealing with violence from non-state actors, such as gangs.[7] An examination of community responses below indicates that perhaps the logic of violence

---

7   The FMLN won the presidential elections for the first time in March 2009. At the time
   of writing, it is too early to measure their policies.

as a functional political tool to combat violence remains. Thus 'violence itself is ignored, justified and, sometimes, stimulated by those who see themselves as upstanding and exemplary citizens, against those they consider the scum of society' (Cruz and Beltrán, 2000: 5). This demands an interrogation of citizen's attitudes towards violence in the communities under study.

Community Justice and the Erosion of Confidence in the Rule of Law

Issues of criminality, state brutality and ineffectiveness, as discussed above, have had deep repercussions in Salvadoran society. El Salvador did not have a strong system of justice before the war and citizen confidence in the new institutions has been steadily undermined by ineffectiveness and ongoing impunity. State ineffectiveness has serious repercussions for the citizens of El Boulevar and La Vía, some of which are voiced in the following narrative. During a particular conflict with a neighbour who threatened him and his sons with a machete, Esteban contacted the police:

> And the policeman replied: 'In the first place, we don't have time for these little family or domestic squabbles, or when neighbours are fighting. We're busy, we don't have time. You see how you can sort it out.' 'And when he's dead?' Then maybe they'll come . . . so one of my sons said to me, 'look dad, we're men, don't be begging anyone'.

Esteban's recollection of the lack of police responsiveness raises several issues for discussion. First, he points to the lack of attention the police give to certain so-called family or community 'squabbles'. Second, the fact that the police were too busy to come to the community risked letting the 'squabble' escalate into something much more serious. Third, his son's comment that they were men and could sort it out is illustrative of the temptation for citizens to fill the void left by the state in terms of administering 'justice'. I will now discuss these three issues, using examples from events that occurred El Boulevar.

In a climate of insecurity, the fact that citizens feel that are not offered protection by state institutions actively dissuades them from reporting crimes. This is particularly acute for the poor who feel that the PNC, the Attorney General's Office (Fiscalía General de la Republica [FGR]) and other such bodies refuse to take them seriously. While I was conducting research in El Boulevar, a well-known gang member threatened one of the elderly residents, a member of the management committee, in the presence of the local government promoter. According to the local promoter: 'Of course, he reported it to the Attorney General's Office, but the Attorney General's Office did nothing.' As a result, the man was now doubly scared. He was worried about the initial threat, and also afraid that the gang member would find out that he had approached the authorities. The perceived ineffectiveness of agents of justice combines with very real fear to deepen a culture of silence whereby citizens do not feel they should seek help from the formal channels of justice. Esteban voices his opinion on the authorities, which he accuses of ignoring the demands of the poor:

> People don't report [crimes] mainly because the reports are filed away. You might report something but it is rare that it is followed up. Reporting is like me going to the sea and throwing salt in. The sea accepts it because it is there. I throw the salt because the water is salty. Someone goes to the FGR, reports a crime but the next day that report doesn't exist because they make lots of excuses, thousands of excuses and what happens? I think that it's because they only work for certain sections of the population. The middle class and the poor have no influence there. When the powerful men in government or those who have economic power report a crime, it appears in the press straightaway, everything that hurt them, what happened to them, et cetera. That's the problem that we have here.

In response to this vacuum of formal justice mechanisms, there have been notable cases where communities have taken 'justice' into their own hands. One resident states: 'When you know the facts, you can act [in response to crime in the community]. Perhaps not through the Attorney General or the justice system, which quite frankly does not help society, that's not protection, it's not protection for citizens' (Beto, El Boulevar). Incidences of 'community justice' have been identified throughout the region with the practice of lynching as its most extreme expression (Moser and Winton, 2002; Goldstein, 2005; Snodgrass-Godoy, 2005; Vilas, 2008). In Guatemala, this not uncommon practice is seen as a symptom of a breakdown of the system of justice. In her study of Guatemala, Angelina Snodgrass-Godoy (2005) avoids such 'obvious' explanations. She suggests that lynching is not just about crime and the absence of formal justice; it is more likely a reaction to high levels of fear and insecurity. Lynching, in this sense, constitutes an extreme expression of 'us' and 'them'.

The practice of lynching does not appear to be as common, or at least as visible, in El Salvador as it is in Guatemala or elsewhere (for example, Goldstein's (2005) account of 'flexible justice' in Bolivia). Nonetheless, the numbers of extra-judicial murders and incidences of summary justice are significant. These include the ongoing presence of social cleansing squads that were discussed in Chapter 2. At a less organised level, there have been cases of family massacres and revenge killings (Moser and Winton,

2002). In the community, residents spoke about receiving death threats from neighbours. Some also hinted that gang members have been hired as *sicarios*, a term adopted from Colombia and now widely used throughout the region to refer to paid assassins. The fact that such practices continue in El Salvador, however isolated, reinforce the necessity of guaranteeing the rule of law for all in these contexts. Snodgrass-Godoy (2005) warns that security can never or should never be purchased at the price of justice. This is especially urgent when we consider that respect for authoritarian measures within Salvadoran society is high.

In El Boulevar, Esteban narrated a particularly brutal episode, reminiscent of Zola's *Germinal*, where some community residents killed a 'thief', hanging his testicles on a pole when they had dismembered him[8]:

> Well, the thief comes and they killed him. The same people from here killed him. They used a woman as a trap to catch him and well, the woman, they went to a solitary spot and the others arrived straight behind them. They killed him in the same way that he killed. They killed him in the same way, they left him in pieces.

Esteban's wife verified this account. The murdered man, who had lived in the community, was said to have terrorised residents for many years. He was allegedly responsible for many murders in and around the community. While this example may be extreme, it is indicative of an endpoint to which communities may resort. It also entails a degree of spectacle that marked the political assassination of previous decades. Both communities demonstrate few alternatives for resolving interpersonal conflict in a non-violent manner, as demonstrated in previously when physical and verbal violence were employed in a community meeting. Violence, in many of its expressions, is not only a cause and consequence of disagreement within communities, but is also seen as a tool for the resolution of conflicts. Several women in La Vía 'thank God' that gang members and thieves have been killed or imprisoned. Their absence means that life is more peaceful. According to Ana María:

> I think that we're okay now because all those, all of them who were thieves here, they're all dead and others are in prison. That guy that lived up beside Don Chepe, the one they called 'The Chicken', he's left here. I mean, thank God, they are killing themselves. There are still some

---

8   In Zola's novel, a shopkeeper is castrated by a starving women. They rip off his genitals and display them at the top of a flag pole.

thieves, not like them though, like those other thieves who went about robbing clothes, hens.

The fact that these young men were engaged in 'anti-social' behaviour excused their violent deaths. They are acting as agents in their own extermination, which is therefore understood as beneficial to the wider community. The death of these young men is understood as an effective way of ridding the community of a problem. The misrecognition of such violence as beneficial hints at the potency of symbolic narratives that criminalise certain groups in El Salvador. It reflects a wider social discourse that seeks to 'other' the perpetrators of violence, yet at the same time these young men are neighbours and relatives of the residents. It is also testament to the seductiveness of narratives that favour the use of violence against certain groups. Despite the privileging of force, it would be wrong to conclude that violence simply breeds more violence. There is a subtle, but salient, reason to argue that alternatives to violence are closed down by the state management of the problem. This is politically different from saying that violence automatically breeds violence. In this context, few options that move beyond the logic of repression have emerged. It therefore places emphasis on the 'counterproductive' (following Aguilar, 2007) and inconsistent contribution of state responses to the problem of violence. It makes forging alternatives difficult and frustrates many attempts to develop strategies to move beyond violence. However, it cannot completely silence them. Importantly, this approach also shifts the gaze back to the state and demands accountability. It is to the different ways of confronting violence that I now turn.

Citizens and Civil Society Confront Violence

Individuals and communities develop a wide range of coping strategies in to survive and resist violence, although the very context of violence limits the options available to citizens. Moser and McIlwaine (2004) distinguish between coping strategies and specific solutions. Strategies of silence and avoiding conflicts were addressed in Chapters 3 and 4, while the discussion above reveals that communities may respond by forging their own channels for 'justice'. These can be both productive and counterproductive. Here, I explore different levels of response to violence by analysing both individual and community strategies, as well as some initiatives promoted by non-governmental organisations (NGOs) and international organisations.

The previous chapters indicate that many citizens respond to violence by modifying behaviours and avoiding spaces that are deemed dangerous. For example, a 2001 survey from El Salvador demonstrates that 81.6

Table 4. Behaviour of Residents as a Result of Fear of Crime in Soyapango[9]

Reaction to crime	Percentage of respondents
Limit shopping	61.5
Limit recreation	60.9
Close business	19.0
Live in closed areas	61.2
Acquire guns	29.4
Move neighbourhood	41.5
Organise neighbours	28.8

Source: Adapted from IUDOP/FUNDAUNGO (2002: 22).

per cent of citizens felt insecure in the centre of their city or village (IUDOP/FUNDAUNGO, 2002: 18). The social panic concerning the 'dangerous stranger' has led to an abandonment of many public spaces and associational life more generally. According to one survey in El Boulevar, 44.6 per cent of respondents testified to not attending an activity at night for fear that something would happen to them outside the community; 69.2 per cent felt that they had to be inside the house early because of problems that occur inside the community. Figures for La Vía demonstrate that 46.4 per cent refrained from attending activities outside the community, while 51.8 per cent felt they have to be inside the house early (see Savenije and Andrade-Eekhoff, 2003). The threat of violence, therefore, not only restricts mobility, but places pressure on family life by confining members to already cramped housing. In light of the earlier discussion of high levels of violence in the home, it is relevant to ask whether there is a connection between this increased pressure on the household and levels of violence within it. Table 4 highlights some of the strategies adopted by individuals as a result of fear of crime in the municipal jurisdiction of Soyapango, where the communities of El Boulevar and La Vía are located. The figures indicate that the most common reaction was to limit interaction in the public realm: 61.2 per cent opted to live in closed areas (*lugares cerrados*); 29.4 per cent acquired guns; 28.8 per cent became involved in neighbourhood organisations and 41.5 per cent moved neighbourhoods.

These patterns are similar to the results of various focus groups in El Boulevar. In the school, students suggested a mix of prevention and repression is needed. In terms of repression, a group of students suggested 'more people on the look out; I mean: more police and more drastic laws'. Other young people demanded accountability: that the police 'do their job', that they investigate crimes. This should be noted in the context that these young people

---

9   For figures from other municipalities, see IUDOP/FUNDAUNGO (2002).

have also reported police harassment simply for being from a community associated with gangs. Among preventative measures, they suggested: increased 'solidarity': 'we should unite, to face the problems, to help each other'. Importantly, the students also recognised the importance of 'example': to 'promote a good example of not using violence' and to 'try to be better, not using violence'. The related issues of solidarity, unity and organisation were all identified as major problems affecting community life in Chapter 3. Adults in El Boulevar strongly advocated the necessity of community participation in forging alternatives to violence, but also that the problem was a community one and, as such, they should all take responsibility in challenging it:

> It is also really important that they give us an opportunity to get involved, you know what I mean? . . . It is important that everyone knows what is going on, it is everyone's problem and it needs to be treated as such because we all live in this community (Gloria, El Boulevar)

Silence, which has been identified as an important coping mechanism, is also recognised as an impediment to moving beyond violence. Students suggested: 'we should speak about it'; 'tell people what we think'; 'forge better communication'; and 'make people think about it'. This intimates the importance of breaking the codes of silence. The need to speak out and to promote conversation was also stressed by adults in community focus groups. According to Esmeralda in El Boulevar:

> Firstly, we need to promote dialogue with the young people; dialogue is very important, dialogue with these people. Also we need to help them, by offering training, in work, for example; teaching them something positive so that instead of destroying, they can build. Look, when a person works, their mind produces something good, but that's why dialogue is needed, right? You know that no one likes it at first, but the more you talk to them, the more you find ways of making them change. It is all a matter of 'finding a way in', as they say . . . because remember every kid who is in those *maras* is a Salvadoran, and whether you like it or not, they're part of our nation . . . [We] can't just get rid of them but we can build something . . .

Esmeralda's words make a direct link to the lack of opportunities available to young people. She also effectively questions society's tendency to 'other' young gang members and view them as disposable. Her son is in the local gang, though he has been trying to 'calm down' or leave the gang since his daughter was born. He no longer found fun (*vacil*) or a sense of belonging with his 'homeboys', since all of his close friends had been murdered. His initial reason for joining the gang had been as a strategy for standing up to local bullies who picked on him because he was smaller. He wanted to leave the gang after several months, but was not allowed and the homeboys in his community threatened to kill him:

> They wanted to kill me because I no longer wanted to have fun [*vacilar*]. I mean I wanted to calm down. I had only been in the gang a little while and that is what they didn't like that I had only been in the gang for two months. (Vladimir, El Boulevar)

To protect himself against the *mara* in El Boulevar, Vladimir joined the small *clika* of MS in the centre of San Salvador. He used the gang as a strategy to protect himself against bullies and then a different *clika* to protect himself against his own homeboys. Several years later when his friends had all been killed, he returned to El Boulevar and was accepted as a member of the local gang. He is very clear that it was his choice to join the gang and now he says that he must face the consequences:

> I looked for this, you know; my mum shouldn't be crying for me. If I looked for this life, I have to stick it out. Maybe you understand me? If I joined the *mara*, I joined so they wouldn't beat me up and if I was sent to jail, it was for the same thing. My mother did not send me to do what I did. I mean my mother has suffered but I tell her that she can no longer make it alright.

Vladimir turned to one set of violent actors to protect himself against another. This generated a vicious circle where violence became his means of protection as well as what he needed protection from. The use of violence to protect or challenge is not uncommon and was discussed above with reference to both state and community levels. This points to the existence of attitudes that not only prioritise the use of force, but see violence as functional and undermine options for those who wish to find alternatives.

At the time of the interview in 2002, Vladimir had decided that he no longer wanted to steal for a living: 'I used to rob but I haven't robbed a thing in eight months . . . I am in a peaceful mood [*me voy en el son pácifico*]'. Instead, he was helping his mother, who sells fruit in the community, by going to the main market to do her shopping, though he was terrified that a member of the Mara 18 would spot him on the bus. This had happened before and they ran after him with a machete. He had a tattoo on his face and even the baseball cap that he wore did not cover this completely.

Women gang members who I interviewed in a different part of San Salvador during 2004 also expressed fear of going outside their neighbourhoods, yet they had no choice because they had to earn an income to support their children. Gendered roles in gangs and the fact that many young women become mothers at a young age mean that women's experience of gang life is precarious. One woman, from the Mara 18, who had a stall in the centre of San Salvador wore long sleeves to work every day to cover her tattoos. She had worked in a *maquila* until they realised that she was a *pandillera*. Once her membership of the gang was known, she lost her job. For these young people, gang membership restricts opportunities to earn a (legal) income: most businesses will not hire tattooed youth and territorial claims mean that they are in danger from rival gangs when they travel across the city to find work. Vladimir's story indicates that joining the gang for protection incurred a debt to his *clika*. He was no longer free to leave once he had signed up and therefore entered a spiralling world of violence. His only options were to become a Christian, or to find a project that would offer him alternatives outside his community.

It is against this challenging web of violence that alternatives must be forged. Organised civil society has developed some limited initiatives to promote training and work opportunities for ex-gang members. These are often developed in conjunction with religious groups or by youths themselves. Examples of these include the Poligano Industrial Don Bosco, which offers formal training and work opportunities for 'at risk' youth. It has managed to forge links with local companies and international donors to promote alternatives for young people (see Carballido Gómez, 2007). MOJE is a youth movement from Ilobasco that offers training in capacity building and markets crafts made by ex-gang members.[10] *Generación XX1* is another youth movement that was created by young people in the municipality of Mejicanos. It brings together youth from both left- and right-wing political standpoints, different religious and spiritual beliefs and varied socio-economic backgrounds. Given the very deep polarisation of Salvadoran society, these groups rarely have a common space in which to interact. As such, the organisation constitutes an important effort to break down ingrained prejudices and fears of the 'other'.

The only organisation to be staffed entirely ex-gang members is Homies Unidos. Set up in El Salvador in 1996, Homies Unidos has faced serious setbacks. In the late 1990s and early 2000s, Homies worked with the Central American University to produce a series of studies on gangs in El Salvador (Homies Unidos and IUDOP, 1998; Santacruz Giralt and Concha-Eastman, 2001). The organisation also promoted efforts to develop peer education among gang members on issues of preventing violence, health care and programmes on sexual health. In an interview with a staff member in 2004, she said that their funding had dried up noticeably after 9/11 because the

---

10 For more information, on MOJE's activities, see: [WWW document]. URL http:// www.mojecasaartesanal.com/moje-5.php (accessed 8 October 2008).

organisation was viewed as an increased 'threat' to security. However, other reasons also accounted for the weakened structure, including the murder and imprisonment of some of its staff (La Prensa Grafica, 2006). In its initial incarnation, the organisation brought together members of rival gangs, but by 2004 most members seemed to have loyalties exclusively to the Mara 18. This was highlighted by a member of the PNC who had previously enjoyed a good working relationship with the organisation but had 'lost trust'.[11] Internal problems and the problem of public mistrust of the organisation have proved a serious obstacle to its development (Cruz and Carranza, 2006).

Mistrust in El Salvador is symptomatic of deeper fault lines in civil and political society, and both a cause and a consequence of ongoing violence. Since the peace accords, spaces for forging political participation and a strong civil society have both opened up and become restricted. The examples offered earlier of the criminalisation of protest bear testament to the continued mistrust and repression of alternative voices. The number of NGOs has mushroomed, especially in the immediate post-war years. This has had both positive and negative effects. NGOs now compete for ever limited sources of funding and their work on a day-to-day basis is challenged by insecurity and violence. On an operational level, their work is challenged by structural constraints placed upon them by the Salvadoran government, such as strict laws that regulate their legal status, the difficulty of forging alliances to work with the state and problems within organisations themselves. Human rights organisations continue to function in the post-war period, though their task has become complex. Historic human rights organisations, such as Tutela Legal and IDHUCA, continue to lobby for an official recognition of past abuses. They also face contemporary challenges posed by ongoing impunity and the continued difficulties presented by contemporary forms of violence (Collins, 2008). Many organisations carry on despite the violence, rather than challenge it directly, or they tackle underlying causes such as inequality and human rights abuses. NGO staff speak about feeling 'overwhelmed' by violence and finding it difficult to forge clear pathways out, particularly given that there seem to be obstacles on multiple levels.

In an attempt to address this, one feminist NGO began dialogue with the local gang in an urban area of Greater San Salvador where it had several projects, including one to challenge gender-based violence.[12] The presence of the gang had a negative effect on the project on a number of levels. First,

---

11   He explained that his trust had been shaken since members of the organisation had allegedly been seen with the supposed leader of the Mara 18, El Viejo Lin.

12   As in other parts of the book, I have chosen consciously to maintain anonymity of the organisation in order to protect the identity of the local promoter. For this reason, I also use the vague term 'urban area'.

some of the communities could only be accessed with police accompaniment to guarantee the safety of NGO personnel and volunteers from surrounding areas. Second, state institutions in the area were overworked because of high levels of criminality, gang violence and domestic abuse. Finally, the gang did not necessarily agree with the aims of the campaign, and so there was a need to talk to the male leadership and to explain the project. The local promoter tried to develop communication with the leadership to talk about the possibilities of working with women members. After several months, she had to give up because she felt unsafe and, crucially, she lived locally. Members of the gang had let her know that they knew where she lived and where her daughter went to school. In this case, the fact that she was from the area made her more vulnerable. Anecdotal evidence suggests that personnel in key institutions such as the police are changed regularly to avoid threats from local criminals, but also to prevent them developing too close links with local criminal actors. The everyday terror that communities are faced with limits the space for resistance for both local residents and the institutions that are there to support them. It is not difficult in this context to understand the pull of silence.

One of the ways in which the pervasiveness of both silence and misinformation have been undermined directly by civil society is via the development of a critical research agenda on violence. Organisations such as the Foundation for the Study and Application of the Law (FESPAD), Instituto Universitario de Opinión Pública (IUDOP; Public Opinion Institute at the Central America University) and FLACSO are attempting to reframe the parameters of the debate on crime and violence in El Salvador and the region at large (Savenije and Andrade-Eekhoff, 2003; FESPAD, 2005, 2006; Cruz, 2006; Aguilar, 2007). Research on issues of youth gangs (Aguilar and Miranda, 2006); legal reform and its weaknesses (FESPAD, 2006) and the limitations of electoral democracy (Cruz, 2001) all provide important critical perspectives with which to challenge dominant government rhetoric and practice of repression. A lot of this research is financed by international donors and much of it has come under the auspices of the UNDP Violence in a Transitional Society Programme.

The UNDP initiative has been in existence since 1998. It brings together different state agencies and civil society organisation to think critically on issues of crime, violence and legal responses. Interviews with UNDP staff reveal that the programme responded specifically to gaps in the approach to rising levels violence and crime in the post-war period. The stated objectives of the programme are:

(i) To contribute to the prevention and control of interpersonal violence, especially against women; neutralise the risk factors that facilitate violence; and to support policy that is inclusive of young people;

(ii) to strengthen the justice and security institutions so that they can respond in an effective way to violence, crime and insecurity; and

(iii) to contribute to the development of knowledge and information to enrich debate about issues of security and justice on local and national levels (UNDP Seguridad Ciudadana, 2007).

Since its inception, research on violence in the country has been strengthened. However, much of this lacks a consistent gender analysis. Pilot projects have encouraged gun-free municipalities, education for peace in schools and public awareness campaigns, though the government has ignored many of its recommendations (Amaya, 2006). A key theme of these campaigns has centred on challenging attitudes to gun ownership and use, including drafting reforms to El Salvador's extremely lax gun laws and campaigns targeted at both adults and children to raise awareness about the dangers of firearms. For example, poster campaigns in 2002 under the slogan *Armas, ni de juguete* ('Guns, not even as toys') were accompanied with a campaign that collected toy guns in exchange for other toys. Linked to this is the development of local-level interventions in targeted areas (often in conjunction with the CNSP) that promote alternatives to violence. One such initiative is the *Menos Armas, Mas Vida* ('Less arms, more life') campaign that seeks to change attitudes and prohibit the use of guns in public spaces. This has piloted in several municipalities including San Martin and Ilopango in 2008, on the outskirts of San Salvador. According to the director of the CNSP, Oscar Bonilla, the results have been overwhelmingly positive and have resulted in a significant reduction in murders (interview with author, May 2008).[13]

Local government is increasingly seen as an important actor in dealing with crime and violence. Since 2006, several municipal governments have set up 'municipal observatories' to monitor crime and violence. This model is currently being rolled out across the region under the auspices of the Observatorio Centroaméricano Sobre Violencia (Central American Observatory on Violence).[14] The rationale behind local observatories lies in the need to maintain accurate databases and encourage inter-institutional cooperation at a municipal level. There is also a strong component of citizen participation. Local residents are encouraged to form neighbourhood groups and to formulate 'risk maps' of the area that highlight particular points of high crime and danger. It is too early to tell whether these interventions have been successful, but interviews with staff in Ahuachapan in late 2007 suggested that they already had some problems in accessing data from local

---

13   For a discussion of the experience, see Dorfillo 2006.
14   For more information on this initiative, see Observatorio Centroamericano, 2007.

state agencies. This points to the crux of the problem: the lack of coherency between different initiatives and no unified understanding of the problem even within the same institution.

An example of this lies in the creation of a new Policia Rural. Although the problem of violence may appear more acute in urban centres, President Saca announced the creation of a specialised police force to guarantee the security of rural areas in 2004. The redeployment of police to this rural force was felt keenly by many working in urban areas that already had very scarce resources and problems of staff retention.[15] Some interviewees felt that the Policia Rural was established merely to protect the commercial interests of landowners because it was deployed along with military personnel at harvest time. To fill the gaps in urban coverage, some military were redeployed in a public security function in the urban areas. One police officer argued that the military involvement in the PNC had brought the force into disrepute, but has also had negative implications for how the force itself behaves: 'Soldiers are not trained in public security, [they] don't work like the police and now there are elements [in the police] behave like soldiers and don't respect human rights' (interview with author, October 2007). Although he and other officers acknowledged that the investigative capacity of the force had been strengthened, he expressed his frustration at the lack of attention paid to prevention within the force at a national level. To counteract this, he said that many officers now worked directly with local government to implement prevention plans.

When agents of the state and citizens are overwhelmed by high levels of crime and violence, it becomes difficult to address all areas effectively. Violence against women or community conflicts, in this case, slip down the institutional agenda. Following an interview in 2008, a male lawyer explained how he agreed that the murder of women was a problem, but could not understand why 'femicide' was singled out when, on average, more men than women were killed. This logic is difficult to counteract unless the specific circumstances and the context in which women are killed is explored. The emphasis on murder also reveals the endpoint of violence, and not the non-lethal abuse that often precedes it in the case of intimate partner violence. Focusing on prevention at this level and the interconnection between different types of violence, rather than responding to its most extreme effects, could provide a useful challenge to violence in all its forms.

---

15 This was mentioned in interviews with members of the PNC in 2006 and 2007. It was also addressed in a newspaper article about crime in the upmarket area of the Zona Rosa (Castro Fagoaga, 2006).

Cumulative effects of violence undermine institutional capacity to deal with it. A doctor in an urban health centre told me in 2007 how she had to negotiate with the local gang leader to be able to work in his community. She was dealing with a particularly brutal case where a woman had been gang raped by twenty members of the local *mara*. The woman did not want to report the rape because she was scared; she also could not leave her house for fear of what the same men (or their *homies*) would do to her. The gang leader approached the doctor to let her know that he was aware that she was dealing with the case. It was not an open threat, but the implication was clear. Nonetheless, the doctor continued to treat the woman. She also pushed forward an agenda within the health centre to detect and advise women survivors of domestic and sexual violence. Against these conditions, many individuals within organisations develop strategies to be able to work with gangs or within the climate of broader insecurity. Important to individuals such as the doctor mentioned here has been contact with networks of women's organisations. The final section of this chapter will address some responses by the Salvadoran women's movement.

Feminist Challenges to Violence

Throughout this book I have argued that feminism has thrown out a challenge to violence in both theory and practice. The women's movement in El Salvador continues to resist and promote alternatives to violence on a daily basis, not an easy task in a violent and deeply patriarchal society. Organisations such as Asociación de Mujeres Salvadoreñas (AMS), Organización de Mujeres Salvadoreñas (ORMUSA), Movimiento Salvadoreño de Mujeres (MSM), Movimiento de Mujeres Mélida Anaya Montes or Las Mélidas (MAM) and Las Dignas forge crucial spaces for women to recognise and name violence. Since the ending of the war in 1992, the Salvadoran women's movement has developed a range of strategies for resisting and transforming violent gender relations. These organisations have lobbied the government collectively and individually to promote the development of new laws that ensure protection for women. They provide legal advice and practical support to survivors of violence, and actively work to promote change in the way violence is interpreted and legislated in El Salvador. I explore briefly three interlinked strategies that reflect the multi-level challenge to violence: the development of safe spaces for women that are free from violence; the engagement of men in challenging violence against women and the development of coordinated approaches across institutions to end gender violence. The importance of education to change both attitudes and raise awareness of women's right to a life free from violence is a cross cutting theme to each of these strategies.

Developing Safe Space for Women Survivors of violence

Throughout the various elements of this research, women talked about a range of strategies they used to resist men's violence. Women often made a distinction between 'dealing with the problem' and seeking justice. The former involved escaping violent partners, seeking temporary refuge with friends and family, or keeping quiet. Seeking justice, on the other hand, meant liaising with the authorities and many women felt they would not be taken seriously or they would only be making their partners angrier. This is not to say that women do not report abuse, but many are aware of the limits of the rule of law in protecting them from violence. Other strategies are about survival, and these may or may not directly confront the violence. Survival includes behaviours such as silence, being a 'good wife', appearing submissive: making sure that the dinner was on the table, 'agreeing with him' and not going out without his permission. The stated aim in these strategies was not to 'provoke' men's anger. Again, this confers the behavioural responsibility on women for managing men's tempers.

At other times, women risked men's anger. When I worked for Las Mélidas in the late 1990s, a woman I knew well suggested that she was going to 'get it' from her husband for attending a meeting without his permission. Nonetheless, she explained that the women's group gave her strength and provided a safe space where she could be herself and speak openly about her life. She used to get up early to do her chores and her daughter supported her attendance by covering for her if she failed to arrive home before her husband. The decision to attend the gender training workshops was not taken lightly. Although this act of resistance had its very obvious costs, she also felt it had direct benefits for her. While I was carrying out research for Oxfam America in 2007, other women echoed such sentiments: Elsa suggested that participating in capacity building workshops helped her enter a dialogue with her husband. Feeling at a very low ebb, her motivation lay in the fact that he had been seeing other women and abusing her:

> When I began with these workshops, it was difficult because he did not want me to go because he liked it if I was in the house ... I suppose, he was used to it. One day, speaking with him, I explained that if he respects me a little, I will not disrespect him but I do have my rights and I benefit from learning new things that are going to help me psychologically. My head is so bad at the minute because of what we are going through. I am depressed, not well. (Elsa, focus group, Ahuachapan)

Working with Men to End Violence Against Women

Challenging her husband's reluctance to give her 'permission' to participate in the workshops had not been easy, but she saw it as necessary for her own survival. She also pointed to the importance of these safe spaces for women. Men's violence has effects beyond the physical. Elsa reveals how psychological abuse and restricting her mobility were important tools used by her husband. Psycho-social services available to women are scant and, where available, poorly resourced. This makes other informal networks important for women to articulate their fears and also to learn from other women's experiences. The self-help group I observed in 2001 – 2002 was part of a state-funded service, although no finances were allocated to the gender programme. Instead, the psychologist in charge of the centre felt that it needed to be addressed and did it in addition to her other duties. Many people like her work quietly and without much in the way of funding or support to challenge violence. The small-scale, and often disparate, strategies may only reach a small number of people, but this does not mean they are not effective.

Many women's organisations have a psycho-social element as central to their work. They recognise the importance of providing targeted assistance to survivors of violence. This is particularly because state assistance is scarce. Las Dignas ran a programme for ex-combatant women throughout the 1990s and continues to offer psychological and legal support to women survivors of violence (Vásquez, Ibañez and Murguialday, 1996). Las Méldias addresses gender violence in a holistic way. Violence against women is a cross-cutting theme of all programmes. For many years, regional offices were staffed with a lawyer, a doctor and a psychologist. This meant that responses for women were coordinated and immediate, though funding for some of these initiatives has been difficult to come by and has meant that at least one clinic has closed down.[16]

Coordinating Approaches and Responses

Recognising the need for a multi-layered approach has been central to the feminist project. As a result of the practical difficulties in maintaining a coherent multi-layered programme to address violence against women, many women's organisations work in networks. These have been successful in promoting legal reform and raising awareness on issues of violence against women. Two examples that work explicitly to end violence against women are Red Feminista frente a la Violencia contra las Mujeres en El Salvador (The Feminist Network to Challenge Violence against Women in El Salvador) and the Oxfam America-funded campaign to end gendered violence *Entre vos y yo: una vida diferente* ('Between you and me: A different life').

---

16   Some of these services have been reduced in recent years. The clinic in San Marcos, for example, which had been an important source of information, and legal and medical assistance to women in the late 1990s, was closed when I returned in 2007. When I asked what had happened, I was told that it shut down because of lack of funding.

The Feminist Network to Challenge Violence against women in El Salvador is made up of three women's organisations, Las Mélidas, Las Dignas and ORMUSA. The network raises awareness about the shortcomings in legal protection offered by the state and specifically challenges institutionalised machismo. Las Dignas, for example, launched a campaign in the run up to the 2009 elections *Ni estado, ni hombre macho* ('Neither a macho state nor a macho man') to draw out the linkages between individual male violence and institutionalised patriarchy. ORMUSA maintains a monthly 'observatory' on violence to demand justice for survivors and victims and raise awareness on violence against women (Observatorio de la Violencia de Género Contra la Mujer, 2008). This is a useful portal for researchers, but also builds evidence to support advocacy and education initiatives.

The second broad coalition of organisations is brought together under the Oxfam America Campaign to end gendered violence, 'Between you and me: A different life'. I conducted research with key stakeholders of the campaign in 2007 and 2008. The campaign brings together NGOs with different institutional remits, such as gender, human rights and rural development. These organisations work in coordination with national- and local-level actors to raise awareness on violence and rights, provide specialist training to personnel in state institutions and to elected representatives, and propose legal reforms that protect women and children. For example, training judges, police, medical staff and other key institutional personnel has been integral to the campaign approach. Staff who receive training are then expected to replicate it in their own institution in order to ensure greater institutional purchase. In addition, the trainees form local networks to replicate training for citizens at a community level. This approach allows communities to meet institutional representatives and also encourages greater coordination between institutions at the local level.

The campaign engages a variety of methods and approaches, both formal and popular. Street theatre, formal university diplomas, educational activities with youth and institutional agreements with state agencies all inform an overall strategy that targets women, men and youth. Bird et al. (2007) stress that working with men is an important element in preventing violence against women (see also Welsh, 2001 on Nicaragua). Interviews with male service providers, such as the PNC, and men who had participated in masculinity workshops in El Salvador suggest that they found these useful in rethinking both their own behaviour and how to deal with men's violence in their working lives.[17]

---

17 This was also addressed in the self-help group that I observed. According to Teofilio, talking about issues in the self-help group was important: 'For me coming here to this

Women associated with the campaign agreed with the need to work with men: 'because if you only train the woman, the man won't believe her, right? He's the violent one, so you need to talk to them both' (Sandra, Ahuachapan). Sandra raises an important point: working with men is crucial, but it should not be to the exclusion of women (see also Pearson, 2000). She has been participating in the Oxfam America training workshops and uses the material that they give her to spread information on women's rights in her community. She has used it creatively: putting posters in her own house, which is at the entrance to he community; sending material to men she knows that have a history of abuse and arranging for some men to attend gender training workshops. She recounts an experience with her son-in-law who expressed surprise that his wife should have information about women's rights:

> I think everything we are doing is working because whenever they give me posters against gendered violence, I take the materials to [my community] and I put up the poster. I live on the edge of the street so I put it in a place where people can see and I sent one to him [a man she knew who used violence against his wife] and I sent one to my daughter because her husband is very strict. He doesn't hit her but he has rules and doesn't allow her out. She is not allowed to go out or visit the family until he comes. So I said to her 'go and give this to Chepe and tell him to read it'. When he arrived, he said, 'What's this poster all about?' He is in the Air Force you see. 'Read it', she said. 'Who gave it to you?' 'My mother; she is going to the workshops', she said. 'I see they're inciting [*avivando*] you too' he said [she laughs]. 'I knew about his stuff but I never thought you would know about it'. 'Well then, stop annoying me or I will report you', she said.

Her words indicate that having access to basic information on their rights is an important first step for women to challenge men's violence. In this way, they can also demand that the state fulfils its function of protection. Access to public data and public services have been central to the demands of the Salvadoran women's movement. Without these, changes in the law are only one step in the struggle for recognition of and struggle for the survivors of violence. Attitudes that normalise male aggression and violence more generally, such as those explored above, are not uncommon and mean that women's space for resistance is all the more limited. This is reinforced

---

place has been a great experience. It really helps. talking about my life . . . is like letting it all out for me and letting out all this stuff that has been oppressing me here inside . . . I used to only let it out when I was drinking and then I would cry. I had no other alternative.'

by the few alternatives to violence in wider society. The role of the state is central to these and its complicity should not be ignored in constructing alternatives. This discussion offers no easy solutions to violence, nor does it attempt to romanticise efforts at resisting it. It does, however, point to some of the tensions in forging alternatives. The more successful strategies that I have articulated here are those that work on multiple levels and that are founded on the principles of prevention and justice.

Conclusion

This chapter has identified important cleavages in the management of violence in El Salvador. I have argued that the present threat to democratic governance should not be viewed solely as the problems presented by violence, but also the responses of both state and citizens. The double-edged sword of state response and ineffectiveness should be viewed as important to the development of violence in El Salvador. The active promotion of a politics of fear marks a worrying indicator of the quality and sustainability of democratic reforms. The combination of the *Mano Dura* logic shapes both the macro and micro politics of managing violence in El Salvador. Much in the same way as previous decades, the state continues to rely on the complicity of upstanding citizens to push forward an exclusionary and elitist agenda. The narrow definition of the problem has led to restricted responses. This sustains the argument that knowledge about violence is generative of material consequences that discipline modes of response. In the longer term, repressive measures fail to address the roots of the problem and serve to divert attention from other urgent priorities, such as the strengthening of local democratic institutions and historic problems of political polarisation and corruption. The alternatives that do exist in this climate of fear are restricted by the hegemonic (dis)ordering of the problem, specifically the demonisation of certain groups such as youth and social movements. Following Arditti (2005: 94), this reveals the 'darker possibilities' of the democratic era in El Salvador, where the promise of peace in the previous decade is being gradually eroded by the 'underside' of democracy. Continuities in elite (mis)management of the state illustrate how those in government are, through a return to repressive measures, expressing their sense of possession rather than occupancy.

I have outlined key feminist alternatives to violence. This is not to suggest that feminism offers the only articulate counterweight to violence, but it does highlight strategies that the women's movement has used to challenge the pervasiveness of violence against women. Throughout, I have argued that responses to violence must be analysed against how violence is defined and conceptualised. Narrow definitions will only generate partial responses.

Given the importance of the family as a space for socialisation and the centrality of violence to hegemonic forms of masculinity, it is vital to unpack the connections between societal violence and abuse within the home. In El Salvador, there is a popular saying: *hay que darle vuelta a la tortilla*, which translates as the need to flip over the corn tortilla (a main dietary staple for Salvadorans). This is appropriately symbolic to express the necessity for a radical change in how violence is understood, recognised and legislated in El Salvador. To do this requires political will. The discussion here highlights the shortcomings in the public security agenda with its focus on repression. It also indicates the sidelining of gendered violence from this debate. Implicit in this critique is a shifting of the parameters of the debate to address strategies of prevention and to think about the linkages between violence in its 'public' and 'private' forms.

Conclusions

The purpose of this book has been to generate critical questions on the subject of violence. I have insisted throughout that the questions we ask are as important as any notional 'answers' that we may develop in the course of our research. Important to this exercise has been the development of a feminist analysis of violence in all its forms. The contribution of this approach to debates on violence can be seen on three principal fronts for discussion in this concluding chapter. First, feminist research roots theory in lived experience. A key finding of feminist research is that women are more likely to be harmed by men that are known to them. This challenges a whole range of normative assumptions about violence that are based in notions of stranger violence. Reframing violence as immediate and familiar places it as an important element of human relations and not as something external. This challenges popular epistemologies of violence that are based on dangerous and prejudiced stereotypes.

Second, the core of this book has been the multiple stories of violence from those men and women who must confront it on a daily basis. Situating my study in the micro politics of everyday life offers important insights as to how citizens negotiate and survive political change and conflict. These subaltern vocabularies of violence foreground critical questions on the limitations of El Salvador's peace, demanding an engagement with matters of political economy, the state and broader civil society. Using the community as a lens, connections are forged between different types of violence.

This focus brings me to my third line of argument. Feminist research has been central to placing women's experiences of violence on national and international political agendas. Legal reforms, service provision and advocacy campaigns have been advanced by feminist activism and scholarship. Nonetheless, there remains an implicit separation of the pervasive abuse of women from debates on crime and more 'public' forms of violence. I have argued here that this is not based on either the scale of the problem or on material harm, but on a privileging of masculinist epistemologies of violence. I have developed the argument that violence–in practice and representation–is embedded in unequal power relations. A central task of this book has been to unpack the ways in which the discursive management of violence is both produced by and productive of these inequalities. In this vein, I have developed the notion of gendered hierarchies of violence that are not based on material harm, but on the differentiated value placed on different forms of violence.

Feminism has posed a challenge to the study of violence on numerous levels. In this concluding chapter, I draw out the contributions of these three central themes to debates on the politics of violence. First, I explore the methodology of situating my study in the politics of El Salvador. I ask how a localised study can inform broader debates on both violence and politics. This leads to the second theme, which is concerned with dismantling the myths and meanings of violence. In particular, I wish to emphasise ways in which the questions posed by feminism illuminate a study of violence that is both immediate and familiar. Such a standpoint necessarily rejects the temptation to 'other' violence and to remove it from everyday social and political relations of power. Finally, I wish to emphasise that there are not only different epistemologies of violence, but that these are based on relations of power. From this standpoint, they stand in competition with each other and in collusion with powerful and disciplining forces of knowledge production that not only silence and shut down divergent interpretations of violence, but actively undermine effective responses to it.

Situating a Politics of Violence in Transition

Transition to democracy and peace-building in El Salvador, as in other parts of the globe, must be understood in the context of its principal drivers: globalisation and structural adjustment (Robinson, 2004). Grugel (2007:244) argues that rather than analyse the return to (or establishment of) institutions *per se*, we need to be alert to the 'terms under which this return took place ... today's institutions have to be judged not against what they replaced but against the yardstick of what democracy should be'. In particular, it demands a critical interrogation of structural forms of violence across time and space. Issues of uneven political economy and the disarticulation of state institutions that is required by neoliberalism are antagonistic to goals of peace and justice. Popkin (2000: 162) argues that El Salvador offers 'an example to be avoided', labelling the process as 'peace without justice'.

There is an emerging literature on the limits of peace processes and democratic transitions in Latin America and across the globe. This localised study does not claim to offer the possibility of generalising across regions, but it does raise critical questions that concern the nature of peace, transition and justice in the post-war context. These questions, posed by an interrogation of subaltern vocabularies of violence, illuminate more critical understandings of peace and violence in both public and private realms and result in practical and political, as well as theoretical, implications. A study that is reliant on situated knowledge does not imply bounded or localised knowledge. Instead, situated and often subjugated voices undermine the generalising and disciplining practices of dominant tendencies in both academic and policy debates. The preceding chapters have been written to extend debates on the political economy of peace-building and, in particular, critical scholarship on the limits of 'liberal' peace and democracy (for example, Richmond, 2006; Pugh, Cooper and McDonald, 2008).

I have situated this study in the politics of El Salvador, a country with a brutal and polarised history, arguing throughout that violence cannot exist in a vacuum. It has been essential to explore the ways in which El Salvador's historical legacies continue to shape contemporary perceptions and interpretations of violence. This emphasises the importance of forging connections across time and space. Such an approach does not suggest that violence has not evolved, nor does it ignore changes in the political scenario, but it does emphasise the importance of rooting the study of violence within historical processes. Within this context, men, women and children have learned to survive and to give meaning to the world around them. There is constant negotiation between structures that frame how individuals understand the everyday, the events that shape it and the popular reactions that give meaning to it. Decades of political oppression, the continued brutality of gendered relations, and an explosion of social and criminal violence have left deep scars on Salvadoran society. Perhaps most dangerously, continued violence has created a society with a huge threshold for tolerating and accepting it as a normal element of the everyday routine. El Salvador's 'peace' has revealed the extent to which violence has become embedded in social and political relations, so much so that many manifestations are not readily identified as violent. One of the most damaging consequences of this context, as illustrated in the preceding chapters, is that violence may be rendered unspoken and unquestioned.

It is against this backdrop that much of this book has been concerned with the struggle over interpretations of violence. A key challenge has been the implicit disjuncture between the discursive management of different types of violence and the material harm that is generated by an individual act. In short, violence is not always judged against its range of material and harmful effects. In particular, I have argued that a gendered hierarchy of meaning operates in order to justify and to legitimise certain types of violence over others. Making explicit these hierarchies, rather than reading them as given, places the role of ideology as central to the interpretation of all violence and not just its more overt political expressions. This approach stands in contrast to analyses of violence that separate its different expressions into bounded categorisations such as political, social, violence against women, or crime. Instead, it underscores the importance of crafting political connections between multiple types of violence in order to make explicit the connections between them in everyday life. The 'minimalist' approach to peace-building in El Salvador has failed to translate into real structural reform of Salvadoran society and the limited advances that have been made are fragile and challenged by ongoing fault lines. The vocabularies of violence of the citizens of El Boulevar and La Vía suggest the need to inflect Galtung's maxim that peace is more than the absence of war. Instead, we should ask what kind of peace is forged when the absence of violence cannot be guaranteed.

Although democratic spaces have opened up in El Salvador, the voices of men and women that are central to this analysis suggest that many conflicts on a micro scale are still resolved in a violent manner. This raises questions about the nature and quality of peace in the country. Democratising forces are directly contradicted by weak institutionality and heavy-handed policing. This is a sobering reminder not to allow our gaze to stray from the role of the state in fomenting the problem of violence. Making connections between different types of violence is essential to the transformation of war and armed conflict that tend to prioritise only direct political manifestations. The 'erasure' of the multiple vocabularies of violence from official 'war stories' neglects the multi-layered effects and consequences of conflict (Nordstrom, 2004).

A general interest in post-war societies as areas of political settlement has been narrowly defined as 'public' and, in the case of El Salvador, as elite. This means that gendered relations have been ignored and so too have the experiences of citizens on a local or community level. Chapter 2 argued that such a narrow focus is counterproductive in that settlements are not only narrow, but actively miss overlapping issues of inequity, historic conflicts and ongoing violence. Chapters 3 and 5 foregrounded ongoing conflicts in both the community and broader civil society that point to continued polarisation and violence. Chapter 4 emphasised the tendency to depoliticise the private realm, leading to a minimising of, or blatant disregard for, experiences of gendered violence in the home. By not restricting this study to the formal political resolution of conflicts, I have observed the continuity of violence in the domestic realm and the many other forms of insidious violence that affect the everyday life of citizens. The incidence and severity of this normalised violence reveals the multi-layered and contested politics of inequality in post-war El Salvador.

The end of the war may have led to a dramatic reduction in politically motivated violence for the citizens of El Salvador. This can only be seen as a positive development. However, this study has also drawn attention to a more difficult aspect of the transition to 'peace'. Ramos (2000) argues that high levels of violence must be understood as symptomatic of other negative forces in society. The everyday lived realities of citizens of La Vía and El Boulevar, as well as many other low-income communities like them, warn against simplistic analyses of peace as a solely positive development. The promise of peace in El Salvador has been compromised on multiple levels. In particular, the political economy of neoliberal governance in the post-war era has closed down economic alternatives for vast swathes of the population. This has created the opportunities for crime and violence to flourish, although simplistic linkages between crime and poverty should be avoided. The stories of violence uncovered in these pages demonstrate that there are very few among the poor who actively reap benefit from crime and violence, although they are most often singled out as the main protagonists.

Challenging the Myths of Violence

Key to the interrogation of myths of violence in this book has been an examination of values and norms as productive of violent power relations based on gender and class. In uncovering the multiple and often contested vocabularies of violence, it has been necessary to analyse how violence is used by both men and women, against both men and women. This foregrounds an analysis of violence as relational, demanding a gendered analysis to contemplate issues of men and masculinities as well as women and femininities. It has been important to grapple with issues of representation and the politics of discourse. In particular, I have been concerned with unsettling dominant myths that are both gendered and gendering. A guiding principle of this research is that unless we understand these processes through which certain types of violence are legitimised, our thinking on violence will always be partial.

Rather than develop a singular and closed definition, my account has engaged with competing and contested interpretations of violence. The tension between narrow definitions and broad frameworks for understanding violence was explored in Chapter 1. There is a tendency, in both literature and popular discourse, to approach violence from a reductionist perspective, limiting it to its physical manifestation, its legal/illegal status or to that which occurs in the public realm. This tendency was explored in literature from a wide range of disciplines and in a variety of empirical contexts. Narrow definitions of violence and a concentration on the public sphere have served to minimise the recognition of violence in the domestic realm or between family members. Through an exploration of life histories, this book has exposed the wide range of violence that affect men and women at different political and social moments.

The extreme brutality of many family relations examined in Chapter 4 highlights that violence continues to be a recourse for many individuals and is seen not only as a normal option in many cases, but an effective one. This raises the importance of analysing the generational dynamics of violence. Empirical data have highlighted the centrality of violence to family life, where it is may be seen as functional and even necessary. Social norms regarding parenting prescribe the use of the *Mano Dura*. Echoing Goldstein (2003), an analysis of violence against children should be analysed within broader patterns of domination. Placing violence against women and children in this broader political framework of power opens up the possibility of forging connections between different levels of violence and dominance. Men often learn to be men through exposure to violence, using violence later to reinforce these expectations of masculinity. An understanding of violence as gendered thus moves beyond a reductive reading of gender as a male–female dyad to foreground the relational interpretation of power and inequality.

Women's use of violence against their children has been explored both from the perspective of women as mothers, and women who have been subject to violence throughout their lives since childhood. In a focus group held in La Vía, participants reflected on one of the indirect effects of violence against women: 'You take it out on your kids. They are the ones who pay and they cannot defend themselves ... when there are problems with your husband, you take it out on your kids.' Women's use of violence remains a relatively understudied area (see Burman, Batchelor and Brown, 2001). Kelly (1996) speaks of the tensions felt by feminists in exposing it, because there is a risk that it will overshadow the enormity and extent of women's repeated subjection to violence at the hands of men. I share these preoccupations, although I also recognise the need to identify and recognise women's participation and the role of the subaltern in reproducing hegemonic practices more generally. This does not mean that women's use of violence should be examined as a separate category. Rather, as this study has done, it is necessary to move beyond a narrow analysis of individual responsibility to analyse the structures that give meaning to violence. The challenge is to dissect the larger systems of oppression and exploitation that allow violence to be an acceptable and routine element of everyday social and political interaction. Throughout the course of the research, men constantly referred to women's violence and its role in reproducing machismo. The process of interpreting violence is closely bound up with a need to apportion blame. Men, in defence of their own actions, often pointed to their mothers as the figure that 'taught' them how to be men.

It is not uncommon for men to blame women for the pervasiveness of machismo and violence in social relations. Indeed, the many examples of men's victimisation at the hands of their mothers points to the centrality of women in reproducing patriarchal power relations. This notion is telling of the tension between agency and structure. On the one hand, individuals are accountable for their behaviour, especially in the perpetration of violence, yet, on the other, patriarchal structures in society justify and normalise such acts. Women are caught up in a contradictory web of gendered myths, where they, in effect, become active agents in their own subordination. This is testament to the very real symbolic power of hegemonic structures. Kandiyoti (1988) has explored women's relationship with patriarchy in Northern India. In her study of mothers-in-law, she explores how women resist and collude with patriarchal relations within the household. The notion of the 'patriarchal bargain' proposed by Kandiyoti offers some insight into why women collude with a gender system that subjugates them and therefore reproduces gender inequalities. In the search for more inclusive frameworks to understand violence, it is necessary to confront how men and women are active in reproducing these structures of domination.

Addressing questions of complicity, hierarchy and surveillance within subaltern communities poses many difficulties, not least of all for politically committed research (Mallon, 1994: 1511). Nonetheless, the alternative action of ignoring intra-community tensions erases power differences, which becomes particularly undermining of a gender analysis of violence. I have chosen to meet this challenge by foregrounding the ambiguities and issues of complicity and collusion among and across communities. I have thus examined power relations within communities, as well as providing an exploration of how individuals and communities collude with and resist dominating forces such as the state. State violence in El Salvador has been reliant on the active collaboration of citizens. This exposes both the immediacy and ordinariness of multiple forms of violence to everyday life and the presence of the state in local worlds, thus undermining a clear separation between state and societal violence. It also locates citizen collusion as both an effect of hegemonic political economy and as the product of limited opportunity and forced conscription. By adopting this approach, I am not ignoring the very real courage, solidarity and heroism of citizens who resisted the state project of repression and exclusion; nor am I ignoring the very real tensions in the politics of representing these communities. I am attempting to contextualise these in a situation of poverty and violence that refuses to ignore or to minimise the misery generated by inequality on multiple levels (see Bourgois, 2003). Positioning the study in this way rejects a tendency to homogenise or romanticise subaltern groups. This does not deny the possibilities of resistance and solidarity, but it does foreground the conditions that make the exercise of forging these alternatives all the more challenging. Colluding with or merely resigning oneself to the perceived inevitability of hegemonic forces is and has been an important survival strategy for many citizens. In order to dismantle these logics, it is important to recognise them.

Competing Epistemologies of Violence: Privilege and Power

Historic mainstream, or 'malestream', epistemologies have privileged the public realms of existence and have ignored the many types of violence that affect women and children. The non-recognition of much of women's subjection to violence is a telling statement about male privilege. The public/private dichotomy remains an important prism through which individuals make sense of the everyday. As Owens (2008: 979) argues: 'Some forms of violence are *made* public and others are *made* private through historically varying ways of organizing and justifying force. There is no such thing as public violence or private violence. There is only violence that is made public or private through political struggle and definition' (emphasis in the original). Chapter 2 highlighted the privileging of the 'public' in the literature on violence in Latin American societies. Such an approach misses the many insidious forms that pervade the everyday lives of many citizens in the region. A conceptualisation of violence from the perspective of 'public' security, it has been argued, has undermined the citizens' rights of women and children within the home. An exploration of the public/private distinction in this book grew out of the minimisation of 'private' violence in interviewees' narratives, as revealed in Chapters 3 and 4. It is also informed by a concern that violence in the public sphere is rarely understood as gendered. An analysis of interviewees' testimonies has uncovered a very clear gradation of violence. I have argued that the series of 'recognition codes' (after Feldman) that society adopts in order to understand violence creates a scenario where different manifestations are tolerated to different degrees. In a very crude sense, these can be categorised as violence occurring in the public realm, on one hand, and in the private, on the other. The latter, in the form of violence against women and children, has not only been left out of legal frameworks in many countries until recent years, but also continues to be invalidated by individual and social discourse.

This process of grading violence is a way of putting some sense of order onto a chaotic world and serves as a survival strategy within it. 'Talk of crime' is reliant not only on stereotypes and mobilising fears, but also on allowing individuals to distance themselves from 'bad' violence. Popular epistemologies of violence are dependent on, and productive of, various guises of 'others'. Good and evil, as Samuel and Thompson (1990) point out, are a classic way to handle fears. Notions of good and bad, however tenuous, offer certainties about the world however unstable or false they may be. Munck (2000: 5), however, cautions against the use of such oppositional categories, suggesting: 'we should perhaps be more open to ambiguity, multiplicity and fragmentation'. The importance of being alert to subjective understandings of violence and its many 'socially approved rationalisations' has been emphasised throughout (Ptacek, 1988: 151). Recognising and dismantling the way in which violence is legitimised is the key to moving beyond violent social relations.

A feminist lens has allowed a multiplicity of voices to emerge, exposing both the lived experience of violence and the meanings ascribed to it. The research has uncovered a world where men and women have different understandings of violence in their everyday lives. Both within and between individual narratives, we have seen a web of contradictions and competitions emerge. I have argued that violence discriminates and that people are differentially located with regard to the politics of naming violence. These experiences, from the act of violence to the act of narration, are refracted through a prism of socially constructed discourse that offers some sense of order and meaning to a difficult world. This is where ontological and epistemological processes interact. They shape how individuals and groups coexist, the questions they ask and their ways of interpreting the social order. The notion of hierarchy is linked to the way social relations and identities are constructed and the reproduction of powerful discourse. Although wary of static conceptualisations, the exploration of how men and women ascribe meaning to the violence of their everyday life has provided an important contribution to the scholarship of violence. This approach is valid for the many types of violence that affect everyday life, moving beyond restrictive frameworks and narrow definitions. It provides a space for the voices of individuals to give meaning to their own lives, but it also questions how these voices have been informed by wider discourses within society.

A key area for consideration has been the process of silencing. The silencing of violence past and present raises important questions on several levels. Silence was an explicit goal of the Salvadoran state in order to close down possibilities for resistance and opposition, and to generate apathy and indifference among citizens. In many instances, its effects were quite the reverse in that it forced a critical opposition to speak out and to resist. Nonetheless, an historical examination of state terror has proposed that its effectiveness lay precisely in the silence, apathy and collusion of citizens in the face of extreme repression. Following Foucault, I have argued that silence is both a reaction to and a strategy of violence. There is no singular silence nor can it be understood solely as what is not said, but should be seen as an integral element in closing down struggles for justice. Widely adopted as a strategy for survival, testimonies reveal that speaking out about violence is dangerous. Citizens must 'learn how to live', as one woman advised, and learning how to live means 'keeping quiet'. Concomitantly, remaining silent generates a whole range of problems on individual and community levels that reinforce processes of violence, inequality and impunity. This has broader repercussions, as Chapter 3 has indicated, for fostering mistrust and isolation within communities.

The vicious circle of silence and violence frustrates possibilities for moving beyond violence. Importantly, it also nourishes processes of impunity because citizens become afraid to speak out against violence and the state is ineffective in its response. The ARENA governments (1989–2009), consistently attempted to suppress the call for justice by its citizens. They refused a minimal recognition of past human rights abuses and fostered impunity in the postwar period by producing particular discourses of fear and panic. This was discussed in Chapter 5 with particular attention to youth gangs. Although many may accept this status quo, many more continue to demand justice.

Without a critical consideration of ambiguity and competition, the researcher risks becoming complicit with the politics of power that discipline knowledge of violence. In this vein, I argue for a theorisation of violence that understands it not just as a discrete act of aggression, but as a process that involves performance, interpretation and response. Positioning a theory of violence that is mindful of the constituting forces of difference, of silence and of power is essential in order to produce and validate forms of knowledge that resist and challenge the exclusionary and polarising ideologies that are so central to prevailing epistemologies. Without challenging the contested and multiple meanings and silences of violence, strategies to move beyond and to resist violence will remain frustrated. Rather than making violence more complex and ambiguous, I believe that this approach moves us towards more comprehensive understandings that narrow definitions cannot contain.

Multiple and often contradictory responses to violence are evident at state and community levels. Despite some isolated exceptions from civil society, no consolidated attempt to move beyond violence has been identified. Public opinion surveys reveal the perseverance of demonising attitudes towards the poor and 'criminal' classes. Communities recognise the need to generate alternative strategies and do this as routine strategies of survival on a daily basis, but these limited alternatives are challenged by few spaces afforded by a political and economic system that continues to foster polarisation and inequality. This does not close down the possibility of challenging violence, but it does render it more difficult. Salvadoran activists have made important advances in the last two decades to place violence against women on a national agenda. I do not wish to overly romanticise such strategies, but their multi-faceted approach is rooted precisely in challenging masculinist myths of violence. Women have worked to challenge the normalisation of domestic abuse, to develop legal and judicial reforms, and to offer advice and protection to survivors of violence. Critical insights on how to challenge violence in all its forms can be learned from these multiple strategies of resistance.

It is hardly coincidental that feminist contributions to the theorising of violence remain, to a large degree, at the sidelines of academic debate. The silencing of these feminist voices is in itself an exercise in shutting down challenges to hegemonic structures of knowledge and practice. By placing feminist concerns as central to this analysis, I address important gaps in contemporary debates on criminality and violence in Latin America. First, developing a gendered analysis of violence refuses the sidelining of violence against women as a 'private' or 'family' matter that is implicitly viewed as a 'lesser' violence. This not only alerts us to the existence of hierarchies of violence but calls us to dismantle them. Second, the critical perspectives of feminism have exposed the immediacy and ordinariness of violence to everyday life. Situating violence within human relations unsettles both sanitising and pathologising accounts that rely on gendered stereotypes and class-based prejudices. Connections must be forged between different types of violence in both public and private arenas. In this way, feminism presents a direct challenge that goes to the heart of exposing the very potent ways in which power relations discipline what we know and how we should respond to different acts of violence. Violence is an evolving phenomenon and one that offers no simple solutions. Nonetheless, without more nuanced understandings of violence as action, as interpretation and as resistance, the task of challenging is rendered all the more distant.

7

References

Acosta, M. (1999) 'Overcoming the Discrimination Against Women in Mexico: A Task for Sisphus "Introduction" ' in J. E. Méndez, G. O'Donnell and P. S. Pinheiro (eds.) *The (Un)Rule of Law and the Underprivileged in Latin America*. University of Notre Dame Press: Notre Dame, 160–180.

Aguilar, J. (2007) 'Los Resultados Contraproducentes de las Políticas Anti-Pandillas'. *Estudios Centroaméricanos* **62**(709–710): 877–890.

Aguilar, J. and Miranda, L. (2006) 'Entre la Articulacio'n y la Competencia: las Respuestas de la Sociedad Civil Organizada a las Pandillas en El Salvador' in J. M. Cruz (ed.) *Maras y Pandillas en Centroamerica, las Respuestas de la Sociedad Civil Organizada*, Vol. IV. UCA Editores: San Salvador.

Aguilar Villamariona, J., Amaya Cóbar, E. and Martínez Ventura, J. (2001) *Información y Gestión Policial en El Salvador*. FESPAD: San Salvador.

Ahnen, R. (2007) 'The Politics of Police Violence in Democratic Brazil'. *Latin American Politics and Society* **49**(1): 141–164.

Alvarenga, P. (1996) *Cultura y Etica de la Violencia: El Salvador1880–1932*. San Jose, Costa Rica.

Alvarez, O. (2004) *Honduran Official*. Quotation in: 'Al Qaida Recruits Central American Gang', Associated Press, October 21, 2004 [WWW document]. URL http://archive.newsmax.com/archives/articles/2004/10/21/152818.shtml [accessed 28 August 2009].

Amaya, E. (2006) 'Security Policies in El Salvador, 1992–2002' in J. Bailey, L. Dammert (eds.) *Public Security and Police Reform in the Americas*. University of Pittsburgh Press: Pittsburgh, 132–147.

Amaya Cóbar, E. and Palmieri, G. F. (2000) 'Debilidad Institucional, Impunidad y Violencia', *PNUD Violencia en una Sociedad en Transición: Ensayos*. PNUD: San Salvador, 75–114.

Amnesty International (2007) *Amnesty International Criticizes El Salvador for Using Anti-Terrorism Laws to Punish Social Protesters* [WWW document]. URL http://www.amnestyusa.org/document.php?lang=e&id=ENGUSA20070718001 [accessed 28 August 2009].

Arana, A. (2005) 'How the Street Gangs took Central America'. *Foreign Affairs* **84**(3): 98–110.

Arditti, B. (2005) 'Populism as an Internal Periphery of Democratic Politics' in F. Panizza (ed.) *Populism and the Mirror of Democracy*. Verso: London 72–99.

Ardón, P. (1998) *Los Conflictos y el Proceso de Paz en Centroamérica*. Oxfam UK and Ireland: Oxford.

Arendt, H. (1969) *On Violence*. Harvest Books: London and New York.

Aretxaga, B. (1997) *Shattering Silence: Women, nationalism and Political subjectivity in Northern Ireland*. Princeton University Press: Princeton.

Aron, A., Corne, S., Fursland, A. and Zelwer, B. (1991) 'The Gender-Specific Terror of El Salvador and Guatemala: Post-traumatic Stress Disorder in Central American Refugee Women'. *Women's Studies International Forum* **14**(1–2): 37–47.

Arriagada, I. and Godoy, L. (2000) 'Prevention or Repression? The False Dilemma of Citizen Security'. *CEPAL Review* **70**: 111–136.

Artiga González, A. (2004) 'El Salvador. Maremoto Electoral en 2004'. *Nueva Sociedad* **192**: 12–22.

Baires Quezada, R. (2007) *Con un muerto menos al día, la Policía prefiere no celebrar* [WWW document]. URL http://www.elfaro.net/secciones/Noticias/20071001/noticias3_20071001.asp [accessed 28 August 2009].

Balán, J. 'Introduction' in S. Rotker (ed.) *Citizens of Fear: Urban Violence in Latin America*. Rutgers University Press: New Brunswick, 1–6.

Bannister, J. and Fyfe, N. R. (2001) 'Fear and the City'. *Urban Studies* **38**(5–6): 807–813.

Benson, P., Fischer, E. and Thomas, K. (2008) 'Resocializing Suffering: Neoliberalism, Accusation, and the Sociopolitical Context of Guatemala's New Violence'. *Latin American Perspectives* **35**(5): 38–58.

Binford, L. (1996) *The El Mozote Massacre: Anthropology and Human Rights*. University of Arizona Press: Tucson.

Binford, L. (2002) 'Violence in El Salvador: A Rejoinder to Philippe Bourgois's "The Power of Violence in War and Peace"'. *Ethnography* **3**(2): 201–219.

Bird, S., Delgado, R., Madrigal, L., Ochoa, J. and Tejeda, W. (2007) 'Constructing an Alternative Masculine Identity: The Experience of Centro Bartolomé de las Casas and Oxfam America in El Salvador'. *Gender and Development* **15**(1): 111–121.

BodyGendrot, S. (2001) 'The Politics of Urban Crime'. *Urban Studies* **3**(56): 915–928.

Boraz, S. and Bruneau, T. (2006) 'Are the Maras Overwhelming Central America?'. *Military Review* 36–40. [WWW document]. URL http://www.findarticles.com/p/articles/mi_m0PBZ/is_6_86/ai_n27084052/?tag=content;col1 [accessed 28 August 2009].

Boserup, E. (1970) *Women's Role in Econonmic Development*. Allen and Unwin: London.

Bourdieu, P. (1977) *Outline of a Theory of Practice*. Cambridge University Press: Cambridge.

Bourdieu, P. (1990) *The Logic of Practice*. Polity Press: Cambridge.

Bourdieu, P. (2001) *Masculine Domination*. Polity Press: Cambridge.

Bourdieu, P. and Wacquant, L. (1992) *An Invitation to Reflexive Sociology*. University of Chicago Press: Chicago.

Bourgois, P. (1996) 'In Search of Masculinity: Violence, Respect, and Sexuality Among Puerto Rican Crack Dealers in East Harlem'. *British Journal of Criminology* **36**(3): 412–427.

Bourgois, P. (2001) 'The Power of Violence in War and Peace: Post-Cold War Lessons from El Salvador'. *Ethnography* **2**(1): 5–34.

Bourgois, P. (2002) 'The Violence of Moral Binaries: Response to Leigh Binford'. *Ethnography* **3**(2): 221–231.

Bourgois, P. (2003) *In Search of Respect: Selling Crack in El Barrio*, 2nd edn. Cambridge University Press: New York.

Burgois, P. and Scheper-Hughes, N. (2004) *Violence in War and Peace: An Anthology*. Blackwell Publishing: Oxford.

Bowker, L. (1998) 'On the Difficulty of Eradicating Masculine Violence: Multisystem Overdetermination' in L. Bowker (ed.) *Masculinities and Violence*. Sage Publications: London, 1–14.

Burman, M., Batchelor, S. and Brown, J. (2001) 'Researching Girls and Violence: Facing the Dilemmas of Fieldwork'. *British Journal of Criminology* **41**: 443–459.

Buvinic, M., Morrison, A. and Shifter, M. (1999) *Violence in Latin America and the Caribbean: A Framework for Action*. Inter-American Development Bank, Sustainable Development Department: Washington, D.C.

Caldeira, T. (2000) *City of Walls: Crime, Segregation and Citizenship in Sao Paulo*. University of California Press: Berkeley.

Call, C. (2003) 'Democratisation, War and State-building: Constructing the Rule of Law in El Salvador'. *Journal of Latin American Studies* **35**: 827–862.

Carballido Gómez, A. (2007) *Cuando la juventud cuenta: sistematización del programa Miguel Magone y Laura Vicuña, polígono industrial Don Bosco El Salvador*. UNDP: San Salvador [WWW document]. URL http://www.ocavi.com/docs_files/file_358.pdf [accessed 27 January 2008].

Cárdia, N. (2002) 'The Impact of Exposure to Violence in Sao Paolo: Accepting Violence or Continuing Horror?' in S. Rotker (ed.) *Citizens of Fear: Urban Violence in Latin America*. Rutgers University Press: New Brunswick, 152–186.

Carranza, M. (2007) 'Los Acuerdos de Paz, 15 anos Después. Una Mirada Desde la Opinión Pública', Problemas de la Paz: Violencia, Impunidad, Deficit Institucional. *Edición Monográfica' Estudios Centroamericanos* **701–702**, March-April, 2007, 219–238.

Castro Fagoaga, C (2006) *Nuevas actividades en la Zona Rosa: homicidio, secuestro y robo a mano armada* [WWW document]. URL http://www.elfaro.net/secciones/Noticias/20060424/noticias5_20060424.asp [accessed 28 August 2009].

Cavanagh, K., Dobash, R. P., Dobash, R. E. and Lewis, R. (2001) 'Remedial Work: Men's Strategic Responses to their Violence against Intimate Female Partners'. *Sociology* 33: 258–281.

Chant, S. (2000) 'Men in Crisis? Reflections on Masculinities, Work and Family in North-West Costa Rica'. *European Journal of Development Research* 12(2): 199–218.

Chant, S. with Craske, N. (2003) *Gender in Latin America*. Latin American Bureau: London.

Chesney-Lind, M. (1986) 'Women and Crime: The Female Offender'. *Signs* 12: 78–101.

Chevigny, P. (2003) 'The Populism of Fear: Politics of Crime in the Americas'. *Punishment and Society* 5(1): 177–196.

Clark, M. (2001) 'Twenty Preliminary Propositions for a Crtical History of International Statecraft in Haiti' in I. Rodríguez (ed.) *The Latin American Subaltern Studies Reader*. Duke University Press: Durham, 241–259.

Cock, J. (2001) 'Gun Violence and Masculinity in Contemporary South Africa' in R. Morrell (ed.) *Changing Men in Southern Africa*. Zed Books: London, 43–56.

Código Penal Republica de El Salvador (2001.) *Códigos Penal y Procesal: ley penitenciaria y su reglamento*. Editorial Jurídica Salvadoreña: San Salvador.

Coleman, L. (2007) 'The Gendered Violence of Development: Imaginative Geographies of Exclusion in the Imposition of Neo-Liberal Capitalism'. *The British Journal of Politics and International Relations* 9(2): 204–219.

Collins, C. (2008) 'State Terror and the Law: The (Re)judicialization of Human Rights Accountability in Chile and El Salvador'. *Latin American Perspectives* 35(5): 20–37.

Concha-Eastman, A. (2001) 'Urban Violence in Latin America and the Caribbean: Dimensions, Explanations, Actions' in S. Rotker (ed.) *Citizens of Fear: Urban Violence in Latin America*. Rutgers University Press: New Brunswick, 37–54.

Connell, R. (1987) *Gender and Power*. Polity Press: Cambridge.

Cornwall, A. and White, S. (2000) 'Men, Masculinities and Development'. *IDS Bulletin* 31(2): 1–15.

Corrin, C. (1999) *Feminist Perspectives on Politics*. Longman: London and New York.

Craske, N. (1999) *Women and Politics in Latin America*. Polity Press: Cambridge.

Crawley, H. (2000) 'Engendering the State in Refugee Women's Claims for Asylum' in S. Jacobs, R. Jacobson and J. Marchbank (eds.) *States of Conflict: Gender, Violence and Resistance*. Zed Books: London, 87–104.

Cruz, J. M. (1999) 'Maras o Pandillas Juveniles: Los Mitos sobre su Formación e Integración' in O. Martinez Penate (ed.) *Sociología General: El Salvador*. Editorial Nuevo Enfoque: El Salvador, 269–277.

Cruz, J. M. (2000) 'Violencia, Democracia y Cultura Política en América Latina'. *Estudios Centroamericanos* 619–620: 511–526.

Cruz, J. M. (2001) *¿Elecciones para qué? El impacto de ciclo electoral 1999–2000 en la cultura política salvadoreña*. Facultad Latinoamericana de Ciencias Sociales (FLACSO): San Salvador.

Cruz, J. M. (2006) (ed.) *Maras y pandillas en Centroamérica. Las respuestas de la sociedad civil organizada, Volumen IV*. UCA Editores: San Salvador.

Cruz, J. M. and Beltrán, M. A. (2000) *Las Armas. de Fuego en El Salvador: Situacio'n e Impacto sobre la Violencia*. IUDOP: San Salvador.

Cruz, J. M. and Carranza, M. (2006) 'Pandillas y políticas públicas. El caso de El Salvador' in J. Moro (ed.). *Juventudes, violencia y exclusión. Desafíos para las políticas públicas*. MagnaTerra Editores: Guatemala.

Cruz, J. M. and González, L. A. (1997) 'Magnitud de la Violencia en El Salvador', *Estudios Centroamericanos* 588: 953–967.

Cruz, J. M., Trigueros Arguello, A. and González, F. (1999a) *El Crimen Violento en El Salvador. Factores Sociales y Económicos Asociados*. IUDOP/UCA: San Salvador (Original version in Spanish).

Cruz, J. M., Trigueros Arguello, A. and González, F. (1999b) *The Social and Economic factors associated with Violent Crime in El Salvador*. IUDOP/ World Bank: San Salvador (English Version).

Cubitt, T. and Greenslade, H. (1997) 'Public and Private Spheres: The End of Dichotomy' in E. Dore (ed.) *Gender Politics in Latin America: Debates in Theory and Practice*. Monthly Review Press: New York, 52–64.

Dalton, J. J. (2007) *Chalchuapa, Territorio del Miedo,'* El Pais. 5 September 2007. [WWW document]. URL http://www.elpais.com/articulo/internacional/Chalchuapa/territorio/miedo/elpepuintlat/20070905elpepuint_4/Tes [accessed 26 August, 2009].

Daniel, V. (2000) 'Mood, Moment and Mind' in V. Das, A. Kleinman, M. Ramphele and P. Reynolds (eds.) *Violence and Subjectivity*. University of California Press: Berkeley, 333–366.

Das, V. and Kleinman, A. (2000) 'Introduction' in V. Das, A. Kleinman, M. Ramphele and P. Reynolds (eds.) *Violence and Subjectivity*. University of California Press: Berkeley, 1–18.

Das, V., Kleinman, A., Ramphele, M. and Reynolds, P. (eds.) (2000) *Violence and Subjectivity*. University of California Press: Berkley.

Dawson, G. (2005) 'Trauma, Place and the Politics of Memory: Bloody Sunday, Derry, 1972–2004'. *History Workshop Journal* 59: 151–178.

De Cesare, D. (1998) 'The Children of War: Street Gangs in El Salvador'. *NACLA Report on the Americas* 32(1): 21–29.

DFID workshop, July (2002) Private Communication.

DIGESTYC (2007) *Resultados del VI Censo de Población y V de Vivienda 2007*. Dirección General de Estadística y Censos: San Salvador.

Dobash, R. E. and Dobash, R. P. (1988) 'Research as Social Action: The Struggle for Battered Women', in K. Yllo and M. Bograd (eds.) *Feminist Perspectives on Wife Abuse*. Sage: London, 51–74.

Dobash, R. E. and Dobash, R. P. (1998) 'Violent Men and Violent Contexts' in R. Dobash, R. Dobash (eds.) *Rethinking Violence against Women*. Sage: Thousand Oaks, 141–198.

Dobash, R. E., Dobash, R. P. and Cavanagh, K. (2003) 'Researching Homicide: Methodological Issues in the Exploration of Lethal Violence' in R. M. Lee and E. A. Stanko (eds.) *Researching Violence: Essays on Methodology and Measurement*. Routledge: London, 49–66.

Dobash, R. P., Dobash, R. E. and Cavanagh, K. (2004) 'Not an Ordinary Killer–Just an Ordinary Guy: When Men Murder an Intimate Woman Partner'. *Violence Against Women* 10(6): 577–605.

Duffield, M. (2001) *Global Governance and the New Wars*. Zed Books: London.

Dunkerley, J. (1982) *The Long War: Dictatorship and Revolution in El Salvador*. Junction Books: London.

Dunkerley, J. (1988) *Power in the Isthmus*. Verso: London.

Dunkerley, J. (1993) *The Pacification of Central America*. University of London ILAS Research Papers.

ECA (1999) 'Valoración del Siglo XX desde los Mártires' *Estudios Centroamericanos* **613–614**: 957–974.

ECA (2003) 'Editorial: La Campaña Electoral de ARENA: Populismo Punitivo', *Estudios Centroamericanos* **657–658**: 655–672.

ECA (2006) 'Los Hombres del Presidente Contra el Estado Salvadoreño: Poderes Paralelos Colapsan la Institucionalidad'. *Estudios Centroamericanos* **696**: 925–938.

ECA (2007) 'Quince años de Paz?' *Problemas de la Paz: Violencia, Impunidad, Déficit Institucional...* Edición Monográfica' Estudios Centroamericanos **701–702**, March-April, 2007, 195–202.

ECA Editorial (2000) 'La Seguridad en Crisis'. *Estudios Centroamericanos* **619–620**: 493–511.

ECLAC (2007) *Social Panorama of Latin America*. [WWW document]. URL http://www.eclac.org/publicaciones/xml/9/30309/PSI2007_Sintesis_Lanzamiento.pdf [last accessed 8 July 2008].

Edkins, J. (2003) *Trauma and the Memory of Politics*. Cambridge University Press: Cambridge.

Ehlers, T. B. (1991) 'Debunking Marianismo: Economic Vulnerability and Survival Strategies among Guatemalan Wives'. *Ethnology* **30**(1): 1–14.

Elson, D. (ed.) (1991) *Male Bias in the Development Process*. Manchester University Press: Manchester.

Enloe, C. (1993) *The Morning After: Sexual Politics at the End of the Cold War*. University of California Press: Berkeley.

Enloe, C. (2000) *Bananas, Beaches and Bases: Making Feminist Sense of International Politics*. University of California Press: Berkeley.

Enloe, C. (2004) *The Curious Feminist: Searching for Women in a New Age of Empire*. University of California Press: Berkeley.

ERIC, IDESO, IDIES and IUDOP (2001) *Maras y Pandillas en Centroame'rica, Volumen I*. UCA Publicaciones: Managua.

ERIC, IDESO, IDIES and IUDOP (2004) *Maras y Pandillas en Centroamérica, Pandillas y Capital Social, Volumen II*. UCA Editores: San Salvador.

Eschle, C. and Maiguashca, B. (2007) 'Rethinking Globalised Resistance: Feminist Activism and Critical Theorising in IR'. *British Journal of Politics and International Relations* **9**(2): 284–301.

Escobar, A. (2004) 'Development, Violence and the New Imperial Order'. *Development* **47**(1): 15–21.

Farmer, P. (2004) 'An Anthropology of Structural Violence'. *Current Anthropology* **45**(3): 305–325.

Feldman, A. (1991) *Formations of Violence: The Narrative of the Body and Political Terror in Northern Ireland*. The University of Chicago Press: Chicago.

Feldman, A. (2000) 'The Prosthetics and Aesthetics of Terror' in V. Das, A. Kleinman, M. Ramphele and P. Reynolds (eds.) *Violence and Subjectivity*. University of California Press: Berkeley, 46–78.

Feldman, A. (2003) 'Political Terror and the Technologies of Memory: Excuse, Sacrifice and Actuarial Violence'. *Radical History Review* **85**(winter): 58–73.

Ferudi, F. (2006) *The Politics of Fear: Beyond Left and Right*. Continuum International Publishing Group Ltd: London.

FESPAD (2004) *Informe Anual Sobre Justicia Penal Juvenil 2004*. [WWW document]. URL http://fespad.org.sv/portal/html/Archivos/Descargas/IPJ2004.pdf [last accessed 22 June 2007].

FESPAD (2006) *Informe Anual Sobre Justicia Penal Juvenil 2005*. [WWW document]. URL http://fespad.org.sv/portal/html/Archivos/Descargas/ESPyJPES2005.pdf [last accessed 22 June 2007].

FESPAD (2008) *Consideraciones Generales en Materia de Seguridad Pública durante la Gestión del Presidente Antonio Saca*. [WWW document]. URL http://fespad.org.sv/wordpress/wp-content/uploads/2008/06/datosviolenciahomicidagestionsaca.pdf [last accessed 30 July 2008].

Flores, F. (2003) *Discurso presidencial*. [WWW document]. URL http://www.elsalvador.com/noticias/2003/07/24/nacional/nacio14.html [accessed 28 August 2009].

Foucault, M. (1977) *Discipline and Punish: The Birth of the Prison*. Penguin English Translation: Harmondsworth.

Foucault, M. (1980) *A History of Sexuality: Vol 1 The Will to Knowledge*. Penguin: London.

Foucault, M. (1990) 'On Power' in L. D. Kritzman (ed.) *Michel Foucault: Politics, Philosophy and Culture Interviews and Other Writings 1977–1984*. Routledge: London, 96–109.

Freedman, E. (2008) *Who's Defending Monsignor Romero?*, Revista Envío 218. [WWW document]. URL http://www.envio.org.ni/articulo/3717 [accessed 26 August 2009].

Fundacion de Estudios para la Aplicación del Derecho (FESPAD) (2005) *Estado de Seguridad Pública y la Justicia Penal en El Salvador, Enero- Agosto 2005*. FESPAD: San Salvador.

Gaborit, M. (2007) 'Recordar Para Vivir: El Papel de la Memoria Histórica en la Reparación del Tejido Social', *Problemas de la Paz: Violencia, Impunidad, Deficit* Institucional Edición Monográfica' Estudios Centroamericanos **701–702**, 203–218.

Gaborit, M. and Santori, A. (2002a) *Cotidianeidad y Poder en la Construcción de la Subjetividad Femenina*. Unpublished manuscript: San Salvador.

Gaborit, M. and Santori, A. (2002b) *Como Invisibilizar a una Persona: Disparidad de Género en El Salvador*. Unpublished manuscript: San Salvador.

Galtung, J. (1969) 'Violence, Peace and Peace Research'. *Journal of Peace Research* **6**(3): 167–191.

Galtung, J. (1990) 'Cultural Violence'. *Journal of Peace Research* **27**(3): 291–305.

Gidwani, V. K. (2009) 'Subalternity' in R. Kitchin and N. Thrift (eds.) *International Encyclopedia of Human Geography*. Elsevier: London.

Goldstein, D. (2003) *Laughter Out of Place: Race, Class, Violence, and Sexuality in a Rio Shantytown*. University of California Press: Berkeley and Los Angeles.

Goldstein, D. (2005) 'Flexible Justice: Neoliberal Violence and 'Self-Help' Security in Bolivia'. *Critique of Anthropology* **25**(4): 389–411.

González de la Rocha, M. (1994) *The Resources of Poverty: Women and Survival in a Mexican City*. Blackwell Science: Oxford.

Government of El Salvador (2006) *Ley Especial Contra Actos De Terrorismo*. [WWW document]. URL http://www.csj.gob.sv/leyes.nsf/c8884f2b1645f48b86256d48007011d2/f50b147ff5914eda0625721f00744c15?OpenDocument [accessed 28 August 2009].

Gramsci, A. (1971) *Selection from the Prison Notebooks*. Lawrence and Wishart: London.

Green, L. (1994) 'Fear as a Way of Life'. *Cultural Anthropology* **9**(2): 227–256.

Green, L. (1995) 'Living in a State of Fear' in C. Nordstrom and A. C. G. M. Robben (eds.) *Fieldwork Under Fire: Contemporary Studies of Violence and Survival*. University of California Press: Berkeley, 105–128.

Greig, A. (2000) 'The Spectacle of Men Fighting'. *IDS Bulletin* **31**(2): 28–32.

Grenier, Y. (1999) *The Emergence of Insurgency in El Salvador: Ideology and Political Will*. Macmillan: London.

Grugel, J. (2007) 'Latin America after the Third Wave'. *Government and Opposition* **42**(2): 242–249.

Guha, R. (2000) 'On Some Aspects of the Historiography of Colonial India' in V. Chaturvedi (ed.) *Mapping Subaltern Studies and the Postcolonial*. Verso: London, 1–7.

Gutmann, M. C. (1996) *The Meanings of Macho: Being a Man in Mexico City*. University of California Press: Berkeley.

Gutmann, M. C. (2003) 'Introduction: Discarding Manly Dichotomies in Latin America' in M. C. Gutmann (ed.) *Changing Men and Masculinities in Latin America*. Duke University Press: Durham and London, 1–26.

Hall, S., Critcher, C., Jefferson, T., Clarke, J. and Roberts, B. (1978) *Policing the Crisis: Mugging, the State, and Law and Order*. Macmillan: London.

Hanmer, J. (1990) 'Men, Power and the Exploitation of Women' in J. Hearn and D. Morgan (eds.) *Men, Masculinities and Social Theory*. Unwin Hyman: London, 21–42.

Harding, S. (ed.) (1987) *Feminism and Methodology: Social Science Issues*. Indiana University Press: Bloomington.

Harvey, P. (1998) 'Feminism and Anthropology' in S. Jackson and J. Jones (eds.) *Contemporary Feminist Theories*. Macmillan: London, 73–86.

Hearn, J. (1998) *The Violences of Men*. Sage: London.

Hernández Reyes, A. P. and Solano, R. M. (2003) *Estudio Sobre la Aplicación de la Ley Contra la Violencia Intrafamiliar*. PNUD and Asociación Cristiana Femenina (ACF)/Comité 25 de noviembre: San Salvador.

Holden, R. H. (1996) 'Constructing the Limits of State Violence in Central America: Towards a New Research Agenda'. *Journal of Latin American Studies* **28**(2): 435–459.

Homies Unidos and Instituto Uinversitario de Opinión Pública (1998) *Solidaridad y Violencia en las Pandillas del Gran San Salvador: Más Allá de la Vida Loca*. UCA Editores: San Salvador.

Howard, D., Hume, M. and Oslender, U. (2007) 'Violence, Fear and Development in Latin America: A Critical Overview'. *Development in Practice* **17**(6): 713–724.

Human Rights Watch (HRW) (2001) *World Report 2001: Special Issues and Campaigns*. [WWW document]. URL http://www.hrw.org/legacy/wr2k1/special/gay.html [accessed 27 August 2009].

Human Rights Watch (HRW) (2007) *El Salvador: Terrorism Law Misused Against Protesters*. [WWW document]. URL http://www.hrw.org/en/news/2007/07/30/el-salvador-terrorism-law-misused-against-protesters [accessed 28 August 2009].

Huezo Mixco, M. (2000) 'Cultura y Violencia en El Salvador', *PNUD Violencia en una Sociedad en Transición: Ensayos*. PNUD: San Salvador, 115–138.

Hume, M. (2004) 'It's as if You Don't Know Because You Don't Do Anything About it': Gender and Violence in El Salvador'. *Environment and Urbanization* **16**(2): 63–72.

Hume, M. (2007a) '(Young) Men with Big Guns: Reflexive Encounters with Violence in El Salvador'. *Bulletin of Latin American Research* (Special Issue) **26**(4): 480–496.

Hume, M. (2007b) 'Mano Dura: El Salvador Responds to Gangs'. *Development in Practice* **17**(6): 725–738.

Hume, M. (2007c) 'Unpicking the Threads: Emotion as Central to the Theory and Practice of Researching Violence'. *Women's Studies International Forum* **30**(2): 147–157.

Hume, M. (2008a) 'The Myths of Violence: Gender, Conflict, and Community in El Salvador'. *Latin American Perspectives* **35**: 59–76.

Hume, M. (2008b) *Yo Sí Tengo una Vida Diferente: Women's Changing Perceptions of Gender Based Violence in Ahuachapan and San Marcos*. Unpublished paper for Oxfam America, San Salvador.

IDHES (2005) *El Informe sobre Desarrollo Humano El Salvador 2005: Una mirada al nuevo Nosotros. El impacto de las migraciones*. PNUD/UNDP: San Salvador.

IDHUCA (2002) *La agenda pendiente, diez años después (de la esperanza inicial a las responsabilidades compartidas)*. [WWW document]. URL http://www.uca.edu.sv/publica/idhuca/agendapendiente.pdf [last accessed May 8, 2008].

IDHUCA (2003,) *Boletín de Derechos Humanos*. UCA: San Salvador.

IDHUCA (2007) 'Llevamos la Fiesta en Paz?' *Problemas de la Paz: Violencia, Impunidad, Déficit Institucional... Edición Monográfica' Estudios Centroamericanos* 701–702, March-April, 2007, 239–262.

de Innocenti, Z. and Innocenti, C. (2002) *El Salvador Explotación Sexual Comercial de Niñas, Niños y Adolescentes: Una Evaluación Rápida*. International Labour Organisation (ILO - IPEC): Geneva.

Inter-American Convention on the Prevention, Punishment and Eradication of Violence Against Women (1994) *Convention of Belem do Para*. (Adopted in Belém do Pará, Brasil, on June 9, 1994, at the twenty fourth regular session of the General Assembly). [WWW document]. URL http://www.cidh.oas.org/Basicos/English/basic13.Conv%20of%20Belem%20Do%20Para.htm [accessed 27 August 2009].

IUDOP (1996) *Sondeo sobre violencia en los centros educativos del Área de San Salvador. Serie de informes 59* . IUDOP-UCA: San Salvador, El Salvador.

IUDOP (1998) 'Solidaridad y Violencia: Los Jóvenes Pandilleros en el Gran San Salvador', *ECA*, San Salvador: UCA: 695–710.

IUDOP (2006) *Encuesta de evaluación del año 2006: Consulta de opinión pública de noviembre de 2006. Serie de Informes 112*. IUDOP: San Salvador. [WWW document]. URL http://www.uca.edu.sv/publica/iudop/Web/2006/informe112.pdf [accessed 28 August 2009].

IUDOP/FUNDAUNGO (2002) *Encuesta Sobre la Percepción de la Seguridad Ciudadana a Nivel Nacional, Municipal y Zonal*. Ministerio de Justicia and Consejo Nacional de Seguridad Pública: San Salvador.

Jabri, V. (1996) *Discourses on Violence: Conflict Analysis Reconsidered*. Manchester University Press: Manchester.

Jackson, C. (2006) 'Feminism Spoken Here: Epistemologies for Interdisciplinary Development Research'. *Development and Change* 37(3): 1–23.

Jacobson, R., Jacobs, S. and Marchbank, J. (2000) 'Introduction: States of Conflict' in S. Jacobs, R. Jacobson and J. Marchbank (eds.) *States of Conflict: Gender, Violence and Resistance*. Zed Books: London, 1–24.

Jansen, G. and Davis, D. (1998) 'Honoring Voice and Visibility: Sensitive-Topic Research and Feminist Interpretive Inquiry'. *Affilia* 13(3): 289–311.

Jelin, E. (1997) 'Engendering Human Rights' in E. Dore (ed.) *Gender Politics in Latin America: Debates in Theory and Practice*. Monthly Review Press: New York, 65–83.

Kandiyoti, D. (1988) 'Bargaining with Patriarchy'. *Gender and Society* 2(3): 274–290.

Keane, J. (1996) *Reflections on Violence*. Verso: London.

Keane, J. (2004) *Violence and Democracy*. Cambridge University Press: Cambridge.

Keen, D. (2000) 'War and Peace: What's the Difference?' *International Peacekeeping* 7(4): 1–22.

Kelly, L. (1988a) *Surviving Sexual Violence*. Polity: Cambridge.

Kelly, L. (1988b) 'How Women Define their Experience of Violence' in K. Yllo and M. Bograd (eds.) *Feminist Perspectives on Wife Abuse*. Sage: London, 114–132.

Kelly, L. (1996) 'When does the Speaking Profit Us? Reflections on the Challenges of Developing Feminist Perspectives in Abuse and Violence by Women' in M. Hester, L. Kelly and J. Radford (eds.) *Women, Violence and Male Power*. Open University Press: Buckingham, 34–49.

Kelly, L. (2000) 'Wars Against Women: Sexual Violence, Sexual Politics and the Militarised State' in S. Jacobs, R. Jacobson and J. Marchbank (eds.) *States of Conflict: Gender, Violence and Resistance*. Zed Books: London, 45–65.

Kelly, L. and Radford, J. (1996) ''Nothing Really Happened': The Invalidation of Women's Experiences of Sexual Violence' in M. Hester, L. Kelly and J. Radford (eds.) *Women, Violence and Male Power*. Open University Press: Buckingham, 19–33.

Kimmel, M. (2000) *The Gendered Society*. Open University Press: New York.

Kinsella, H. M. (2007) 'Understanding a War That Is Not a War: A Review Essay'. *Signs: Journal of Women in Culture and Society* 33(1): 209–231.

Kooning, K. and Kruijt, D. (1999) 'Introduction: Violence and Fear in Latin America' in K. Kooning and D. Krujit (eds.) *Societies of Fear: The Legacy of Civil War, Violence and Terror in Latin America*. Zed Books: London, 1–30.

Kooning, K. and Kruijt, K. (2003) 'Latin American Political Armies in the Twenty. First Century'. *Bulletin of Latin American Research* 22: 371–384.

Kooning, K. and Kruijt, D. (eds.) (2004) *Armed Actors: Organised Violence and State Failure in Latin America*. Zed Books: London.

Kooning, K. and Kruijt, D. (eds.) (2007) *Fractured Cities: Social Exclusion, Urban Violence and Contested Spaces in Latin America*. Zed Books: London.

La Prensa, Grafica (2006) *PNC captura a director de ONG*. [WWW document]. URL http://archive.laprensa.com.sv/20060517/nacion/492936.asp [accessed 28 August 2009].

Lauria-Santiago, A. (2005) 'The Culture and Politics of State Terror and Repression in El Salvador' in C. Menjívar and N. Rodríguez (eds.) *When States Kill: Latin America, the US and Technologies of Terror*. University of Texas Press: Austin, 85–114.

Lawrence, B. and Karim, A. (2007) *On Violence: A Reader*. Duke University Press: Durham, NC and London.

Lechner, N. (1992) 'Some People Die of Fear: Fear as a Political Problem' in J. E. Corradi, P. Weiss Fagen and M. A. Garretón (eds.) *Fear at the Edge: State Terror and Resistance in Latin America*. University of California Press: Berkeley, 26–35.

Levine, M. (2003) 'Researching Violence: Power, Social Relations and the Virtues of the Experimental Method' in R. M. Lee and E. A. Stanko (eds.) *Researching Violence: Essays on Methodology and Measurement*. Routledge: London, 126–136.

Liebling, A. and Stanko, B. (2001) 'Allegiance and Ambivalence. Some Dilemmas in Researching Disorder and Violence'. *British Journal of Criminology* **41**: 421–430.

Lindo-Fuentes, H., Ching, E. and Lara-Martinez, R. A. (2007) *Remembering a massacre in El Salvador: The Insurrection of 1932, Roque Dalton, and the Politics of Historical Memory*. University of New Mexico Press: Albuquerque.

Lister, M. R. (1997) *Citizenship: Feminist Perspective*. Macmillan and New York University Press: London and New York.

Londoño, J. L. and Guerrero, R. (1999) *Violencia en América Latina: Epidemiología y costos*. Working Paper R-375. Inter-American Development Bank: Washington, DC.

Lorde, A. (1984) *Sister Outsider: Essays and Speeches*. Crossing Press: Berkeley.

Lundy, P. and McGovern, M. (2006) 'The Ethics of Silence: Action Research, Community "Truth-Telling" and Post-Conflict Transition in the North of Ireland'. *Action Research* **4**(1): 49–64.

Macauley, F. (2005) 'Judicialising and (De)Criminalising Domestic Violence in Latin America'. *Social Policy and Society* **5**(1): 103–114.

MacKinnon, C. (1982) 'Feminism, Marxism, Method, and the State: An Agenda for Theory'. *Signs: Journal of Women in Culture and Society* **7**(3): 515–544.

MacKinnon, C. A. (1983) 'Feminism, Marxism, Method, and the State: Toward Feminist Jurisprudence'. *Signs: Journal of Women in Culture and Society* **8**(4): 635–658.

Mallon, F. E. (1994) 'The Promise and Dilemma of Subaltern Studies: Perspectives from Latin American History'. *The American Historical Review* **99**(5): 1491–1515.

MAM (1999) *Participación e incidencia de las mujeres en los procesos de desarrollo local: Experiencia de la gestión de una demanda en las comunidades del municipio de San Marcos*. Movimiento de Mujeres Mélida Anaya Montes: San Salvador.

Marcuse, P. (1997) 'Walls of Fear and Walls of Support' in N. Ellin (ed.) *Architecture of Fear*. Princeton Architectural Press: New York, 101–114.

Martín-Baró, I. (1983) *Acción e Ideología: Psicología Social desde Centroamérica*. UCA: San Salvador.

Martín-Baró, I. (1989) 'Political Violence and War as Causes of Psychological Trauma in El Salvador'. *Journal of La Roza Studies* **2**(1): 5–13.

Martín-Baró, I. (ed.) (1990) *Psicología Social de la Guerra: Trauma y Terapia*. UCA Editores: San Salvador.

Mason, T. D. (1999) 'The Civil War in El Salvador: A Retrospective Analysis'. *Latin American Research Review* **34**(3): 179–196.

McClintock, C. (1998) *Revolutionary Movements in Latin America: El Salvador's FMLN and Peru Shining Path*. Institute of Peace: Washington, D.C.

McCoy, J. (2006) 'International Reaction to Democratic Crisis in the Americas, 1990–2005'. *Democratization* **13**(5): 756–775.

Mc Laughlin, E. (2002) 'Political Violence, Terrorism and States of Fear' in J. Muncie and E. Mc Laughlin (eds.) *The Problem of Crime*, 2nd edn. Sage and Open University Press: London: 284–330.

McIlwaine, C. (1998) 'Contesting Civil Society: Reflections from El Salvador'. *Third World Quarterly* **19**(4): 651–672.

McIlwaine, C. (1999) 'Geography and Development: Violence and Crime as Development Issues'. *Progress in Human Geography* **23**(3): 453–463.

McWilliams, M. (1997) 'Violence Against Women and Political Conflict: The Northern Ireland Experience'. *Critical Criminology* **8**(1): 78–92.

McWilliams, M. (1998) 'Violence Against Women in Societies Under Stress' in R. E. Dobash and R. E. Dobash (eds.) *Rethinking Violence Against Women*. Sage: Thousand Oaks, 111–140.

Melara, M. (2001) 'Los Servicios de Seguridad Privada en El Salvador'. *Estudios Centroamericanos* **636**: 907–932.

Melhuus, M. and Stølen, K. A. (eds.) (1996) *Machos, Mistresses and Madonnas: Contesting the Power of Latin American Gender Imagery*. Verso: London.

Méndez, J. E. (1999) 'The Problems of Lawless Violence: Introduction' in J. E. Méndez, G. O'Donnell and P. S. Pinheiro (eds.) *The (Un)Rule of Law and the Underprivileged in Latin America*. University of Notre Dame Press: Notre Dame, 19–24.

Menjívar, C. and Rodríguez, N. (2005) 'State Terror in the US-Latin American Interstate Regime' in C. Menjívar and N. Rodríguez (eds.) *When States Kill: Latin America, the US and Technologies of Terror*. University of Texas Press: Austin, 3–27.

Miranda, J. L. (2000) 'Sicología y Violencia', in *Violencia en una Sociedad en Transición: Ensayos*. PNUD: San Salvador, 49–74.

Moffett, H. (2001) *Entering the Labyrinth: Coming to Grips with Gender War Zones – The Case of South Africa*. Working Paper Series on Men's Roles and Responsibilities in Ending Gender Based Violence, Vol. 5. INSTRAW: New York.

Mohanty, C. T. (1991) 'Introduction: Cartographies of Struggle, Third World Women and the Politics of Feminsim' in C. T. Mohanty, A. Russo and L. Torres (eds.) *Third World Women and the Politics of Feminism*. Indiana University Press: Indianapolis, 1–50.

Mohanty, C. T. (1998) 'Under Western Eyes: Feminist Scholarship and Colonial Discourses' in C. T. Mohanty, A. Russo and L. Torres (eds.) *Third World Women and the Politics of Feminism*. Indiana University Press: Indianapolis, 51–80.

Monaghan, R. (2008) 'Community-Based Justice in Northern Ireland and South Africa'. *International Criminal Justice Review* **18**(1): 83–105.

Montobbio, M. (1999) *La Metomorfosi del Pulgarcito: Transición Política y Proceso de Paz en El Salvador*. Icaria/FLACSO: Barcelona.

Moodie, E. (2006) 'Microbus Crashes and Coca-Cola Cash: The Value of Death in "Free-Market" El Salvador'. *American Ethnologist* **32**(1): 63–80.

Moore, H. (1994) 'The Problem of Explaining Violence in the Social Sciences' in P. Harvey and P. Gow (eds.) *Sex and Violence: Issues in Representation and Experience*. Routledge: London, 138–155.

Morgan, K. and Thapar Björkert, S. (2006) 'I'd Rather You'd Lay Me on the Floor and Start Kicking Me': Understanding Symbolic Violence in Everyday Life'. *Women's Studies International Forum* **29**: 441–452.

Moro, B. (2000) 'Introducción', *Violencia en una Sociedad en Transición: Ensayos*. PNUD: San Salvador.

Morrell, R. (2001) 'The Times of Change: Men and Masculinity in Contemporary South Africa' in R. Morrell (ed.) *Changing Men in Southern Africa*. Zed Books: London, 3–40.

Moser, C. O. N. and Clark, F. (eds.) (2001) *Victims, Perpetrators or Actors? Gender, Armed Conflict and Political Violence*. Zed Books: London.

Moser, C. and McIlwaine, C. (2000a) *Urban Poor Perceptions of Violence and Exclusion in Colombia*. The World Bank: Washington, D.C.

Moser, C. and McIlwaine, C. (2000b) *Violence in a Post-Conflict Context: Urban Poor Perceptions from Guatemala*. The World Bank: Washington, D.C.

Moser, C. and McIlwaine, C. (2004) *Encounters with Violence in Latin America: Urban Poor Perceptions from Colombia and Guatemala*. Routledge: London.

Moser, C. O. N. and Shrader, E. (1999) *A Conceptual Framework for Violence Reduction*. Urban Peace Program Series LCR Sustainable Development Working Paper No. 2. World Bank: Washington, D.C.

Moser, C. O. N. and Winton, A. (2002) *Violence in the Central American Region: Towards and Integrated Framework for Violence Reduction*. ODI Working Paper 171. Overseas Development Institute: London.

Muncie, J. and Mc Laughlin, E. (2002) 'Introduction: Reading the Problem of Crime' in J. Muncie and E. Mc Laughlin (eds.) *The Problem of Crime*, 2nd edn. Sage and Open University Press: London: 1–7.

Munck, R. (2000) 'Deconstructing Terror: Insurgency, Repression and Peace' in R. Munck and P. de Silva (eds.) *Post-modern Insurgencies: Political Violence, Identity Formation and Peacemaking in Comparative Perspective*. Macmillan: London, 1–13.

Munck, R. (2008) 'Deconstructing Violence: Power, Force, and Social Transformation'. *Latin American Perspectives* **35**: 3–19.

Nordstrom, C. (1997) *A Different Kind of War Story*. University of Pennsylvania Press: Philadelphia.

Nordstrom, C. (2004) *Shadows of War: Violence, Power and International Profiteering in the Twenty First Century*. University of California Pres: Berkeley.

O'Brien, P. and Cammack, P. (1985) *The Generals in Retreat: The Crisis of Military Rule in Latin America*. Manchester University Press: Manchester.

Observatorio Centroamericano sobre Violencia (OCAVI) (2007). [WWW document]. URL http://www.ocavi.com [accessed 28 August 2009].

Observatorio Centroamericano sobre Violencia (OCAVI) (2009) *Cantidad de Homicidios Registrados por Año en El Salvador (1999–2008)*. [WWW document]. URL http://www.ocavi.com/docs_files/file_418.pdf [accessed 26 August 2009].

O'Driscoll, C. (2008) 'Fear and Trust: The Shooting of Jean Charles de Menezes and the War on Terror'. *Millennium: Journal of International Studies* **36**(2): 149–170.

O'Hanlon, R. (2000a) 'Recovering the Subject: Subaltern Studies and Histories of Resistance in Colonial South Asia' in V. Chaturvedi (ed.) *Mapping Subaltern Studies and the Postcolonial*. Verso: London, 72–115.

O'Hanlon, R. (2000b) 'After Orientalism: Culture, Criticism and the Politics of the Third World' in V. Chaturvedi (ed.) *Mapping Subaltern Studies and the Postcolonial*. Verso: London, 191–219.

Orellana, V. A. and Arana, R. E. (2003) *El Salvador: Masculinidad y Factores Socioculturales Asociados a la Paternidad*. UNFPA: San Salvador.

ORMUSA (2008) *Observatorio de Violencia de Género Contra la Mujer*. [WWW document]. URL http://observatoriodeviolencia.ormusa.org/principal.html [accessed 28 August 2009].

O'Sullivan, C. (1998) 'Ladykillers: Similarities and Divergences of Masculinities in Gang Rape and Wife Battery' in L. Bowker (ed.) *Masculinities and Violence*. Sage: London, 82–110.

Owens, P. (2008) 'Distinctions, Distinctions: "Public" and "Private" Force?'. *International Affairs* **84**(5): 977–990.

Oxfam America (2007) 'Situación de la Violencia De Género y su Prevención', *Campaña de Prevención de la Violencia de Género*. Oxfam America: San Salvador.

Oxhorn, P. (2008) 'Editor's Foreword: Pioneering Multidisciplinary Research on Latin America'. *Latin American Research Review* **43**(2): 3–5.

PAHO/WHO (1998) *Violence Against Women in the Americas*. Pan American Health Organization/World Health Organization, Subcommittee on Planning and Programming of the Executive Committee. [WWW document]. URL http://www.paho.org/english/gov/ce/spp/spp31_6.pdf [accessed 28 August 2009].

Paige, J. (1994) 'History and Memory in El Salvador: Elite Ideology and the Insurrection and Massacre of 1932'. Paper delivered at the Annual Meetings of the Latin American Studies Association, Atlanta.

Pain, R. (2001) 'Gender, Race, Age and Fear in the City'. *Urban Studies* **38**(5–6): 899–913.

Pain, R. (2003) 'Youth, Age and the Representation of Fear'. *Capital and Class* **60**: 151–171.

Pateman, C. (1987) 'Feminist Critiques of the Public/Private Dichotomy' in A. Phillips (ed.) *Feminism and Equality*. Blackwell Science: Oxford, 103–126.

Pearce, J. (1986) *Promised Land Peasant Rebellion in Chalatenango El Salvador*. Latin American Bureau: London.

Pearce, J. (1998) 'From Civil War to 'Civil Society': Has the End of the Cold War Brought Peace to Central America?' *International Affairs* **74**(3): 587–615.

Pearson, R. (2000) 'Which Men, Why Now? Reflections on Men and Development'. *IDS Bulletin* **31**(2): 42–48.

Pécaut, D. (1999) 'From the Banality of Violence to Real Terror: The Case of Colombia', in K. Kooning and D. Kruijt (eds.) *Societies of Fear: The Legacy of Civil War, Violence and Terror in Latin America*. Zed Books: London, 141–167.

Pereira, A. and Davis, D. (2000) 'New Patterns of Militarized Violence and Coercion in the Americas'. *Latin American Perspectives* **111**(27): 3–17.

Phillips, N. (2007) *Migration as Development Strategy? The New Political Economy of Dispossession and Inequality in the Americas*. IPEG Papers in Global Political Economy no. 27, May 2007. [WWW document]. URL http://www.bisa.ac.uk/groups/18/papers/27%20Phillips.pdf [accessed 20 July 2008].

Pickering, S. (2001) 'Undermining the Sanitized Account: Violence and Emotionality in the Field in Northern Ireland'. *British Journal of Criminology* **41**: 485–501.

Pinheiro, P. S. (1996) 'Democracies without Citizenship'. *NACLA* **030**(2): 17–33.

Popkin, M. (2000) *Peace without Justice: Obstacles to Building the Rule of Law in El Salvador*. Pennsylvania State University Press: University Park, Pennsylvania.

Portillo, E. (2005) *FBI y Saca discrepan sobre relación entre maras y Al Qaeda*. [WWW document]. URL http://www.elfaro.net/secciones/noticias/20050228/noticias4_20050228.asp [accessed 28 August].

Portillo, E. (2006) *San Martín reduce a la mitad promedio de homicidios*. [WWW document]. URL http://www.elfaro.net/secciones/Noticias/20060710/noticias5_20060710.asp [accessed 28 August 2009].

Prieto-Carrón, M., Thomson, M. and Macdonald, M. (2007) 'No More Killings! Women Respond to Femicides in Central America'. *Gender and Development* **15**(1): 25–40.

Pryse, M. (2000) 'Trans/Feminist Methodology: Bridges to Interdisciplinary Thinking'. *NWSA Journal* **12**(2): 105–118.

Ptacek, J. (1988) 'Why Do Men Batter their Wives?' in K. Yllo and M. Bograd (eds.) *Feminist Perspectives on Wife Abuse*. Sage: London, 133–157.

Pugh, M. (2006) 'Post-war Economies and the New York Dissensus'. *Conflict, Security and Development* **6**(3): 269–289.

Pugh, M., Cooper, N. and McDonald, M. (eds.) (2008) *Whose Peace? Critical Perspectives on the Political Economy of Peacebuilding*. Palgrave Macmillan: London.

Radford, J. and Kelly, L. (1998) 'Sexual Violence Against Women and Girls: An Approach to an International Overview of Research' in R. E. Dobash and R. P. Dobash (eds.) *Rethinking Violence against Women*. Sage: Thousand Oaks, 53–76.

Radford, J. and Stanko, E. A. (1996) 'Violence Against Women and Children: The Contradictions of Crime Control Under Patriarchy' in M. Hester, L. Kelly and J. Radford (eds.) *Women, Violence and Male Power*. Open University Press: Buckingham, 65–80.

Ramazanoglu, C. (1992) 'What Can You Do With a Man? Feminism and the Critical Appraisal of Masculinity'. *Women's Studies International Forum* **15**(3): 339–350.

Ramos, C. G. (2000) 'Marginación, Exclusión Social y Violencia', in *Violencia en una Sociedad en Transición: Ensayos*. PNUD: San Salvador, 7–48.

Ramos, C. G. and Loya, N. (2008) 'El Salvador: Quince Años de la Firma de los Acuerdos de Paz'. *Revista de Ciencia Política (Santiago)* **28**(1): 367–383.

Reguillo, R. (2002) 'The Social Construction of Fear: Urban Narratives and Practices' in S. Rotker (ed.) *Citizens of Fear: Urban Violence in Latin America*. Rutgers University Press: New Brunswick, 187–206.

Renzetti, C. M., and Lee, R. M. (eds.) (1993) *Researching Sensitive Topics*. Sage: London.

Ribbens, J. and Edwards, R. (1997) *Feminist Dilemmas in Qualitative Research: Public Knowledge and Private Lives*. Sage: London.

Richmond, O. (2006) 'The Problem of Peace: Understanding the "Liberal Peace"'. *Conflict, Security and Development* **6**(3): 291–314.

Richardson, D. and May, H. (1999) 'Deserving Victims?: Sexual Status and the Social Construction of Violence'. *Sociological Review* **47**(2): 308–331.

Rivas Martínez, M. (2005) *No más violencia contra las mujeres EL SALVADOR: Casos de llamamiento*. [WWW document]. URL http://www.amnestyusa.org/document.php?lang=s&id=ESLAMR290052005 [accessed 26 August 2009].

Roberts, H. (ed.) (1981) *Doing Feminist Research*. Routledge: London.

Roberts, S. (2004) 'Government Strategy: Increasing Community Safety or Courting the 'Decent' Majority'. *Criminal Justice Matters* 57(Autumn). [WWW document]. URL http://www.crimeandsociety.org.uk/articles/file9.html [accessed 20 June 2007].

Robinson, W. (2003) *Transnational Conflicts: Central America, Social Change, and Globalization*. Verso: London.

Robinson, W. (2004) 'Global Crisis and Latin America'. *Bulletin of Latin American Research* 23(2): 135–153.

Rodgers, D. (1999) *Youth Gangs and Violence in Latin America and the Caribbean: A Literature Survey*. Latin America and the Caribbean Region Sustainable Development Working Paper, The World Bank: Washington DC.

Rodgers, D. (2001) *Making Danger a Calling: Anthropology, Violence and the Dilemmas of Participant Observation* Crisis States Programme Working Papers no. 6. London School of Economics and Political Science: London.

Rodgers, D. (2006) 'The State as a Gang: Conceptualising the Governmentality of Violence in Contemporary Nicaragua'. *Critique of Anthropology* 26(3): 315–330.

Rodgers, D. (2007) 'Joining the Gang and Becoming a Broder: The Violence of Ethnography in Contemporary Nicaragua'. *Bulletin of Latin American Research* 26(4): 444–461.

Rodgers, D. and Moser, C. (2005) *Change, Violence and Insecurity in Non-Conflict Situations*. Overseas Development Institute Working Paper ODI: London.

Rotker, S. (ed.) (2002) *Citizens of Fear: Urban Violence in Latin America*. Rutgers University Press: New Brunswick.

Saca, A. (2005) *Press Conference*. [WWW document]. URL http://www.casapres.gob.sv/presidente/declaraciones/2005/12/dec2701.html [accessed 21 June 2007].

Said, E. (1978) *Orientalism*. Routledge and Kegan Paul: London.

Said, E. (1986) 'Orientalism Reconsidered' in F. Barker, P. Hulme, M. Iversen and D. Loxley (eds.) *Literature, Politics and Theory*. Methuen: London, 210–229.

Salas, Y. (2002) 'Imaginaries and Narratives of Prison Violence' in S. Rotker (ed.) *Citizens of Fear: Urban Violence in Latin America*. Rutgers University Press: New Brunswick, 207–223.

Salvadoran Truth Commission (1993) *From Madness to Hope: Report of the Truth Commission for El Salvador*. United Nations Publications: New York.

Samuel, R. and Thompson, P. (1990) 'Introduction', in R. Samuel and P. Thompson (eds.) *The Myths We Live By*. Routledge: London, 1–22.

Santacruz Giralt, M. (2005) 'Creciendo en El Salvador: Una Mirada a la Situación de la Adolescencia y Juventud en el País'. *Estudios Centroamericanos* 685–686: 1079–1099.

Santacruz Giralt, M. and Concha-Eastman, A. (2001) *Barrio adentro. La Solidaridad Violenta de las Pandillas*. IUDOP-UCA/OPS-OMS: San Salvador.

Saraga, E. (2002) 'Dangerous Places: The Family as a Site of Crime' in J. Muncie and E. Mc Laughlin (eds.) *The Problem of Crime*, 2nd edn. Sage and Open University Press: London: 191–239.

Savenije, W. and Andrade-Eekhoff, K. (eds.) (2003) *Conviviendo en la Orilla: Violencia y Exclusión Social en el Area Metropolitana de San Salvador*. FLACSO: San Salvador.

Savenije, W. and Van der Borgh, C. (2004) 'Youth Gangs, Social Exclusion and the Transformation of Violence in El Salvador' in K. Kooning and D. Kruijt (eds.) *Armed Actors: Organised Violence and State Failure in Latin America*. Zed Books: London, 155–171.

Sawicki, J. (1991) *Disciplining Foucault: Feminism, Power, and the Body*. Routledge: New York.

Scheper-Hughes, N. (1992) *Death without Weeping: The Violence of Everyday Life in Brazil*. University of California Press: Berkeley.

Scheper-Hughes, N. (1995) 'The Primacy of the Ethical: Propositions for a Militant Anthropology'. *Current Anthropology* **36**(3): 409–420.
Scheper-Hughes, N. (1998) 'Un-Doing: Social Suffering and the Politics of Remorse in the New South Africa'. *Social Justice* **25**(4): 114–142.
Scott, J. C. (1985) *Weapons of the Weak: Everyday Forms of Peasant Resistance*. Yale University Press: New Haven.
Scott, J. C. (1990) *Domination and the Arts of Resistance: Hidden Transcripts*. Yale University Press: New Haven.
Scott, J. W. (2004) 'Feminism's History'. *Journal of Women's History* **16**(2): 10–29.
Segal, L. (1997) *Slow Motion: Changing Masculinities, Changing Men*, 2nd edn. Virago: London.
Shirlow, P. and Pain, R. (2003) 'The Geographies and Politics of Fear'. *Capital and Class* **80**: 15–26.
Shope, J. (2006) "You Can't Cross a River Without Getting Wet': A Feminist Standpoint on the Dilemmas of Cross-Cultural Research'. *Qualitative Inquiry* **12**(1): 163–184.
Shrader, E. (2001) *Methodologies to Measure the Gender Dimensions of Crime and Violence*. World Bank, Gender Unit, Poverty Reduction and Economic Management, Latin American and Caribbean Region: Washington, DC.
Silva Avalos, Claudia. (2003) 'Violencia y Desarrollo Humano en el Gran San Salvador: Un estudio de La Vía' in W. Savenije and K. Andrade-Eekhoff (eds.) *Conviviendo en la Orilla: Violencia y Exclusión Social en el Area Metropolitana de SanSalvador*. FLACSO: San Salvador, 207–262.
Slim, H. and Thompson, P. with Bennett, O. and Cross, N. (1998) 'Ways of Listening' in R. Perks and A. Thompson (eds.) *The Oral History Reader*. Routledge: London and New York, 114–125.
Smutt, M. and Miranda, L. (1998) 'El Salvador: Socialización y Violencia Juvenil' in C. G. Ramos (ed.) *América Central en los Noventa: Problemas de Juventud*. FLACSO Programa El Salvador: San Salvador, 151–188.
Snodgrass-Godoy, A. (2004) 'When 'Justice' is Criminal: Lynchings in Contemporary Latin America'. *Theory and Society* **33**(6): 621–651.
Snodgrass-Godoy, A. (2005) 'La Muchacha Respondona: Reflections on the Razor's Edge Between Crime and Human Rights' *Human Rights Quarterly* **27**(2): 597–624.
Snodgrass Godoy, A. (2006) *Popular Injustice: Violence, Community and Law in Latin America*. Stanford University Press: Stanford.
Sparks, R., Girling, E. and Loader, I. (2001) 'Fear and Everyday Urban Lives'. *Urban Studies* **38**(5–6): 885–898.
Spivak, G. (1988.) 'Can the Subaltern Speak?' in C. Nelson and L. Grossberg (eds.) *Marxism and the Interpretation of Culture*. Macmillan Education: London, 271–313.
Stanko, E. A. (1988) 'Fear of Crime and the Myth of the Safe Home: A Feminist Critique of Criminology' in K. Yllo and M. Bograd (eds.) *Feminist Perspectives on Wife Abuse*. Sage: London, 75–89.
Stanko, E. A. (1990) *Everyday Violence: How Women and Men Experience Sexual and Physical Danger*, 2nd edn. Pandora: London.
Stanko, E. A. (1994) 'Dancing with Denial: Researching Women and Questioning Men' in M. Maynard and J. Purvis (eds.) *Researching Women's Lives from a Feminist Perspective*. Taylor and Francis: London, 93–105.
Stanley, W. (1996) *The Protection Racket State: Elite Politics, Military Extortion and Civil War in El Salvador*. Temple University Press: Philadelphia.
Stanley, W. (2006) 'El Salvador: State-building Before and After Democratization, 1980–1995'. *Third World Quarterly* **27**(1): 101–114.
Stanley, L. and Wise, S. (1990) 'Method, Methodology and Epistemology in Feminist Research Process' in L. Stanley (ed.) *Feminist Praxis: Research Theory and Epistemology in Feminist Sociology*. Routledge: London, 20–62.

Stanley, L. and Wise, S. (2000) 'But the Empress Has No Clothes! Some Awkward Questions about the "Missing Revolution" in Feminist Theory'. *Feminist Theory* 1(3): 261–288.

Taussig, M. (1987) *Shamanism, Colonialism, and the Wild Man: A Study in Terror and Healing*. University Of Chicago Press: Chicago.

Taussig, M. (1989) 'Terror as Usual: Walter Benjamin's Theory of History as a State of Siege'. *Social Text* 23: 3–20.

Tedesco, L. (2000) 'La Ñata contra el Vidrio: Urban Violence and Democratic Governability in Argentina'. *Bulletin of Latin American Research* 19(4): 527–545.

Tiano, S. (1984) 'The Public-Private Dichotomy: Theoretical Perspectives on 'Women in Development'. *Social Science Journal* 21(4): 11–28.

Tickner, J. A. (2005) 'Gendering a Discipline: Some Feminist Methodological Contributions to International Relations'. *Signs: Journal of Women in Culture and Society* 30(4): 2173–2188.

Toch, H. (1998) 'Hypermasculinity and Prison Violence' in L. Bowker (ed.) *Masculinities and Violence*. Sage Publications: London, 168–178.

Tombs, D. (2006) 'Unspeakable Violence: The Truth Commissions in El Salvador and Guatemala' in I. Maclean (ed.) *Reconciliation, Nations, and Churches in Latin America*. Ashgate: Aldershot, 57–84.

Torres-Rivas, E. (1999) 'Epilogue: Notes on Terror, Violence, Fear and Democracy' in K. Kooning and D. Kruijit (eds.) *Societies of Fear: The Legacy of Civil War, Violence and Terror in Latin America*. Zed Books: London, 285–300.

Torres-Rivas, E. (2000) 'Sobre el Terror y la Violencia Política en América Latina', *PNUD Violencia en una Sociedad en Transición*. PNUD: San Salvador, 46–59.

Towers, M. and Borzutzky, S. (2004) 'The Socioeconomic Implications of Dollarization in El Salvador'. *Latin American Politics and Society* 46(3): 29–54.

Townsend, J. and Zapata, E. (1999) 'Introduction' in J. Townsend, E. Zapata, J. Rowlands, P. Alberti and M. Mercado (eds.) *Women and Power: Fighting Patriarchies and Poverty*. Zed Books: London, 1–18.

Trigueros Martel, R. (2006) 'Las Maras Salvadorenas: Nuevas Formas de Espanto y Control Social'. *Estudios Centroamericanos* 696: 957–980.

United Nations (1995) *The United Nations and El Salvador 1990–1995, Blue Book Series*, Vol. 4. United Nations: New York.

United Nations Development Programme (UNDP) (2000) *Violencia de Género en El Salvador*. PNUD/UNDP: San Salvador.

UNDP (2007) *Seguridad Ciudadana*. [WWW document]. URL http://www.pnud.org.sv/2007/sc/content/view/7/81/ [accessed 28 August 2009].

UNODC (2007) *Crime and Development in Central America: Caught in the Crossfire*. United Nations Publications: New York.

UTEC (2001) *Oscuridad de la Casa: La Realidad Escondida del Abuso Sexual, el Maltrato Infantil y sus Efectos Psicológicas en El Salvador*. Universidad Tecnológica: San Salvador.

Vásquez, N., Ibañez, C. and Murguialday, C. (1996) *Mujeres- Montaña: Vivencias de Guerrilleras y Colaboradoras del FMLN*. Horas y Horas: Madrid.

Velado, M. (2001) *Violencia Intrafamiliar y Delitos Contra la Libertad Sexual* Las Mélidas: Mélidas: San Salvador.

Vilas, C. (2008) 'Lynchings and Political Conflict in the Andes'. *Latin American Perspectives* 35(5): 103–118.

Walby, S. (1990) *Theorizing Patriarchy*. Basil Blackwell: Cambridge.

Waylen, G. (2006) 'You Still Don't Understand: Why Troubled Engagements Continue between Feminists and (Critical) IPE'. *Review of International Studies* 32: 145–164.

Websdale, N. and Chesney-Lind, M. (1998) 'Doing Violence to Women: Research Synthesis on the Victimization of Women' in L. Bowker (ed.) *Masculinities and Violence*. Sage Publications: London, 55–81.

Welsh, P. (2001) *Men aren't from Mars: Unlearning Machismo in Nicaragua*. CIIR: London.

Whitehead, S. and Barrett, F. J. (2001) 'The Sociology of Masculinity', in S. Whitehead and F. J. Barrett (eds.) *The Masculinities Reader*. Polity: Cambridge, 1–26.

Wickham-Crowley, T. (1992) *Guerrillas and Revolution in Latin America: A Comparative Study of Insurgents and Regimes Since 1956*. Princeton University Press: Princeton.

Widgery, L. (1972.) *Report of the Tribunal Appointed to Inquire into the Events on Sunday, 30 January 1972, which Led to Loss of Life in Connection with the Procession in Londonderry on that Day*. HMSO: London.

Williams, R. (1977) *Marxism and Literature*. Oxford University Press: Oxford.

Williams, R. (1985) *Keywords: A Vocabulary of Culture and Society*. Hogarth Press: London.

Williams, P. J. and Walter, K. (1997) *Militarization and Demilitarization in El Salvador's Transition to Democracy*. University of Pittsburgh Press: Pittsburgh.

Winton, A. (2004) 'Young People's Views on How to Tackle Gang Violence in "Post-Conflict" Guatemala'. *Environment and Urbanization* 16(2): 83–99.

WOLA (2006) *Youth Gangs in Central America: Issues in Human Rights, Effective Policing, and Prevention*. [WWW document]. http://www.wola.org/media/gangs_report_final_nov_06.pdf [accessed 23 June 2007].

Wolf, S. (2008) 'Contesting Mano Dura: Human Rights Advocacy in El Salvador' paper presented at *JISLAC conference, Regional Seminar in the West, 22–23 February 2008*. University of Bristol, UK.

Wood, E. J. (2003) *Insurgent Collective Action and Civil War in El Salvador*. Cambridge University Press: Cambridge.

Yllo, K. (1988) 'Political and Methodological Debates in Wife Abuse Research' in K. Yllo and M. Bograd (eds.) *Feminist Perspectives on Wife Abuse*. Sage: London, 28–50.

Young, I. M. (2003) 'Feminist Reactions to the Contemporary Security Regime'. *Hypatia* 18(1): 223–231.

Zalewski, M. (1995) 'Well, What is the Feminist Perspective on Bosnia?' *International Affairs* 71(2): 339–356.

Zilberg, E. (2007) 'Gangster in Guerrilla Face: A Transnational Mirror of Production between the USA and El Salvador'. *Anthropological Theory* 7(1): 37–57.

Zinecker, H. (2007) Cuánto cambio requiere la paz? Las experiencias de El Salvador y sus enseñanzas' in *Problemas de la Paz: violencia, impunidad, déficit institucional. Edición Monográfica Estudios Centroamericanos*. **701–702**: 315–325.

Žižek, S. (2008) *Violence*. Profile Books: London.

Zschaebitz, U. (1999) *La situació de las comunidades tugurizadas en el AMSS: ensayo de caracterización*. Fundación Salvadoreña de Desarrollo y Vivienda Mínima: San Salvador.

8

Index to BLAR book on violence